SIMPLY
GENIUS!

Hay House Titles of Related Interest

YOU CAN HEAL YOUR LIFE, the movie,
starring Louise L. Hay & Friends
(available as a 1-DVD program and an expanded 2-DVD set)
Watch the trailer at: **www.LouiseHayMovie.com**

THE SHIFT, the movie,
starring Dr. Wayne W. Dyer
(available as a 1-DVD program and an expanded 2-DVD set)
Watch the trailer at: **www.DyerMovie.com**

♪♪♪

THE 8TH CHAKRA: What It Is And How It Can Transform Your Life,
by Jude Currivan

COSMOS: A Co-Creator's Guide To The Whole World,
by Jude Currivan & Ervin Laszlo

*IN MY OWN WORDS: An Introduction to My Teachings and
Philosophy,* by His Holiness the Dalai Lama; edited by Rajiv Mehrotra

*THE MAP: Finding the Magic and Meaning
in the Story of Your Life,* by Colette Baron-Reid

*MODERN-DAY MIRACLES: Miraculous Moments and Extraordinary
Stories from People All Over the World Whose Lives Have Been
Touched by Louise L. Hay,* by Louise L. Hay & Friends

*THE MOTHER OF INVENTION: The Legacy of Barbara Marx
Hubbard and the Future of YOU,* by Neale Donald Walsch

*WHAT HAPPENS WHEN WE DIE: A Groundbreaking Study
into the Nature of Life and Death,* by Sam Parnia, M.D., Ph.D.

♪♪♪

All of the above are available at your
local bookstore, or may be ordered by visiting:

Hay House UK: **www.hayhouse.co.uk**
Hay House USA: **www.hayhouse.com**®
Hay House Australia: **www.hayhouse.com.au**
Hay House South Africa: **www.hayhouse.co.za**
Hay House India: **www.hayhouse.co.in**

SIMPLY GENIUS!

And Other Tales from My Life

An informal autobiography by

ERVIN LASZLO

HAY HOUSE

Australia • Canada • Hong Kong • India
South Africa • United Kingdom • United States

First published and distributed in the United Kingdom by:
Hay House UK Ltd, 292B Kensal Rd, London W10 5BE. Tel.: (44) 20 8962 1230;
Fax: (44) 20 8962 1239. www.hayhouse.co.uk

Published and distributed in the United States of America by:
Hay House, Inc., PO Box 5100, Carlsbad, CA 92018-5100. Tel.: (1) 760 431 7695 or
(800) 654 5126; Fax: (1) 760 431 6948 or (800) 650 5115. www.hayhouse.com

Published and distributed in Australia by:
Hay House Australia Ltd, 18/36 Ralph St, Alexandria NSW 2015. Tel.: (61) 2 9669
4299; Fax: (61) 2 9669 4144. www.hayhouse.com.au

Published and distributed in the Republic of South Africa by:
Hay House SA (Pty), Ltd, PO Box 990, Witkoppen 2068.
Tel./Fax: (27) 11 467 8904. www.hayhouse.co.za

Published and distributed in India by:
Hay House Publishers India, Muskaan Complex, Plot No.3, B-2, Vasant Kunj,
New Delhi – 110 070. Tel.: (91) 11 4176 1620; Fax: (91) 11 4176 1630.
www.hayhouse.co.in

Distributed in Canada by:
Raincoast, 9050 Shaughnessy St, Vancouver, BC V6P 6E5. Tel.: (1) 604 323 7100;
Fax: (1) 604 323 2600

Copyright © 2011 by Ervin Laszlo

The moral rights of the author have been asserted.

Editorial supervision: Jill Kramer • *Project editor:* Lisa Mitchell
Interior design: Tricia Breidenthal
Interior photos: All of the photos are courtesy of the author
unless otherwise indicated.

The author of this book does not dispense medical advice or prescribe the use of any technique as a form of treatment for physical or medical problems without the advice of a physician, either directly or indirectly. The intent of the author is only to offer information of a general nature to help you in your quest for emotional and spiritual wellbeing. In the event you use any of the information in this book for yourself, which is your constitutional right, the author and the publisher assume no responsibility for your actions.

A catalogue record for this book is available from the British Library.

ISBN 978-1-84850-337-3

Printed and bound in Great Britain by TJ International, Padstow, Cornwall.

The title of this book was inspired
by an episode recounted in the first chapter.
Ten-year-old Ervin, a child prodigy on the piano,
insisted on learning a piece that is said to call
for great maturity on the part of the performer.
The way he played this sonata—the "Appassionata"
by Beethoven—prompted his mother to take him
to a renowned professor of the Academy
of Music in Budapest to get his opinion.

When little Ervin finished playing,
the professor threw up his hands and said,
"Simply genius!" The saying resonated with Ervin
for the rest of his life. Whenever he attempted
something that on first sight seemed nearly
impossible, he would say to himself, "Perhaps it's
simply genius!" And then he would try.

CONTENTS

PART III: THE QUEST

PART IV: THE THREE CAPSTONE PROJECTS

FOREWORD

by DEEPAK CHOPRA

In a skeptical age when doubters sit by the side of the road saying no to every new idea, Ervin Laszlo said yes. At a time when even the most brilliant minds are satisfied to conquer a single field, he refused to divide himself into pieces. That is what makes this book such a delightful read. You get to wander to the far frontier of speculative thinking, the very Everest of human knowledge, where the air is thin and exhilarating. And instead of being scared, you look down from that height and murmur, "What a glorious view."

Ervin Laszlo is a one-man human-potential movement, and when reading his life story, it's easy to feel left behind. He sailed through a career in music so swiftly that a lesser talent would still be practicing, vaguely hoping for a career. He consumed the principles of science and was showered with degrees and recognition. His journey couldn't stop until it expanded onto the world stage with his forays into the Club of Rome and the United Nations.

Where does such a remarkable trajectory lead?

It could have led to a crash back to Earth, like Icarus. It could have become entombed in libraries or lost in the maze of philosophy. But it was inevitable, looking back, that Ervin Laszlo voraciously consumed so many areas of accomplishment in order to gain a view of the whole. After beauty, knowledge, acclaim, social prestige, and philosophy had made their contributions, he looked around and asked the same questions every child does: *Who am I? Why am I here? What does life mean?*

Unlike a child, however, Laszlo felt that he could answer these primal questions. In so doing, he did something that was easy for him but incredibly courageous for most others. He betrayed his class—the priesthood of science—and the worldview of materialism. I first encountered his exploration of the Akashic field years ago. It is a concept as old as human wisdom and as outrageous to a materialist as anything can get.

According to ancient Indian beliefs, the world is created from five elements known as the *Tanmatras:* earth, air, fire, water, and space. The Sanskrit word for "space" is *Akasha.* Yet since every particle of creation is alive and conscious, the Vedic seers, or *rishis,* declared that space was not empty, inert, or lifeless. Akasha is consciousness waiting to be filled with objects and events. And when those objects and events pass away, Akasha doesn't forget them; instead, the field of Akasha serves as an invisible memory bank of creation. More than that, it links all happenings—from the subatomic to the big bang—just as our personal memory links every event in our lives to form a whole person. It takes past, present, and future to unfold who we are and who we will be; yet anything that occurs in space and time is secondary to Akasha, the mind that serves as the invisible womb of the universe . . . and of each life as we live it.

When Laszlo hit upon the concept of the Akashic field, all of his past knowledge came to bear, and he had an "Aha!" moment, as major breakthroughs are often called. Having mastered so many aspects of life, he saw existence as a whole. Einstein declared that without a sense of awe and wonder when contemplating the infinite mystery of Nature, no important scientific discovery can be made. But he should have added that nothing else will cause scientists to shake their heads and believe that one of their own has been lost to mysticism.

In defiance of that, Laszlo has turned his insider's knowledge of science back on itself. This is not mysticism, he asserts. It is meta-science, a science that goes beyond. And with great urgency, he proposes that unless science goes beyond, the planet cannot sustain itself. It is a powerful argument.

The modern world has pushed the envelope to the point that every technological breakthrough is as potentially destructive as it is constructive. Creativity has its diabolical side, as atomic weapons and newer means of mechanized death demonstrate. Communications link every corner of the globe, but those bent on terror and havoc can take advantage as never before. Billions of the dispossessed who starved in poverty for centuries now see the chance to rise in India, China, Africa, and South America; but with their rise comes an exponential jump in pollution and ecological peril.

Laszlo has woven into his life story this urgent theme to redefine ourselves and learn to live as whole beings. He foresees a world shift that will take place not externally, but in consciousness. In that regard, he is not unique. From all sides we hear about tipping points and critical mass. With the sense of an ending comes the hope for a beginning. What makes Laszlo's tale unique is that he has come full circle as few have before. He has traveled into the abstract world where science quantifies experience, and then he has journeyed back to say, "You cannot quantify life and reduce it to data and mathematics. Eventually, you must see yourself as human and life as a mystery."

This mystery encompasses every moment of Ervin Laszlo's long, remarkable adventures. But every sword begins with a hand, a scabbard, a hilt, and a blade—finally to end in a single point. This book presses that point home with force, and because we trust the guiding hand, the point cannot be escaped.

♪♫♪♫♪♫♪

PREFACE

This book has an unusual history. It started with a refusal—by me. When my friend and literary agent, Bill Gladstone, suggested that I write about how I went from music to science and philosophy, then to the United Nations and my commitment to a global "worldshift," I said no. I had neither the time nor the inclination to write my memoir. But Bill insisted: mine has been an unusual life, or even several "lives," and it would surely be of interest to many people.

I finally relented and wrote down some of the incidents I've most often been asked about (and were therefore clear in my mind), beginning with the "love story": how I met my wife. Then I went on to recount my American debut as a fifteen-year-old pianist (my "Big Day" in New York City), my professional debut at the ripe age of nine in Budapest, and the "Simply genius!" episode less than six months later.

But Bill persisted. "How did you shift from music to science and philosophy?" he asked. That required jotting down my spontaneous resolution one New Year's Eve in the Alps, together with the story of my unexpected encounter with an editor in Holland. Thanks to Bill's initial push, other recollections followed; it appeared that my life was full of unexpected twists and turns.

Soon I had nearly two dozen "lived stories" on my desk. They were fun to recollect and to write about. I looked at what I had compiled and thought: *All right, let me see what would be needed to make this into a reasonably complete account of at least the major phases and episodes of my life.*

Then came a surprise. Upon putting the individual episodes together, something surfaced that I had sometimes suspected but had never bothered to look into. The stories turned out to have an underlying leitmotif—in fact, several of them had intertwined, much as in a fugue in music. Each leitmotif appears to have evolved on its own and to have led logically, even if unexpectedly, to the others.

There is a tongue-in-cheek saying: "I don't know what I mean until I say it." Here it turned out that I didn't know what meaning there was to my life until I wrote about how I had lived it.

The first two dozen stories took just six weeks to draft, but it took as many months to realize what they meant, and even more to spell out clearly. I was assisted in this endeavor by my family, my strongest supporters and also my most severe critics. My wife, Carita (whom I call Marjorie in these stories because that, too, is one of her names, and she had been called by that name when we met and for quite some time after that), could vouch for everything that concerned my life since I had met her in my mid-twenties. And our sons, Christopher and Alexander, could complete the stories that concerned them, although they vowed that they had no idea of many of the things that had taken place while they were children. My heartfelt thanks goes to them, with double and triple thanks to Carita/Marjorie for her patience in reading draft after draft and making careful comments on each.

My wonderful Hungarian friends Maria Sági and Ivan Vitányi recalled for me many of the events and developments that marked my ongoing "romance with my roots" in my native city, which then led to the founding of the Club of Budapest. I owe deep gratitude to them, for they, too, made many important suggestions, having read half a dozen drafts of the book, while paying special attention to the episodes and developments in which they played a major part.

When the various stories coalesced into a meaningful whole, I told my great friend Deepak Chopra about it, and he immediately offered to write the Foreword—just as, several years previously, he had spontaneously written a brilliant endorsement of my major work *Science and the Akashic Field*. I am grateful to him both for his deep insight and his enduring friendship.

Before going to press, I received valuable pointers on how to best phrase my account of the various events that marked my life from William Simon who, unlike I, had vast experience in writing in this genre. My thanks go to both Bills for launching, and then helping bring to fruition, this unexpected but very happy adventure.

Just as I thought the manuscript was ready for publication, having received the enthusiastic endorsement of Kim McArthur of McArthur & Company, the book's Canadian publisher, the editorial team at Hay House, headed by Jill Kramer under the watchful eye of president Reid Tracy, came into the picture. Editors Alex Freemon, Patrick Gabrysiak, and Lisa Mitchell pressed me to follow up on the leitmotifs they said were implicit but not sufficiently explicit in the story of my life, and urged me to go back for a second look. I did, and I believe that it was very much worth the effort. My sincere thanks to all of them.

And what can I say about the outcome of this attempt to write "an informal autobiography"? Looking back on all the stories that marked key turning points in my life, it has become clear to me that my life was, and is, unconventional: a life "beyond the box." But being beyond the box doesn't mean being at sea. All these tales recount episodes along the way—a complex and eventful way, one that took me to where I am today. First to my surprise, and then to my satisfaction, my life path turned out to have real meaning. It has brought me into the wonderland of the reality that is currently emerging at the cutting edge of the natural sciences, as well as face-to-face with the exciting world of our unstable and unsustainable but already rapidly changing civilization.

"May you live in exciting times" is a familiar saying in China, where it is often wished on one's worst enemies (in China, "exciting times" were often bloody times). I would, however, wish exciting—but not violent—times on my best friends. Because there is nothing more challenging and fascinating than to live at a turning point in history—a point where one age ends, and another begins.

This is where we are today. There could hardly be a greater and more exciting challenge in life than to lend a hand in the shaping of a world that is about to be born. Except, of course, to explore the deeper nature of that world, and of the universe in which it came to be.

These are the twin destinations to which my "life beyond the box" has taken me. Reading the tales that made up the main stations along the way could help you, dear reader, to retrace my steps and relive my adventures, and reach some of the insights and enjoyments they had afforded to me.

I wish you a good journey—a journey that is meaningful, as well as fun.

— **Ervin Laszlo**
Montescudaio, Tuscany

♪♫♪♫♪♫

PART I

THE
GRAND
ADVENTURES

CHAPTER ONE

SIMPLY GENIUS!

"Yippee!"

My yell would have made Winnetou—the brave Apache chief I had much admired in Karl May's popular Wild West stories— proud. My outburst on that particular day escaped full force from my throat when, walking home from school, I spotted what I was looking for. It was at the corner of Aréna-út (the wide street that fronts the Városliget, the Budapest City Park) and a smaller street with shops—and with posters. There it was, across the street on a large cylindrical column intended to display bills for upcoming events. I was glad that I had taken this route, for normally I would walk along the Fasor, a quiet avenue lined with a double row of chestnut trees on each side . . . but with no posters.

Running across the street for a closer look, I unfortunately didn't notice that one of the stones in the cobblestone pavement was displaced. My foot got caught in the hole and I fell, leaving my knee skinned and badly bruised, with blood running down to my sock. But never mind, my discovery was worth it.

The reason for my exuberance were the two posters right in the middle of the wide column, one under the other. The one on top was large and horizontal, the usual format for concerts in Budapest: it announced that the Budapest Symphony Orchestra, conducted by Miklos Lukács, would perform the following day. The piano soloist, the poster proclaimed in fat red letters, would be Ervin Laszlo—*me*. I had been hunting for these posters on the streets of Budapest over the course of the past week, ever since they had first been put up, but until now hadn't found one so close to home—and also close to school, where both my parents and my friends would see it.

"My" poster was just above another that I had also hunted down, because I enjoyed seeing it, although I couldn't quite say why. It advertised a play at a downtown theater, a comedy titled *A Meztelen Lány* (*The Naked Girl*). I didn't know anything about that play, but somehow it was nice to see the poster and say the title aloud. The theater poster, in the usual smaller format, was just below mine; and this seemed to me to be an excellent arrangement.

The date was March 1942, and I was nine years old. Contrary to what my glee upon seeing the juxtaposition of the two posters might suggest, I was a piano prodigy, not a sex prodigy. I had no interest in girls. If anything, I considered them a nuisance. I didn't waste any time thinking about them, but seeing *The Naked Girl* under my name intrigued me.

I paid dearly for my careless dash across the street, because the next day I had to walk onstage with a big bandage around my knee. (Boys in those days wore knee pants even in the evening and on dressy occasions. Wearing long pants would have made me look like an undersized grown-up.)

The concert took place in the festive Vigadó, the famous ballroom and concert hall on the shores of the Danube. My appearance was greeted with gasps by the audience members—not because of the bandage around my knee, but because there had been no mention in the announcement that the soloist would be so young. I had been playing private or semi-private concerts in literary and artistic clubs and salons in the city for the past two years, but this was my formal debut on a major stage, and I had been looking forward to it for months.

Still, part of my delight on that special day in my young life was due to something entirely different. It was the prospect of getting a particular kind of candy that I especially liked but seldom received: candied tropical fruits, packed in a large and colorful metal box. One of those boxes, I figured, would last me for several weeks, and then there would be another concert and perhaps another box. At my earlier appearances, I had been receiving more ordinary candies of many kinds, and even some laurel wreaths with colorful ribbons imprinted with my name and the date of the performance, but those rewards were of much less interest.

I knew the person who was most likely to bring me the desired candy, and it worried me that I didn't see her backstage before the concert. (This lady was to play a major role in my life as a musician, as I shall recount later.)

Having duly listened to all kinds of last-minute injunctions about looking at the conductor and waiting for his cue before starting—and above all, keeping still while the orchestra played without a piano solo part—I at last walked onstage, bowed to acknowledge the first hesitant and then surprisingly prolonged and happy applause, and embarked on my piece, Mozart's Concerto in A Major. All went well until the middle of the first movement, the part where the opening theme returns and then continues in a different key. Just as I launched into the theme for the second time, a movement off to the right in the audience caught the corner of my eye. A lady was entering the first row. Was she the awaited candied-fruit conveyor?

Another look confirmed that she was. My heart gave a thump and my spirits soared considerably. Unfortunately, her appearance also distracted me. I forgot that we were not playing the main theme for the first but for the second time, so instead of continuing in the tonic key, I continued with the dominant. I went my way and the orchestra went its way, and that produced a discordant, disturbing sound. The conductor must have thought that I had lost my way, so he picked up the bulky orchestral score and leaned over to show it to me. I ignored him—I was not great at reading even a simple piano score, much less the complex score of a whole orchestra. In any case, I didn't need to see it; I knew what was wrong and how to put it right. I switched immediately to the correct tonality, and we continued without a hitch.

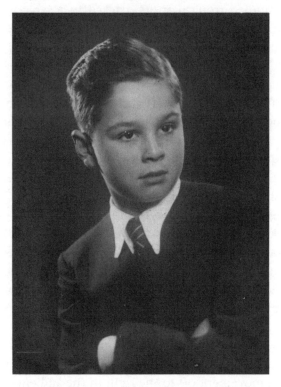

A photographer's "serious" picture of me taken around the time I began to study piano with Mother.

Nobody noticed anything, other than that the conductor had picked up the score and then quickly put it back again. I gulped— that was a close call. I decided to "live myself back into the music," as Mother would say, and stay there.

As always, living myself into the music made everything else disappear—the conductor, the orchestra, even the public. There was only the music flowing, pulsing, and taking me into the land of Mozart—a place that was both tender and friendly, and loving yet rigorous.

There was a standing ovation when I finished the concerto, and many hugs and handshakes—first onstage with the conductor and first-row players, and then with friends and crowds of well-wishers backstage. The lady from the front row showed up, and sure enough, she had a large metal box in her hands. She hugged me and handed it over. I could hardly wait for her and everyone else to leave so I could open it. It was the candy I had hoped for!

♪♪♪

"Living myself into the music" was how I learned to play piano. My first piano teacher was my mother. She had started me out when I was four, but I didn't take well to instruction; she later told me that I insisted I knew better about everything. At five I was more willing to listen, and soon acquired quite a repertoire. I never looked at the score; indeed, I didn't learn how to read a score until years later—and even then, not very readily. I just listened to Mother play a piece, and then I would play it myself. This wasn't learning the score or mimicking my mother. Rather, it was absorbing the music through my whole being.

Once I began to play a piece by a great composer, I would spontaneously continue it—to me it seemed the music couldn't have been otherwise than the way it was. I was not playing the score, not touching keys in the order prescribed by the composer. I was in another world, where everything had to be the way it was, and where everything made sense. This was what (in Hungarian) Mother and I called *bele élni magamat a zenébe*—"living myself into the music."

One day my father showed up with a new phonograph, featuring a light pickup arm and a fine chrome needle. It didn't scratch as much as the one we'd had before, and I would spend hours listening to records. Although we had a fairly large collection, my parents knew that for me, getting a new record was always a great joy. On every Christmas and birthday, and even on my name day (the day in which the saint I was named after is celebrated in church), my collection would grow, sometimes by leaps and bounds.

On my tenth birthday, Father came home with Wilhelm Backhaus's recording of Beethoven's famous sonata known as the *Appassionata*. (This is the Piano Sonata no. 23 in F Minor, considered one of Beethoven's most tempestuous works for the piano. It was composed the year Beethoven came to grips with his deafness and reflects the turbulent emotions he experienced during this period.) I wanted very much to play it, but Mother said it wasn't appropriate for me; rather, it was a piece for grown-ups. I didn't agree with her at all. I told her that now that I'd turned ten, I had two numbers to my age. I would have two numbers until I passed ninety-nine. All the great pianists had two numbers, I was almost sure. Therefore, I could play whatever they were playing. I was very impressed with my venerable age.

My mother didn't comment on my reasoning, but in the end, she agreed to teach me the *Appassionata*. I learned the majestic first movement in a few days, and it carried me into a land full of unknown wonders, far beyond where the other pieces had "taken" me. I loved to play the piece—and I played and played it. Mother listened, and decided to get a second opinion.

She took me to Professor Arnold Székely, a renowned professor at the Franz Liszt Academy of Music, who, in his late seventies, was in retirement but was always ready to offer an opinion. He agreed to listen to me. The professor lived on the upper floor of a stately old building overlooking the Danube on the Pest side of the city.

We climbed the marble staircase and were greeted by the professor's housekeeper, an elderly woman wearing a crisp white apron. She said that the professor was expecting us and told us to go right in. The room we entered was large and sunny, with a breathtaking view of the historic buildings across the river, on the Buda side of the city. There was no time to take it all in, though, for the professor got right to the point.

"Welcome. And what will you be playing?"

Mother answered for me, as I felt a bit embarrassed.

"We have worked on several Mozart sonatas, and even Beethoven's First Piano Concerto—all pieces with beautiful, simple melodies," she said.

"Ervin likes them all, but then he heard Wilhelm Backhaus play the *Appassionata* on his new recording, and he fell in love with it. I told him that it's not for him—he must grow up to really understand it—but he doesn't want to listen. He learned the first movement by heart and is practicing it every day, just as soon as he sits down at the piano."

Professor Székely raised his eyebrows but didn't say anything—he just pointed to his pianos. He had two beautiful grands side by side. Just looking at them was like gazing into the most amazing toy store I'd ever seen. I briefly tried both and then chose the Blüthner, which had a wonderful, mellow sound. Playing it didn't feel like playing an instrument; it felt like playing with a friend. I began the first movement, and soon forgot about Professor Székely, Mother, and everything else around me. I was in the wonder world of the *Appassionata*.

When I finished, Mother looked inquiringly at Székely. The venerable professor stood, threw up his hands, and declared: *"Egyszerüen zseni!"* ("Simply genius!"). My mother nodded. Nothing more was said, and we went home.

The saying stuck. It stuck not just with Mother and me, but also became a family legend. Whenever I would contemplate undertaking something that on first sight seemed implausible—if not downright impossible—I would say (but only to myself): *Perhaps it's simply genius!* And then I would try.

♪♪♪

It was eleven years later that I had a chance to meet Wilhelm Backhaus, who had been the unwitting cause of my infatuation with the *Appassionata*. This was in the summer of 1953. The great pianist had been living in Lugano, in southern Switzerland, since 1930, and was sixty-nine at the time. I was twenty-one, and already an internationally recognized virtuoso. I had a small apartment in Lugano, a place I could call home while touring Europe. It was in a part of the town called "Paradiso"—a quiet suburb then; a fashionable resort with dozens of luxury hotels today. Backhaus had an apartment in an old house on the waterfront, with a fabulous view of Lake Lugano, framed by Monte San Salvatore on the right, Monte Brè on the left, and the snowcapped Alps in the distance.

We reminisced: Backhaus, looking back on more than fifty years of his musical career (he gave his first concert at sixteen); and I on twelve years, of which the last six were taken up by American-style whirlwind touring. Backhaus shook his head.

"In my time," he remarked, "we would set a date for a concert; and for weeks beforehand, I would concentrate my feelings, my energies, and my time in preparing for it. When it was over, I would take a break and rest, and then start to prepare for the next concert. But today, as you yourself are experiencing, one just plays one concert after another, as if one were on an assembly line.

"I never did that," he added, "and never will."

Backhaus was true to his resolve, playing but a few concerts a year, although he made many recordings. By the end of his life in 1969, he had recorded almost all of the piano works of Beethoven.

When we finished our tea, I gathered my courage and told him about my experience with his recording of the *Appassionata*. I had a decidedly immodest proposal in mind.

"Your recording has made such an impression on me," I told the world-famous artist, "that it changed my life. I will never forget it." Then I came out with my daring request.

"Would you play it for me? Just the first movement."

Backhaus did, and that was one performance I would never forget.

♪♫♪♫♪♫

CHAPTER TWO

WALKS WITH
UNCLE PIPPA

I had a happy childhood. We lived in a large house composed of many apartments on four floors. Ours was on the top floor, and as the house across the street had only three stories, we could look out over its roof to see the sky above and the municipal park off to the side.

My parents and I lived in a spacious apartment, and my grandparents lived in a similar apartment one floor below us. My uncle and aunt lived on our floor facing the park; and my family's shoe factory was on the ground floor, its entrance directly below us.

The house was owned by a trade union affiliated with the Social Democratic Party and was inhabited, for the most part, by prosperous middle-class families with a liberal orientation. My parents had many friends, many of whom had children, so we formed a close-knit group of our own. I never lacked for company, and I don't remember ever being bored.

The daily routine was simple and seemed to be an unchangeable law of nature. It started with breakfast of hot cocoa with many kinds of bread, brought to my room by one of a succession of peasant women who came to town to find employment as household help (all the apartments in our building had an extra room just for this purpose).

As of the age of five, my morning routine included an hour or two of sitting with Mother by the piano, and by the age of six, I would walk to school by myself. Both the grammar and high schools were within walking distance.

During the first days at school, I was petrified when my mother would leave me, although the lady with the gray specks in her eyes, who was to be my teacher for the first four years, was kind and understanding. On the first day, she had to park me outside for an hour on the sunny upper terrace to dry out . . . my shorts were badly in need of it. But I soon made friends among my classmates and was well regarded by the teachers and parents as the boy who gave great piano performances at the Christmas and Easter shows put on by the schoolchildren.

My afternoons were spent at Budapest City Park (the famous Városliget), first "driving" my toy cars and fire engines, and later joining the soccer matches that would spontaneously form during the spring and summer. During the winter, I would go to the city's open-air ice rink and play hockey. The greatest joys of my life were getting a full-size leather soccer ball, a scaled-down but nearly professional hockey stick, and a beautiful silver-chromed bicycle.

In the summertime, my family would go to Lake Balaton, Hungary's "inland sea." First we stayed at our own house, but then Father sold it and bought a car instead—in those days, a car cost almost as much as a house. For once, my father had backed the wrong horse: he thought that the Nazis would sooner or later take away the house, but he figured that he could hide the car.

Actually, they found the car right away, whereas, after the war we could have had the title to the house returned to us.

These were wonderful three-month vacations, spent mostly on the beach, in the water, and on my bicycle. But I did enjoy getting back to town just as much: I remember hearing the clang of the streetcars on our street the first morning back home and thinking: *Now I will see my friends again and start a new class at school!*

My parents were totally devoted to me. Mother would later admit that before I was born, she and Father used to walk hand in hand, imagining they were holding my hands between them, although it was still months before "little Ervin" would arrive in the flesh. They never doubted that they would have a boy, and chose the name Ervin not because somebody in the family had it, but because no one did. They weren't opposed to tradition—they just wanted to give me a name that was special.

My mother was a city girl, born and raised in Budapest. She was a passionate music lover and wanted to be a professional concert pianist, but by the time she convinced her parents to get a piano and allow her to attend the Academy of Music, she was thirteen and that was too late. Concert pianists need to start training their fingers as early as five or six. When she had me, she was determined not to make the same mistake.

Father was born in Nagyszeben, a town in Transylvania that was part of Hungary until the end of World War I and was then annexed to Romania. He came to Hungary in his early twenties and enrolled in the law school of the University of Pécs. While still a graduate student, he married my mother and decided to settle in Budapest. When he got his law degree, Grandfather asked him to join the management of the shoe factory—his own son ("Uncle Pippa," about whom I shall have more to say in a moment) had no real interest in business of any kind. Father was first in charge of sales and traveled all over the country, and then after my grandfather's passing, he took over the general running of the factory.

I don't have many memories of my grandfather—he died of a heart attack when I was four. I only remember a kind white-haired gentleman with a big white mustache who would always give me a large handful of candies even though Mother would always chide him—and me—saying that I wasn't supposed to have more than a few at a time. Grandfather was raised in a village not far from the capital and came to the city as soon as he could. He opened a small shoe-repair shop and built it into the Graziosa shoe factory, a recognized leader in high-quality shoes for women.

The factory was on the ground floor, and I would visit whenever I could. It was a fascinating place with its whirling machines, rapid-fire hammering, and people busily scurrying about. Ladies' shoes made of beautiful shiny leather were displayed in a glass case by the entrance. One of my favorite pastimes during walks in the city was to look for shoe stores and find "our" shoes displayed prominently in the window.

♪♪♪

The walks I would take with my uncle, *Pippa bácsi,* were important parts of my life. His real name was Pista (pronounced "Pishta," the diminutive of Stephan), but when I first started speaking, I pronounced it "Pippa." He liked it so much that he insisted we all call him that. Uncle Pippa's life passions were philosophy and music. Mother told me later that he would sit at his desk in the shoe factory and write philosophical treatises on Nietzsche and Freud. The factory was run entirely by Father.

Uncle Pippa and I would often walk in the Városliget, the park across from our house. We would take smaller, quieter paths and I would listen to him talk about the many joys of nature and the special wonder of having been born a human being. He said he could never understand how people could go through life without recognizing the miracle of existence and looking for their true mission in life.

When World War II broke out—I was seven at the time—Uncle Pippa would comment on the tragic mistakes made by individuals and entire societies when they attacked and wanted to kill or dominate each other, instead of learning to live in harmony. He could not understand, he told me, how a nation that had produced such writers and thinkers as Goethe, Nietzsche, Schiller, and Schopenhauer and musicians such as Bach, Beethoven, and Brahms could also produce a man such as Hitler, who was so full of hate that he could only sow destruction. But my uncle remarked that he wasn't really surprised that there were people who would put that man on a pedestal and consider him their supreme leader.

Uncle Pippa was a pessimist when it came to human nature, but he was filled with a nearly religious fervor when it came to the "nature of nature"—the essence of the whole universe. There the rule was order and harmony, whereas in human society, we had disorder and discord. The great exception about humans was their ability to create art—especially poetry, literature, and music. In this realm, the human spirit could rise above petty conflict and bloody violence.

One of these walks started with a dramatic episode: I was almost killed! As we set out on our usual route, I remembered that I'd made a date with friends to play soccer that afternoon. As our "stadium" was on the opposite side of the park, I thought I would take my bike—I was happy to have an excuse to ride it anyway. I asked my uncle if it was okay for me to walk with the bike next to me, and he said yes. So I rushed back across the street to our shoe factory, where my precious silver-chromed bike was kept in a corner of Father's office.

I got on the bike right by the door of the factory and rushed back across the road where Uncle Pippa was waiting. I was so happy to have a chance to show off my riding skills that I sped off and didn't see the motorcyclist coming on the left. He, too, must have been in a hurry because he came at me with enormous speed. When at last I saw him—and he saw me—it was almost too late. He jammed on the brakes and both his wheels locked; he was sliding toward me sideways, with a tremendous screech of tires. I had a vision of a screaming devil hurtling at me, and had only a fraction of a second to decide whether to brake and let it pass in front of me or try to speed up and hope he would pass behind.

I chose to put on some speed. That was lucky. The sliding motorbike missed my rear tire by a hair. The rider regained control, and with a muffled shout, he disappeared down the street.

I was safe and sound, but shaken up. Above all, I was very ashamed. Here was Uncle Pippa seeing firsthand how I'd managed to almost kill myself on my bike. I was also worried that he would tell my father—which may have led to a quarantine for the bike in the depths of the shoe factory, at least for the foreseeable future. But Uncle Pippa didn't tell on me, neither that day nor any day after.

During our walk, I was rather subdued, and Uncle was even more thoughtful than usual. He spoke about chance and destiny, and although I didn't understand everything he said, I did realize that there is no such thing as pure chance. In other words, everything happens for a reason. In my near collision, for example, the reason I didn't get killed must have been that I needed to grow up in order to fulfill my life's mission. A moment's inattention couldn't possibly cancel that out. But, my uncle remarked, "It is better not to tempt fate. Before crossing the street, just look both left and right." I was happy to agree with that.

Uncle Pippa's other passion was music. He was a dedicated violinist. With his friends, he formed a string quartet that met in his study at the same hour every week. I could hear the music in my room from the floor below, and as soon as I would hear it, I would run down and sit quietly in a corner. There I would enter the same wonderland that opened for me when I was playing the piano.

String quartets by Mozart, Schubert, and Brahms were their favorites; and hearing the "Pippa quartet" play them made a great impression on me. It was an impression just as lasting as my walks in the park, even if on those walks I would only comprehend a third of what Uncle Pippa was telling me.

But the veneration of the harmony that Uncle said was everywhere in the cosmos—a harmony that I could experience firsthand in playing the piano and listening to music—stayed with me throughout my life.

♪♫♪♫♪♪♫

CHAPTER THREE

SURVIVING IN BUDAPEST

It was into this ordered and sunny existence that the Nazi invasion of Hungary burst through.

It was March 1944 and I was eleven years old. The weekly children's paper, *Mattie the Gooseboy* (*Ludas Matyi*), which was printed, as always, on pink paper, carried an enormous but odd headline that took up most of the first page: "Hold on, Mattie— Here Comes the Curve." I looked inside to see what it meant but couldn't find any clues. I always read this popular paper as soon as it appeared on the newsstand because it was full of humorous stories and cartoons.

I showed the strange headline to my parents to find out what it meant, but they didn't say anything—they just looked at each other and went into the next room. They talked in hushed tones, and then Mother came back and said that Father would have to go to the country for a while. Not to worry, she assured me; he would be back soon.

In the middle of that night, there was a banging on our front door. I woke from a deep sleep and saw large men in heavy boots shine a flashlight into the room and then into my eyes. They were looking for my father. They even searched under the beds. Mother told them that he was in the country, and she didn't know when he would return. At last they went away. The next morning it felt like I had dreamed the whole thing, but it was real.

World War II was moving into its final phase. The Russian Red Army was nearing the Hungarian border in the East, and the German high command decided it was time to move into the country from the West in order to stem the Russian advance. During the night of March 20, 1944, a convoy of tanks and troop carriers thundered across the Austro-Hungarian border. By daybreak it had reached the capital. At dawn, German storm troopers surrounded the home of the Hungarian prime minister, Miklós Kállay, as Gestapo agents entered his apartments. But he had already fled to the Turkish diplomatic mission, where he was given refuge.

At the same time, Gestapo-led frontline troops dispersed throughout the city, rounding up the civilian opposition. They had informers and a list of names. Father was on the list. Like Kállay, he and many others had gotten away: the local underground managed to inform them in the nick of time. *Mattie the Gooseboy* was one of the channels it used. (Mattie, after whom the paper was named, was a well-known folk character: a charming but mischievous boy in charge of herding geese on the farm. He was always getting into trouble and was the subject of many folktales.) Father was on the Nazi blacklist because he had some Jewish forebears in his family, as well as distinct leftist leanings that he didn't bother to hide.

He managed to weather the initial raids and a few days later returned home in the middle of the night.

♪♪♪

My parents knew what was in store for us but didn't want to worry me ahead of time, so I never knew that we had some Jewish blood in our family. Mother was very upset when I began to repeat the anti-Semitic slogans that were heard on the radio or bandied about at school.

One day my physical-education teacher, who was a fanatic anti-Semite and member of the Hungarian Nazi party, grabbed me by the neck in the gym and told me to stay away: I had no right to be there. I went home crying. Mother explained the facts of life to me and told me that I should expect to be treated in a special way, at least for a while. I cried even harder; I didn't like this at all. I had been raised as a Protestant, first attending a Calvinist grammar school run by the Dutch Queen Juliana Foundation and then a Lutheran high school that counted John von Neumann, Eugene Wigner, Béla Bartók, and other world-famous Hungarians among its alumni. But when my parents told me that many of them would have been treated the way I would be, I was much less upset.

The very next day, an order was published in all the papers and was proclaimed every thirty minutes on the radio: Everyone who was not 100 percent Aryan was to be considered a second-class citizen, with strongly restricted rights. Those with Jewish blood anywhere in the last three generations had to wear a large yellow star—the six-pointed Star of David—on their chest.

Mother and Grandmother made several yellow stars using fine shiny silk and stitched them on my shirts and jackets. I quite liked the look of it; wearing this seemed like a decoration. My mother was concerned about what I would experience in school, but she need not have worried: much to everybody's surprise, and to my hardly concealed delight, the best students in class, including most of my friends, showed up at school wearing the star. We looked at each other with fresh respect and a new sense of fellowship.

Then came a time when people who wore yellow stars were periodically rounded up in the streets and herded into an unused brick factory, where they awaited deportation to the concentration camp in Auschwitz. In addition, we were forced to move to specially designated houses. These were scattered all over the city—some of them even in fine neighborhoods. Father managed to secure a place for us on one of the best streets. We packed our belongings and moved to a very nice house on Abonyi Street (Abonyi-utca), not far from where we had lived. It had three floors and three comfortable apartments on each floor, facing a large garden.

The house was soon crowded with all the people who had to move in from other parts of town. There was a family camping out in every room and even in the hallways. But they were quiet, intelligent people, with a keen sense of solidarity as they faced the shared adversity. I don't recall ever witnessing a conflict or argument among the adults, despite the close quarters. I had a fine time with two dozen or so young people, many of them my age or a bit older. We played soccer in the garden, told stories to each other, and repeated in hushed voices the rumors that circulated around town. It was exciting, and rather fun.

We also put on a play. The older children built a stage in the lobby, and we brought down all the chairs we could find. Everyone attended. The play, which took place in a castle, was a comedy by a famous Hungarian writer. It opened with the butler carrying a broom and announcing that the guests, the count and the countess, were arriving. I was the butler. I had a few lines at the beginning of the first act, and after that only a brief appearance to announce that dinner was served, but I learned my lines and rehearsed them conscientiously. It was thrilling to be in a real play.

One day, having just been in a great soccer game in the garden, I had to go to the bathroom urgently and rushed upstairs. We shared our apartment with five families and so also shared the bathroom; everybody was expected to knock before entering. But I was in such a hurry and so euphoric about having scored the winning goal that I just burst in. There in the center of the room was Nikki, a remarkably pretty girl of sixteen, standing in front of the mirror vigorously rubbing shampoo into her hair. She was wearing nothing at all. I mumbled an apology and quickly closed the door. I was sure that Nikki would reproach me and perhaps even tell my parents, but the next time I saw her, she didn't say anything. She just smiled at me as if we now shared a secret, and I smiled back.

After that, Nikki would come into the room where I practiced the piano—the apartment next door had a baby grand I was able to use in the mornings—and would sit on the floor, listening with her eyes closed. Although I usually kept away from girls, I didn't mind her presence at all. With Nikki in the room, it was easy to "live myself" into the music.

Before falling asleep at night, I would imagine that I was incredibly rich and famous, and traveled the world with Nikki at my side. It was a pleasant daydream, and I didn't have any trouble sleeping soundly afterward.

♪♪♪

The good life ended in September when German soldiers accompanied by Hungarian Nazi collaborators began to raid the Star of David–designated houses on our street. They loaded the inhabitants onto trucks and took them to the brick factory where they would await the cattle trains that would transport them to Auschwitz. My parents confronted the possibility—indeed, the overwhelming probability—that we wouldn't survive in these conditions. They were determined to ensure that I would live, even if they didn't.

Father had a plan. He knew a young couple who lived outside the city in Visegrád. This was a historic town at the famous "Danube bend," north of the city, the picturesque site where the great river changes direction, heading south toward Budapest. The couple didn't have political leanings and were not of Jewish origin, so they weren't being persecuted by the Nazis. And Visegrád had no strategic value and, therefore, wasn't likely to be bombed or heavily fought for.

Father offered the couple a large sum of money if they would adopt me as their son, even if there was no way to do so legally. They agreed, and we quietly left the house in Abonyi-utca to meet them. The meeting took place in a safe house, the apartment of an older couple in town who were not in danger of persecution by the Nazis. There the money changed hands . . . and so did I. The young husband and wife took me by the hand, and we boarded the train to Visegrád.

There followed the worst days of my whole life—I still shudder when I think of them. The house was nice, with an open backyard and a view of the Danube. The couple's daughter, who was a few years younger than I was, was a bit jealous of the new addition to the family, but I could handle that. The hardest part was that I felt alone—dreadfully alone.

And even worse than the overwhelming loneliness was the specter that hung over me. Sirens would sound in the village indicating that an air raid was about to start. The four of us—the young couple, their daughter, and I—would quickly leave the house and move to a large cavern on the side of the hill above the river. This was the closest air-raid shelter, and it was relatively safe.

I would stand at the mouth of the cavern and look up at the sky. First nothing would be heard, and the sky remained empty. Then a deep droning would arise somewhere in the distance, becoming louder and louder. Finally, a whole cloud of shiny toylike, yet strangely sinister objects would appear, moving slowly southeast toward Budapest. They were propeller-driven aircraft—the heavy bombers of the Allied powers. When they disappeared in the direction of the capital, silence reigned again. We would stay put in or near the cavern, waiting for the spectacle to recur. It invariably did, coming from the opposite direction.

After an hour or so, the droning would be heard again, but it would be less strong than before. The silver planes would reappear, and they would be less numerous. Once they vanished toward the west, my foster parents would cross themselves, and we would walk back to the house. The daughter would play happily in the backyard, and I would sit looking at the sky, wondering whether my parents were still alive.

After a month of this life, I couldn't take it any longer. I begged the young couple to take me back to the city to meet with my parents. I explained that I absolutely had to see them, not daring to say that I'd had enough and wanted to return. The couple finally agreed, and we met with my parents at the safe house in the city. There I told my mother and father that I was going with them. They replied that it was out of the question because my life would be in danger.

"I don't care!" I cried. "I am coming back. I want to be with you!" They looked at each other and hugged me. We walked out of the apartment, hand in hand, and returned to Abonyi-utca. I had never been so happy in my life.

I was united with my family again, but the danger remained as well. It would only be a matter of days before the fateful truck would pull up in front of the house, and we would be taken away—perhaps never to return.

We had to escape. My parents told me about another plan, and I was happy to go along with this one. We were to visit Ernst von Dohnányi, the renowned composer, pianist, and conductor, who had been my mentor since I was seven. He was also the rector of the Franz Liszt Academy, the first conductor of the philharmonic, and the director of the opera. A charming and naïve man who enjoyed collecting important positions, Dohnányi was offered the post of "Minister of Culture" in the Nazi-imposed puppet government of Ferenc Szálasi; and without giving it a second thought, he accepted.

Mother took me by the hand, and we went to see Dohnányi. We went "incognito," not wearing the Star of David—if we had been caught, we would have immediately been taken to the sinister brick factory. However, walking unobtrusively without the star was less dangerous than wearing it.

Our gamble paid off. We were not accosted, and as soon as Dohnányi heard what could happen to his star pupil, he picked up the phone and called the Spanish ambassador. The ambassador agreed to issue a certificate declaring that our family belonged to the Spanish diplomatic mission. We could then move into one of the two houses in the city that carried the sign "Under Spanish Diplomatic Protection." The Germans respected the immunity implied by this status since Spain was an ally of Nazi Germany, a part of the Axis powers. These "Spanish houses" were the safest places in all of Budapest.

We said good-bye to our friends and sneaked out of the Abonyi Street house under the cover of darkness. This was a twofold risk, because not only did we not wear the yellow stars again, but we also violated the city curfew—*nobody* was supposed to be out after dark. We each carried a small bag with the barest necessities, including pillows and blankets. Ducking into the nearest doorway as soon as we saw anyone, we managed to reach our destination.

The Spanish house, a five-story modern building on a narrow street, was in the center of the city. The many families who were already taking refuge there were not really pleased to see us, but no one complained; we were all in this together. Living space was found for us in the hallway of an apartment on the fifth floor. Those from the neighboring rooms had to maneuver around us whenever they went to the kitchen or bathroom, but we were satisfied. We were now comparatively safe. We put our blankets and pillows on the floor and settled in.

♪♪♪

By December 1944, the Red Army had completely surrounded the city. A three months' siege was under way, with intense fighting on street after street. The city was in shambles. In addition to the heavy, powerful bombs that dropped from American and English long-distance planes, there were now a great many light Russian planes that cruised permanently in the sky, launching small bombs that looked like confetti.

I remember standing on top of the staircase at the back of the house where I could see a wide expanse of sky. There were many things going on—it was a grand, unceasing spectacle. Heavy planes were giving off a deep, monotonous drone as they moved in tight formation; and light planes were crisscrossing in all directions. Antiaircraft projectiles streamed up into the sky like festive fireworks and exploded into white mushrooms around the planes.

When dusk fell—and as it was December, it fell early—dozens of "fingers" of light explored the night sky. Every so often, they would light up a silver "insect," and then several fingers would converge upon it. Sometimes the insect broke apart and started falling to the ground. Below it a parachute would blossom and float majestically toward the earth.

It was fascinating to witness this, and I would watch the sky for hours. I was not particularly worried about what seemed like small packages dropping toward the ground—they would never harm me. The "packages" made a whistling sound as they approached. I was told that if I heard that sound, the package wouldn't land next to me. But if I saw one coming toward me without making a sound, I was to immediately run inside and lie flat on the floor.

Late one afternoon as I was at my lookout post in the back, there was a tremendous bang. I didn't see any package coming toward me nor did I hear any whistling sound. It turned out that the house across the street had received a direct hit. The bomb made contact on the top floor, which was directly across from our fifth-floor apartment. The reason I didn't see it was because I was on the covered staircase, looking toward the back; and the bomb made no sound, since it was coming almost directly toward me.

In the next instant, there was screaming, and a stampede of people rushed from the apartments and headed toward the cellar. My parents appeared at the door of our apartment and, seeing me safe and sound, heaved a sigh of relief and grabbed me by the hand. We joined the rush to the cellar. On the landing below us, there was something strange on the floor, and blood spurted from it. A woman stood in the doorway, screaming wildly, with eyes staring in horror. Mother cried, "Don't look!" and practically dragged me down the stairs.

The explosive that had hit across the street was a so-called shrapnel bomb, intended to fly apart on impact and spread thousands of metal pieces in all directions, like many bullets making contact at once. The front of our house was riddled with holes. All of the windows that weren't already broken had shattered, and inside our apartment even the opposite wall was pockmarked with small but deep holes. Some pieces of shrapnel had actually crossed the room. How my parents avoided being hit was a miracle.

In the cellar, Mother and Father found a place to sit in the storage compartment that belonged to our apartment. It was small, and since there were three families sharing that apartment, there wasn't enough room for anyone to lie down.

We spent three days and three nights down there. During the day, I would wander around the cellar, and at night sleep across my parents' laps. I didn't share the fear of the grown-ups, who listened with dread for the sound of trucks stopping above us. That could have meant soldiers coming to take us away—the end.

There was hardly anything to eat and very little water to drink. Occasionally some men would volunteer to go outside to see if there was anything to be had nearby. A public fountain was said to still be producing water, and a brave baker a few streets away was rumored to still be making bread. I knew this bakery and volunteered to run over to get a few loaves. Mother was not happy with this arrangement, but others welcomed my one-boy expedition, and my parents didn't object. We all had to do our best.

I was told to run flat against the houses that lined the streets and to duck into every doorway that offered shelter. I was to cross to the other side only when I was certain that there were no tanks or soldiers in sight. And I was to run as fast as I could. I followed these instructions and made it to the baker and back. I burst into our cellar with several loaves clutched under my arm and felt like a real hero. It was a fantastic adventure.

Early on the morning of the third day, we heard heavy rumbling above us. Tanks were moving down our street. Were they German tanks or Russian tanks? If they held German soldiers, our lives would be in danger, for our part of town would still be in the hands of the increasingly desperate German and Hungarian troops. The sign that declared that our house was under Spanish diplomatic protection would no longer deter them from entering. Like those in the unprotected yellow-star houses, we would be marched to the river and machine-gunned into the water. On the other hand, if the tanks were Russian, we would be saved.

A few minutes later we had the answer. The cellar door flew open, and five grinning Cossacks burst in, shouting, *"Drastutye!"* ("Hello!"). The street was in Russian hands. We were free to leave anytime and could go anywhere we chose.

♪♪♪

When our house was "liberated" by the Russian soldiers, the danger to our lives was over. But not the nightmare. We could leave the cellar and go up to our fifth-floor hallway, yet I couldn't face going upstairs. The scene on the staircase stayed with me, and so did the sound of the screams. The image of the strange shape on the staircase with blood streaming from it floated before my eyes whenever I would shut them. Until that moment, I'd had the innocent childish belief that something bad couldn't happen to me. But that was now gone.

My parents decided that we should return to our own apartment across the park. Great idea! We found an abandoned two-wheeled handcart, put our bags on it, and started the journey home.

The trip was surreal: the streets were littered with dead horses, and here and there I spotted the body of a dead soldier. The Cossacks, who made up the Red Army, came from the southeast regions of Siberia, and although they carried automatic rifles, they arrived on horseback and horse-drawn carriages. Mother was on the lookout, as she was afraid that my staircase trauma would be reinforced by the sight of bloody corpses. Whenever she saw a dead soldier or a dead horse, she would cry, "Look to your right!" or "Look to the left!" and shove me forward.

Rumor had it that the parts of town we were to cross were already in Russian hands, but this was not the case. Sometimes tanks blocked our way, and at other times soldiers would cut across the street in front of us, pulling two-wheeled guns. There was constant machine-gun fire, and we often had to turn around or make a wide detour.

After several hours, we made it back to our house on Aréna-út. The familiar house was still standing, with walls pockmarked by bullet holes and shrapnel. The one bomb that made a direct hit produced a big hole in the roof, but it was a dud: it didn't explode.

We climbed up the stairs to our old apartment on the fourth floor. Another family was living there now, an older woman and her married daughter. They had moved in when their own house had been destroyed. They were accommodating—everyone had to be in these difficult times. They kept two of the four rooms, and we took the other two. Luckily for me, one of them was my own room, so I felt right at home again.

We unpacked our belongings and hugged each other. We were home. We had survived.

♪♫♪♫♪♫♪

CHAPTER FOUR

COMING BACK TO LIFE

The day after we returned to our apartment on Aréna-út, Father asked our new neighbors if he could borrow a screwdriver. Then he said that he would show them something in their room. He walked over to the window and calmly unscrewed the brass plate on the wall, which covered the mechanism of the roll shutters for the windows. He reached into the opening and pulled on a string. Attached to it was a linen bag, and inside the bag was a wad of money! It was the nest egg Father had prepared for the eventuality that we would come back to our old apartment.

The two ladies who were now our co-tenants just stared in shock; they couldn't believe their eyes. All this time there had been a small fortune right under their noses, and they'd had no idea.

We were at home and no longer under the threat of Nazi persecution, but we couldn't quite come back to life yet. The city was far from safe, with fighting still going on in the hills of Buda. Life was especially dangerous for women. For three days, the soldiers of the Red Army had been given unrestricted freedom to sack the city—a kind of compensation for the danger to which they were exposed and the casualties they had suffered.

The Siberian Cossacks came not only from another place, but they also seemed to come from another time—a different period in history. They were simple folk with a great love of music; they would strum their balalaikas and sing lustily. They also exhibited deep compassion for children and would share whatever food they had with a mother who needed it for her baby. But they did possess two dangerous passions: wristwatches and women.

People quickly learned to keep at least one wristwatch with them at all times. When a soldier accosted them, he would smile in a friendly way and take it for his collection. Soldiers would be quite capable of sticking their bayonets into those who refused to hand over their watches. Many soldiers wore them on both arms, all the way up to their armpits.

Where women were concerned, however, the soldiers' passions could lead to violence. During the three days of unrestricted sacking, many of them hunted for young women. They became very good at it, even when a woman would hide in a cellar or disguise herself as an old hag. The disguises more often hurt than helped: the soldiers would tear off the women's garments unceremoniously, and when they discovered a good-looking young woman, a great shout would go up and she would be dragged away. Often the unfortunate woman would return the following day or even days later.

Mr. Grosz, a distinguished and well-respected lawyer, was our next-door neighbor on the fourth floor of our house. When we returned, he and Father had a great reunion, each recalling how they'd managed to escape the Nazi terror. His wife could not have been more than twenty at the time, and was extraordinarily vivacious and charming. She never walked, but danced, and always had a smile on her face. I was twelve going on thirteen, and she was the first woman I really felt attracted to. I loved to see her laugh and dance, and really enjoyed being in her company.

One evening during the sacking spree, Mr. Grosz rushed over in a very agitated state. A group of soldiers began to pillage the building next to ours, and the shouts and screams were coming dangerously close. This was bad news, but it wasn't unexpected. Father quickly took a ladder and helped my mother up to a wide but almost hidden shelf behind the tank of the toilet. She crouched down as he covered her with old rags. Mr. Grosz hid his young wife in the cellar, where she curled up on an old mattress in a corner under a pile of blankets.

Mother made it, but Mrs. Grosz didn't. The Cossacks didn't think to look above the water tank of the toilet, but they knew to look for women in cellars. They discovered Mrs. Grosz and dragged her away. It was not difficult to imagine what a great find she must have been for the soldiers.

Three days later, Mrs. Grosz showed up in the middle of the night. She was hysterical and hardly able to walk, but had somehow managed to crawl up the four flights of stairs to their apartment. Her husband nursed her all through the night, and toward the morning, she finally fell asleep. Mr. Grosz then threw himself out of the fourth-floor window.

♪♪♪

In our own small family, everyone had survived. Two days after the tragedy involving the couple next door, I woke up to loud cries coming from the next room. They were joyful shouts, coming from my parents, grandmother, and Aunt Katalin, Uncle Pippa's wife. Curious, I opened the door and stuck my head in.

I found them all hugging and kissing a man in a tattered German uniform with the insignia torn off. He had an unkempt beard and long hair, and wore combat boots. I couldn't imagine who he was and why the family was so delighted to have him . . . until I got closer and saw his eyes. It was Uncle Pippa! Half a year ago, he had been drafted into the "work camp" reserved for Hungarian intellectuals of partly or wholly Jewish descent and of questionable loyalty to the Nazi cause. He was then shipped to Serbia to serve in the German army in their fight against the Russians.

Uncle Pippa told us what had happened. One day as his platoon was being marched across a clearing in a forest, a group of armed men materialized all around them, brandishing assorted rifles and submachine guns. The weapons had only one thing in common: they were all aimed at the German commanders in charge of the platoon. The Germans threw down their arms and were quickly taken prisoner. The Hungarians were then offered a choice: either leave in peace, or come and fight with them. My mild-mannered, introverted philosopher-uncle chose to fight. But he fought in his own way: although he was given a rifle, he refused to fire it at any human being. So he was assigned to watch over the German prisoners, with instructions to fire a warning shot if there was any trouble. With that assignment, he was content. Having to fire into the air, he said, he was sure not to hurt anybody. And, he added with a smile, he was also sure not to miss.

Uncle Pippa was part of Marshal Tito's resistance force for nearly six months, until the German army was fully removed from the Yugoslav territory. Then he was discharged and told that he could go home. He did so, but the journey to Budapest was not easy. It had to be covered mostly on foot, although he occasionally hitched a ride on a bullock cart or a horse-drawn carriage. It took him nearly three weeks. The last leg, from the periphery of the city to our house, was especially dangerous, since a German division was still fighting in the area. Uncle Pippa had to travel on foot under the cover of darkness, but was able to make it home just as dawn was breaking.

With the family happy and complete, we resumed the business of living. Eventually, the entire city came back to life. The first step to law and order was dramatic: after the three days of unrestrained pillaging, the regular Red Army simply shot anyone who was found to be out of line. For a day, the streets were littered with dead bodies, mostly Siberian Cossacks, but also some regular Red Army and a few civilians.

Life did go back to normal, but it remained adventurous. A German battalion was in possession of the hilly Buda part of town. From their elevated vantage point, the Germans fired heavy artillery shots into Pest, where the majority of people (including my family) were living. Day or night, the shots would appear out of nowhere and wreak destruction.

As I no longer held the naïve belief that I was immune from artillery fire, I began having frequent nightmares. I also developed a deep-seated fear of walking in open-air corridors that connect most apartments in the city. I felt as if they would give way at any moment. (To this day, I'm still apprehensive when encountering an open gangway on a higher floor or even stepping onto a balcony jutting out over the street. Old fears die hard.)

Despite the daily hazards, life normalized at an amazing pace. Emergency repairs were made to living quarters, shops were re-opened, and colorful neon signs over cafés and stores sprang up everywhere. Local residents went about greeting one another with smiling faces.

One day I woke to the familiar sound of "tap, tap" from below. Our ground-floor ladies' shoe factory was coming back to life!

Most people (except of course the former Nazi collaborators) were buoyed by a new life and vibrant spirit spreading throughout the city. Thousands had been deported and additional thousands had perished, but for the survivors, being alive was pure joy. People would get together, swap escape stories, and celebrate. I was not particularly interested in talking about what had happened, but I had a wonderful time meeting up with old friends and making new ones.

Shortly afterward, I went to see the Music Academy. The main concert hall had a gaping hole in the ceiling—another bomb that didn't explode. But the academy itself had been miraculously spared.

Under Mother's loving guidance, I went back to practicing the piano. The cataclysm was over. I celebrated my city's rebirth in my

own way, "living myself" into the music of my favorite composers
. . . Bach, Prokofiev and, above all, the great Hungarian composers
Bartók and Kodály.

♪♫♪♫♪♫

CHAPTER FIVE

A TALE OF TWO COMPETITIONS

The first music competition in which I ever took part was beset by mishaps. It was, it seems, doomed from the beginning.

It all started when I missed the chance to be selected as part of the official team sent by the Franz Liszt Academy. The music competition was the 1946 Concours International Marguerite Long–Jacques Thibaud (the International Marguerite Long–Jacques Thibaud Competition) in Paris. I was fourteen years old and had a special dispensation to participate—the lower age limit was fifteen. This was because I already had a notable music career behind me, having performed in numerous public concerts since I'd made my debut at the age of nine.

With permission from Paris in hand, my parents entered me in the auditions for the official team. At that time, Hungary was part of the Soviet bloc but was not yet a Communist state. The current Socialist regime was proud of the country's accomplishments in music, literature, and the arts and intended to showcase these achievements to bolster the country's status in the world. So the regime leaders decided to send an "official" team to the competition in Paris.

I learned the pieces I was to perform at the auditions—they were the same ones that were prescribed for the first round of the competition in Paris. I rarely referred to the score: Mother would play a piece for me, and I would then play it myself. I soon had the prescribed pieces committed to memory.

Mother and I showed up at the Franz Liszt Academy at the appointed time, and we waited until it was my turn to be called. This came after several hours, and I was getting impatient. The whole setup irritated me. I didn't like auditions; I was used to being onstage. But here the applicant sat in a curtained-off part of the room so that the jury wouldn't know who was playing. We were told not to speak or make any noise—just play the selection requested by the jury.

When my name was finally called, I sat at the piano and waited in silence. Finally a voice came from behind the curtain: "Play the Liszt Concert Étude no. 6." This was a mystery to me . . . I hadn't heard of that piece. I spread my arms out and looked at the other people in the hall for enlightenment. I had no such piece in my repertoire. I did prepare the Paganini Étude, but not the Liszt Concert Étude no. 6. The officials in the hall whispered vigorously for a while, and then one of them went behind the curtain to speak to the jury. A minute later, the voice behind the curtain said, "All right. Play Chopin's Fantasy in F Minor." This was not a problem, as it was one of the selections I had prepared.

I started playing. It so happens that this piece has a fairly long opening section that's *pianissimo* and *adagio*—that is, very soft and slow. I liked it, but this time I was not comfortable playing it. The incident had disturbed me, and I couldn't live myself into the music. Before I could get into the lively parts and show what

I could really do, the voice behind the curtain said, "Thank you. Next." The whisperers told me that I was to get up and leave.

Outside I told Mother what had happened, and she revealed that the Concert Étude no. 6 was in fact the Paganini Étude. The full and correct name of the piece was "No. 6 of the Great Violin Études of Nicolò Paganini transcribed for the pianoforte by Franz Liszt." At home, Mother simply called it "the Paganini Étude," and since I never looked at the score, I had no idea what its full name was.

Needless to say, I was not selected. We went home to tell Father, and he told us to go to Paris anyway. I could still enter the competition even though I wasn't on the official team representing Eastern Europe. Father said that he would come up with the funds for the trip, although this was not easy. The country had just emerged from the aftermath of World War II, and the economy was only beginning to show signs of life. The shoe factory founded by Grandfather was back up and running, but it didn't generate much of a profit yet. But Father insisted, Mother was all for it, and I could hardly wait for the adventure to start.

♩♩♩

The awaited adventure started soon. Mother and I embarked on the train bound for Paris, equipped with the travel documents issued for this particular occasion: a Hungarian national passport that was valid for two weeks, and a French entry visa authorizing a stay that could not be longer than the validity of the passport. Only three pianists were selected by the jury. One of them was Hédi Schneider, an attractive young lady in her twenties who made no bones about admitting that she had no real interest in the competition; nor did she desire a musical career—she just wanted to see Paris. Her real interests were to find a husband and have children. This admission was greeted with amusement and a bit of condescension by Mother, for whom music was the highest value in life and making a name on the concert stage the highest achievement.

I remember going to the Salle Gaveau in Paris to enter the first elimination test. The piano was on the stage, and the jury was sitting in the first row. I immediately felt at home and had no worries. Playing in public was always something I looked forward to and enjoyed, and playing for the jury members in this beautiful concert hall was no different.

I was given the choice to start with any of the pieces in the required repertory, and I chose the famous Paganini Étude, if for no other reason than to be able to play it at last. Besides, it was a real virtuoso piece, designed to show off the skills of the performer. I would show the jury that I could play it in a way few other pianists—and probably none of the other participants in the competition—could. So I started with a flourish. Instead of reaching the high A in the opening passage with the little finger of the right hand—which was relatively safe but produced a weak sound—I adopted the acrobatic solution of leaping over my right hand with my left and hitting the note with the left's strong middle finger.

This was in the spirit of the piece, since Paganini himself had been a fabulous virtuoso and evidently wrote this score to show what he could do on the violin. Liszt, himself a highly skilled performer, had also liked to show off his own technique on the piano and would hardly have objected to it being performed in this way.

This time, however, the unexpected and almost unthinkable had happened: *I missed*. I came down on the high B key instead of the high A. I was shocked! Although I quickly recovered, I couldn't really live myself into the music, and after a little while, I heard the polite but definite announcement from the jury: "Merci. Le prochain, s'il vous plaît" ("Thank you. Next, please").

There was nothing to do but get up and leave. Once again I wasn't selected. Hédi was more careful. She started with the Chopin Fantasy, a piece that didn't call for technical bravura, which gave her a good opportunity to express the romantic feelings that went well with her long blonde hair and blue eyes. Not only did she get through the first round, but she ended up winning first prize.

Later we heard that the organizers were keen on giving the top award to someone from behind the Iron Curtain to show that the competition was truly international, embracing young musicians from Eastern Europe for the first time since the war. And we were also told that Marguerite Long, the co-founder of the competition, had me in mind for first prize, but when I messed up the opening, she couldn't advance me to the next round. She said to Mother, "Bring him back next year."

The long train ride from Paris back to Budapest was again shared with Hédi, who now felt quite differently about her mission in life. She spoke of devoting herself to music and skyrocketing to fame as the great Hungarian piano genius. Actually, she got married soon after returning to Hungary and wasn't heard from again in the world of music.

♪♪♪

So ended my first experience of the wide world beyond my native Hungary. Up until then, my perspective had been limited to Budapest, the city capital, and an occasional summer vacation on the shores of Lake Balaton. I soon forgot the negative outcome of the adventure, and set forth my day-to-day routine, attending high school in the morning, practicing with Mother in the afternoon, playing ice hockey or soccer in the Városliget across from our house, and going for "philosophical" walks with Uncle Pippa. I was much in demand in Hungary, and gave concert after concert in Budapest as well as in the provinces, including my favorite town, Szeged.

1944. Jan. 16. **HARMONIA** Tisza szálló

ÉVAD 1943/44.

LÁSZLÓ ERVIN

ZONGORA-EST

MŰSOR:

1. J. S. B A C H Kromatikus Fantázia és Fuga

2. BEETHOVEN Szonáta Es-dur op. 31. No. 3.
   Allegro
   Scherzo
   Menuetto (Moderato e Grazioso)
   Presto con fouco

3. C H O P I N Grande Valse As-dur
   Bölcsődal
   Etüd Ges-dur

S Z Ü N E T

4. S C H U M A N N Papillons

5. DELIBES-
   DOHNÁNYI Coppélia valse
   LISZT:
6. Manók tánca

Ára 60 fillér

Febrnár 15. FARAGÓ GYÖRGY BEETHOVEN-EST (III. bérlet)

BARTOS NYOMDA

A typical recital program. Here I performed at the age
of eleven in Szeged, Hungary's second-largest city.

In June of '47, I became the youngest person ever to receive the coveted "Artist Diploma," the highest degree of the Franz Liszt Academy of Music. This required that I pass a theory exam, consisting of memorizing nearly two hundred Hungarian folk songs compiled by Béla Bartók and Zoltán Kodály. I had to recite some of the text, sing the main motifs, and analyze the origin and structure of each song. This was a feat I was able to perform for the examiners following a month of intense cramming, but would not have been able to repeat a week later. In any case, after listening to me sing for a while, the examiners mercifully dispensed with that part of the test—at fourteen years old, my voice was changing, and the sounds I was producing were surely not music to their ears.

The "practical" part of the exam consisted of a full recital in the great hall of the academy that was open to the public. Performing wasn't a problem for me, and nobody was surprised when the jury announced at its conclusion that they had unanimously decided to award the Artist Diploma to me. But they didn't hand over the Diploma right away but waited until the 14th of June. I turned fifteen on the 12th, and to the august members of the jury awarding it to a fifteen-year-old—still by far the youngest ever to receive it—was more acceptable than handing it to a mere fourteen-year-old.

After the recital, which was in the afternoon and was over by evening, my parents took me to Budapest's famous light-opera theater to see a colorful production of *The Merry Widow*. I remember sitting in the front row, looking at the beautiful leading lady dancing and singing, and clutching in my hand the shiny leather wallet I'd received as a present from my parents. This, I felt, was as close to perfect happiness as anyone could possibly get.

Unfortunately, this happy period didn't last long. A few days later, I was called to my father's study and told that there was worrisome news on the grapevine. The Moscow-trained Hungarian Communist Mátyás Rákosi was said to be ready to seize power in our country and establish a Stalinist dictatorship. What this meant was clear to Father: Even if our shoe factory was relatively small— it had less than a hundred workers in the best of times—and even if they were all union members and Father himself was a leading member of the Social Democratic Party, we would still be considered capitalists, and enemies of the people. Our factory would be nationalized, and my father wouldn't even be permitted to be an employee of his own company. He told me that we had to get out while we still could—before the descending Iron Curtain closed off all possibilities of escape.

Perhaps the last chance to get out legitimately—rather than being smuggled through the border at great risk—came when the Geneva-based Concours International d'Interprétation Musicale (International Competition of Musical Interpretation) was announced at the Franz Liszt Academy. It was the second time this competition had been held. The first one, the previous year, had been won by Friedrich Gulda, the Viennese pianist who was already widely known and would later achieve world fame. Young musicians who were at least fifteen years old were asked to audition for the official team, and I could qualify, as by then I had passed my fifteenth birthday.

But I'd had quite enough of trying out for the "official team," and Mother fully understood that. Once again, Father agreed to fund our trip so I could try out on my own instead. As registered participants in the *Concours*, we could obtain a Hungarian passport as well as a Swiss visa.

Before leaving, we had a short but memorable vacation in a bathing resort in the Eastern part of Hungary. I remember enjoying every minute of it, being keenly conscious that a far greater adventure than ever before would soon open up for me. I would be out in the wide world and this time there was no coming back.

So it came about that in September, I was back on the westbound express with Mother, this time headed for Zurich and then Geneva. This trip had a very different feel. We had two bulky pieces of luggage with us, and also a third—the really heavy one, which was crammed full with the scores of my musical repertoire. Our shoes were heavy as well: Father got the trusted workers of the factory to make shoes for us with double soles. Between the two layers of leather, we had stuffed all the Swiss francs that my father could buy for exorbitant prices on the black market. They had to be hidden, because other than a small amount to cover daily costs for the duration of the competition, it was illegal to possess foreign currency.

As the train pulled into Hegyeshalom, the border station, and the border guards came aboard, we sat holding our breaths and offering a silent prayer. One could never know if one would be searched; and discovering our stashed nest egg would have spelled an end to this grand adventure . . . and very likely prison for Father.

When the train gave a welcome lurch and crossed no-man's-land into Austria, we heaved a sigh of relief. Mother got into a conversation with the Austrians who boarded the train, and to my great surprise, I could follow what they were saying. I didn't know that I could speak German! I didn't speak it, in fact, because no more than a handful of words occurred to me, but I could understand most of what was said. When I told Mother, she reminded me that Franziska, an Austrian girl, had been with us as a *Kindermädchen*, or nanny, for several years. She'd been told to speak German to me, and while I would mostly reply in Hungarian, her German had evidently rubbed off. But then I turned six and was enrolled in first grade, and I told my parents that I had no further need for a nanny. Franziska was dispatched back to Vienna. All this came back to me as I listened to the soft Viennese lilt of the German spoken by our fellow passengers.

We changed trains in Zurich and boarded a swift and silent Swiss electric train. We crossed the Alps toward Geneva in the evening as a sight came into view that I have never forgotten: Lake Geneva, ringed by golden yellow lights along the shore, set off against the myriad twinkling silver lights of the city just above. This would be the first stop of my new life in the great wide world.

Our hosts in Geneva helped us find suitable accommodations and took us to a modest but scrupulously clean apartment not far from the lake. Our hostess was a white-haired, simple, and kind lady who only spoke French. She had a turtle named "Madame la Tortue" (*tortue* is French for "turtle") and implored us to be very careful not to step on her pet. Madame la Tortue was allowed to roam freely all over the apartment, including our room.

The apartment didn't have a piano, so our first concern was to find a place where I could practice. The Conservatory of Music provided it, and for the next several days I spent half the day at the conservatory and half exploring Geneva, not understanding a word of what people were saying. My newly discovered familiarity with German was no help at all here. But Mother got along well enough in French, and we looked forward to participating in the Concours.

I showed up for the first round of tests, having learned by heart the correct names of all the pieces that I could be asked to play. I passed the elimination rounds with flying colors and found myself in the finals. This was a public performance in Salle Victoria, with an international audience packing every seat. Having just turned fifteen, I was by far the youngest competitor and, therefore, became the center of attention. Journalists interviewed me, and Swiss radio aired the finals live. I was to perform Beethoven's *Emperor Concerto* accompanied by the world-renowned Orchestre de la Suisse Romande.

The performance went well. The orchestra was excellent, the hall was beautiful, and the public was attentive and appreciative. I was deep into the music, and the entire performance seemed to pass in a flash.

That evening the jury announced that I had won the grand prize. The only disappointment was that it was going to be shared by another pianist nearly twice my age (rumor had it that he had been promised the prize in the previous year's competition). I was interviewed extensively and had my hand shaken and back patted innumerable times.

I was a celebrity, but no one could tell us where we should, or even could, go from here. It was assumed that we would return to Hungary.

A return was not an option, however; the Iron Curtain was descending and the imposition of a Stalinist dictatorship seemed imminent. It began, in fact, a few months later, in January 1948.

What next? Our passport was only valid for two weeks and so was our Swiss visa. We could always apply for political asylum, but if we stayed away, what would happen to Father in Budapest? Everyone knew that the families of dissidents were harshly punished, and could even be imprisoned until the dissidents returned. But this threat was soon removed.

The Hungarian consul in Geneva came to see us in the apartment where we were staying. Our hostess greeted him enthusiastically, as she had followed my progress at the competition with rapt attention, and introduced him to Madame la Tortue. The consul then presented me with a medal. It was inscribed "For the Victory at Geneva" and was signed "Zoltán Tildy, President of Hungary." I have kept it to this day; it sits on a bookshelf next to my desk.

The consul told us that our passports had been extended, and we could travel anywhere in Europe—we just had to get the necessary visas. I was now a feather in the cap of the Hungarian State, and nobody would even think of harming Father or any other relative of mine. The following day Mother and I went to the French consulate and had a six months' visa stamped into our passport.

The great adventure was becoming a reality. We were out in the wide world . . . and we were there to stay.

♪♩♪♩♪♩

CHAPTER SIX

WINTER IN PARIS

It was late September in the year 1947 when I again found myself with Mother on the train bound for Paris. This time the train departed from Geneva, and our visit promised to be very different from the first. After all, I had recently received an international prize as well as an official decoration, and had Hungary's most prestigious music degree in my pocket.

Upon arrival, we decided to visit Marguerite Long, the head of the music school that conducted my ill-fated stint in the competition the year before. Mother recalled that Madame Long had invited me to take part in the competition the following year and implied that I'd have a very good chance of winning first prize. But now that I'd won the competition in Geneva, everything had changed. I was already a star and was treated as such in the "master classes" that Mme. Long invited me to attend.

During these classes, two or three students would perform before a very elegant, exclusive audience. Mme. Long, dressed in flowing robes with an enormous hat that was all feathers and flowers, would sit in an armchair that looked more like a throne. She was dressed to the hilt and looked amazing. Nobody could guess her age, but it was certain—and public knowledge—that she had been the longtime mistress of the French composer Maurice Ravel. Several of Ravel's famous pieces had been written for her.

When a student's performance ended, Mme. Long would comment on it and offer a few words of advice—as much for the benefit of her adoring audience as for the student. Then everyone would applaud, and the next performer would take a seat at the piano. Her comments to me were in such flowery French that I hardly ever understood a word, although I'd picked up everyday expressions rather quickly. I did grasp, however, that she was enthusiastic and complimentary. She was grooming me for the prize the next fall.

I never did win the International Marguerite Long–Jacques Thibaud Competition. This wasn't because I was unable to qualify or for any lack of goodwill; it was simply due to the fact that I was no longer in Paris when the competition took place. I was in America, playing three or four concerts a week and fighting my own battle . . . but that's another story altogether.

♪♪♪

The way Mother and I lived in Paris was quite remarkable. We had no money other than the cash we carried in our shoes, and that didn't go very far. I did receive a modest fee for the concerts I was asked to give, and I enjoyed a certain celebrity status as the Hungarian prodigy who won the prize in Geneva. But several people came to our help. A kind man whose wife was Hungarian offered us a free room above his shop. The location was fabulous— in the heart of Paris, just off the famous Avenue de l'Opéra and two steps from the Louvre—but the room wasn't exactly the top of the line. It had no real bathroom (there was a toilet down the hallway), and there was just one small window high up on the side. It was dark and dingy. In addition, since the shop below sold fish, the apartment didn't exactly smell like eau de cologne. But it didn't cost anything and was in a prime location, so we moved in.

Once we had our lodging settled, our next problem was to figure out where I could practice. I needed about three hours a day at a reasonably good grand piano. This was solved in a single stroke by an elegant lady who approached me one day after one of Mme. Long's master classes. She was tall and slender and had clear, kind eyes, a youthful face, and prematurely gray hair. She also smelled wonderful—she, I realized, was a real *grande dame*. She told me that I could use her piano whenever I wished and for as long as I wished.

The generous lady turned out to be the Baroness Alix de Rothschild, the wife of Baron Guy de Rothschild of the great banking family. They had a mansion on a property that extended from the luxurious Avenue Foch to the fashionable Avenue Victor Hugo. The baroness had a studio on the Victor Hugo side and would visit it every so often to read and paint. It also had a grand piano that she rarely touched, and it was now at my disposal, day or night.

I was given the key to the mansion and another key to the studio in a separate building in the Rothschilds' private park. The studio smelled like paint and varnish, which didn't bother me, but it was also very chilly inside. You can't play the piano with cold, stiff hands. There was a kerosene stove in the corner, and the baroness made sure it was always full, but it couldn't burn continuously because it was a fire hazard. As a result, the studio was cold the first hour and warm and smelly during the second. But the piano was great, and the setting calm and inviting. Most important, I could come by and practice whenever I wished.

Posing for a portrait taken by Baroness Alix de Rothschild
in her studio on Avenue Victor Hugo.

Every once in a while the baroness would show up. She would sit quietly and listen, and then leave just as quietly as she came in. I liked having her around; when she was there, I could instantly live myself into the music. Sometimes she would ask me if everything was well or if I was hungry. If I said that I was a bit hungry, which was often, she would invite me to the house when I finished practicing. There my meal was served by a uniformed footman in a small dining room on the first floor.

Sometimes I'd be invited to a dinner given by Baron Guy de Rothschild. These were gala occasions, held in the main dining room. The butler, assisted by several footmen, would serve one course of delicacies after another. The sommelier, who presented the various wines, was unsure if he should serve me the first time I was there. Perhaps he thought I was too young, but the baroness winked at him, indicating that it was all right. So the sommelier treated me just as he did the other guests, showing me various bottles and whispering the name of each. One bottle was called *Chablis,* and that sounded interesting, so I chose that. Both my host and hostess watched this episode, and smiled approvingly. It was a good choice. I was advanced to the status of standard guest at the Rothschild mansion.

After the meal, having been escorted downstairs along with the other guests by the baron, I would pass by the chauffer-driven limousines at the main door and let myself out at the Victor Hugo entrance. I would walk over to the métro station down the street and take the train to the Avenue de l'Opera. My home address in the fashionable first arrondissement was approved by the baroness, but of course, she was unaware that it was a dark, smelly room above a fish shop.

Our existence was distinctly bohemian. I didn't go to school, and we had no regular income—it was a temporary existence. But for me it had a magical feel: days spent in the luxurious salons of Paris; nights in a kind of garret; all of Paris at my doorstep; and daily practice sessions at the Rothschild studio, often followed by dinner at the mansion.

At the town house of the Marquise de Talhouët in Paris.

One of the great aristocrats we had met, the Marquise de Talhouët, adopted me as her protégé and also took Mother under her wing. She insisted that Mother go with her to her favorite designer, and bought her a gown that became Mother's pride and joy. She would wear it for many years, and always when she accompanied me to my concerts.

Our friendship with the marquise and her husband was enduring. In the following years whenever I would come to Paris, I would stay at their town house off the Champs-Élysées. When I was newly married, my wife and I would visit them during the summer at their famous Chateau de Cirey, where Voltaire had lived from 1734 to 1749 as the guest of the Marquise du Chatelet.

It was not a bad interlude at all. I seemed to have "won" in Paris, too . . . without having even entered a competition.

♪♫♪♫♪♫

CHAPTER SEVEN

MY BIG DAY IN NEW YORK

The letter was unexpected. It was signed Baroness Erzsébet (Elisabeth) Weiss de Csepel, and was addressed to Mother in care of our Hungarian émigré friends in Paris, who duly delivered it to her. The writer of the letter was the special lady who attended my debut in Budapest: *the lady with the candy.* She was the daughter-in-law of Baron Manfred Weiss, the largest industrialist in Hungary. The baroness wrote to invite me to New York City for a debut recital in the United States.

The Weiss family, wealthy and of Jewish origin, was a prime target for the Nazis. Knowing this, they made sure to get out in time. They'd transferred as much of their wealth as they could to Swiss banks, and they themselves fled to Switzerland right before the German invasion. Soon after the war, they emigrated to the

United States and settled in New York. Once settled, the Baroness Weiss decided that she was not going to sit around idly, living off the family wealth, but would earn her own living. She had a degree in psychology from Hungary, and she intended to qualify as a practicing psychoanalyst in New York. After several tries and failures (the number of psychoanalysts recognized in the state was strictly limited, and there were many more applicants than could be admitted), she finally succeeded. The baroness was a remarkable woman and a dedicated patron of the arts. She'd never forgotten about me, and when she heard about my current achievements in Geneva and Paris, she decided that I must come to America.

The year was 1948, and Europe was still war torn. Artists, scientists, and those who had the means to travel—or were lucky enough to be invited by someone who did—flocked to the U.S.

Baroness Weiss went to see a concert agency in New York and asked if they would invite me for a U.S. debut. They agreed to do so, but they needed someone to guarantee the costs. The baroness quickly took out her checkbook and settled it on the spot.

With the arrangements concluded and a concert date set, she wrote to her friends in Paris to contact Mother. A concert stage was waiting for me in New York, the letter stated: the prestigious Town Hall. My American debut was scheduled for the 17th of April. The baroness would send the transatlantic tickets and reserve a room for us in town. Would we come?

This is Mother and me in Paris, just as we were leaving for New York.

Without a moment's hesitation, Mother said yes. She had always dreamed of my touring the world, going from city to city and triumph to triumph. Now this was about to begin with my debut in New York.

We said good-bye to the Baroness Rothschild (it appeared that I was going from one baroness to another), packed our two suitcases and the extra case with my musical scores, and boarded the train to the port city of Le Havre.

We arrived in the evening just as the sun was setting. As we looked out over the harbor, a fantastic sight met our eyes: an enormous ocean liner standing rock still on the mirror-smooth waters. It was lit up like a Christmas tree, and bits of music drifted to our ears. The ship, the SS *America,* didn't come into the harbor, since port facilities hadn't been reconstructed yet. Instead, the ship sent launches to the shore to pick up its handful of passengers from the French side. The great majority of passengers had embarked in Southampton and was already aboard.

As we approached the great ship, it towered over us. It was an enormous palace, with myriad round portholes on many levels. One of them opened, and a smiling face appeared. Next to it a door opened and a ramp was let down, and Mother and I clambered up. We found ourselves on a different planet: shining decks, flowers everywhere, and elegant uniformed stewards showing us the way. We were already in the New World.

Our cabin was modest, but we had it to ourselves—the baroness had made sure of that. Still, we ended up moving the following day. Mother, resourceful as always, asked to speak with the captain and told him about my background, and that I was on my way to a brilliant debut in New York. The captain said that he would gladly provide a superior passage, and asked if I would be willing to play a short concert one evening for the passengers. Mother agreed, and we were immediately moved to a luxurious cabin and invited to sit at the captain's table. This, truly, was paradise.

After my enthusiastically received concert, a well-dressed gentleman approached our table and asked if he could join us. He was of Hungarian origin and lived in New York. Frances, his pretty teenage daughter, was traveling with him. Although neither she nor I were yet sixteen, she was far more mature than I was, and was delighted to be in the company of a shipboard celebrity. She appeared to be quite taken with me, but this was not really reciprocated. I liked her, but we had nothing to talk about. This was partly because I knew only a few words in English . . . and partly because Frances seemed interested only in clothes, jewelry, and horses.

Frances's father wanted to seize the opportunity for a brilliant match for his daughter. At the end of the five-day trip, he proposed to Mother that they agree to a kind of pre-engagement between Frances and me—one that we would convert into a formal engagement when we reached eighteen (we were almost exactly the same age). Mother thought all of this was rather fantastic—a truly American way of doing things—and said, "Thank you, but no thank you." However, she and Frances's father agreed to stay in touch so that the teenagers could get better acquainted.

I did meet with Frances again—just once—at a memorable excursion to a ranch in the Catskill Mountains, north of New York City. She was decked out in a brand-new riding outfit and was very pretty and proud. She cantered gaily ahead, and my horse followed as best it could, with me clinging desperately to its neck. I'd never ridden before, and when I managed to dismount in one piece, I vowed that I would never do so again. And I certainly didn't in the days that followed, for I had other things on my mind.

♪♪♪

The 17th of April, the magical date of my American debut, was approaching. Mother and I counted first the days and then the hours. This was not the joyous anticipation I usually experienced; it was more like waiting for Judgment Day. We had nice rooms on the West Side near Central Park, but I didn't enjoy walking in the park or roaming the streets of Manhattan—my every waking moment was taken up with thinking about and preparing for the Big Day.

The approach of the Big Day had cast a shadow over everything. It deepened with each passing day, and my heart was beating faster and faster. The Hungarian emigré clan in the city filled our heads with the crucial importance of my New York debut, until it seemed that my entire life depended on it. If I failed, we would have to go back to the room above the fish shop in Paris, dragging with us the embarrassment that couldn't be ignored. I would be back to attending the master classes of Madame Long, but I would no longer be a star. And perhaps I also wouldn't have much of a chance of winning first prize at her next competition.

Mother did her best to distract me by playing cards and talking about neutral subjects. She even played gin rummy with me in the dressing room backstage at the Town Hall, right up until the very last moment. Then she gently pushed me onstage and went to hide in a faraway room. She was so nervous that she couldn't bear to hear how I played.

The excitement leading up to this critical day tuned all of my senses to the highest pitch. I lived myself into each piece, and the two-hour recital seemed to take only a few minutes.

Afterward, we returned to our room on the West Side and I slept late the next morning. Whatever the outcome, the nagging uncertainty would soon be over.

After breakfast, we went to see the people at the concert agency on 57th Street. When we arrived, we were shocked. As soon as the elevator door opened on the 14th floor, flashbulbs popped and a whole troop of reporters rushed at me—it had seemed that sentinels were dispatched to await my arrival. The manager, who had been nice if rather distant beforehand, greeted us with a big smile, bearing flowers for Mother and a pitcher of Coke and cookies for me. There were secretaries and other people all over the place, waiting to catch sight of me.

After a photo session, the reporters were told to wait outside while the manager talked to Mother. What was going on?

A publicity photo taken immediately after my debut in New York.

It turned out that the great dailies of the time—*The New York Times*, the *New York Herald Tribune*, and the *New York World-Telegram and Sun*—carried what people afterward told us were rave reviews. The *Times* had titled its review: "Hungarian prodigy scores in debut recital" and said straight out: "He has few peers

MUSIC

WITH QUIET SATISFACTION VETERAN MAESTRO BRUNO WALTER LOUNGES

WHILE LISTENING TO YOUNG ERVIN LASZLO PLAY BACH AND CHOPIN

HUNGARIAN PRODIGY

Music critics call 15-year-old Ervin Laszlo the equal of almost any pianist, young or old

New York's music critics are notoriously jaded listeners. When they show evidence of wakefulness, something unusually good is apt to be happening. Last month they nearly jumped out of their seats at the debut of a dark-haired, 15-year-old Hungarian named Ervin Laszlo, who tackled the piano with a flawless technique and a mature understanding that caused the *Times* to place him "among the outstanding keyboard artists of the present time" and the *Herald Tribune* to say "he has few peers among pianists of any age, young or old." Concert managers and musicians rushed to hear Laszlo. For Bruno Walter the boy gave a private concert (*above*). "You play beautifully," said the great conductor.

CONTINUED ON NEXT PAGE

Life magazine's report on my New York debut.

BENDING OVER THE PIANO, spreading his large hands over the keyboard, Laszlo plays with an intensity that mesmerizes audience and himself.

HE IS AN EARNEST, INTENSE BOY

Ervin Laszlo is earnest, extremely boyish even for 15 and not noticeably affected by the tributes of Manhattan's critics, one of whom described him as "the most remarkable young pianist encountered in 20 years." When such bigwigs of American pianism as Horowitz, Schnabel and Serkin paid their respects, he hoped, shyly, that he might be able to continue studying with one of them. Laszlo was not, in fact, unaccustomed to success. Son of a Budapest shoe manufacturer and a piano-playing mother, he had started studying the piano when he was 5, had given a concert with the Budapest Symphony when he was 9 and had begun a triumphant European career. This was abruptly halted when the Nazis came in 1944. His Jewish father was put in a concentration camp and Ervin took refuge with a Swedish diplomat. Columbia Artists Management Inc. brought him and his mother to the U.S. last March. When the excitement of his Town Hall debut was over he embarked on a round of Manhattan sightseeing, visiting the circus, eating hot dogs at the Central Park Zoo and making a special trip to the Statue of Liberty, which he had missed seeing on his arrival.

WITH HIS MOTHER Ervin Laszlo grins as he clutches a hot dog on the terrace of the cafeteria in Central Park Zoo. His father is arriving this summer.

among pianists of any age." Other reviewers compared me to the greatest artists of the world and did not spare superlatives in describing my performance.

A Hollywood-style whirlwind started, with paparazzi on every corner, a manager assigned to me as a personal guide, and well-publicized meals at fashionable restaurants. *Time, Newsweek,* and other newsmagazines carried the story illustrated with photos.

Two days later, in a voice hushed with awe, my manager announced that *Life* magazine wanted to do a major spread. They would send reporters and photographers, and we were to go with them to the places they selected.

The editors of *Life* had arranged for Bruno Walter, the German-born conductor of the New York Philharmonic, to be photographed listening to me in his Park Avenue apartment. Very likely quite put out by this invasion of reporters and photographers, the famous maestro managed to smile benignly while I pretended to play on his piano. There was no time to actually play anything, since as soon as I started, the flashbulbs went off and I was told, "Okay! Let's go on to the next place!"

The next stop was Central Park, where we looked at the animals and then dined at the open-air restaurant. The photographers kept snapping away. The photos and story ended up in a May 1948 issue of *Life*.

After having been courted by other concert agencies with competitive offers, we signed a favorable three-year contract with Columbia Artists Management (called at the time Columbia Concerts), the leading U.S. concert bureau.

Mother, on the advice of our newfound friends and well-wishers, insisted that I was not to be overworked and exploited. Thus, the contract guaranteed a generous monthly income independent of the number of concerts I would actually perform. We moved into a full-service, furnished apartment on Central Park West; and the Steinway company, having signed me on to play their instruments exclusively, shipped us a brand-new grand piano.

It was springtime, and I was free to do whatever I pleased. Everybody around me advised that I should take some time to relax and enjoy myself. The paparazzi invasion ceased, but people would often stop me on the street and ask if it was my picture that they had seen in *Life*. It was all very strange, yet also very wonderful. Despite all of this attention, I grew depressed and felt worse than I'd ever felt in my whole life. I was convinced that I was mortally sick.

♪♫♪♫♪♫

CHAPTER EIGHT

OH LORDIE, LORDIE!

"Lordie! Come back, Lordie!" I shouted. But Lordie didn't seem to hear me. The blond cocker-spaniel puppy kept barking excitedly at the tree where the chipmunk had disappeared. There was no way that I could distract him and make him stop barking. Two elderly ladies watched disapprovingly.

"You should train your dog better," one said.

"And don't call him 'Lordie,'" added the other woman. "You cannot use the name of our Lord for a dog!"

This amazed me. When thinking of names for the excitable puppy we'd just acquired, I thought of dignified English lords. Calling him "Lordie" seemed like a fun idea. At this point, I had been in America all of six weeks and had picked up English fast, but I was far from being proficient. It never occurred to me that

God could be called Lord, and that giving a puppy the name Lordie would be to take His name in vain.

"Okay," I replied, "so I shall call him 'Goldie.' Goldie, come!" I cried, but still to no avail. Eventually, Lordie/Goldie got tired of trying to catch the chipmunk and decided to return to me. The elderly ladies nodded in approval, and Goldie and I walked back to our apartment on Central Park West.

I was supposed to be happy, enjoying my laurels and new life . . . but I wasn't. I was certain that I'd developed brain tumors of the worst kind. My days were numbered.

♪♪♪

It all started a week or so after my tumultuous New York debut. Reporters were kept away, and friends and well-wishers were screened, and I was told to explore Central Park or go shopping on Fifth Avenue and not to have a worry in the world. There was no need to even practice regularly. My next concert performance wasn't until the fall, and there was the whole summer before us. All I had to do was relax and have fun.

But I was not enjoying myself. The events of the past weeks and months had led to something close to a nervous breakdown. Weeks of waiting for the "Big Day" and the Hollywood-style celebrity whirlwind that followed were the last straw. When I was left with nothing to do but try to enjoy myself, all the stresses and excitements seemed to have caught up with me.

The trauma of the war wasn't that far removed, although it felt like what had happened in Budapest was from another lifetime. That was in early 1945, and now we were in the late spring of '48. I'd survived the blast of a real bomb, and then I'd "bombed" myself in one international music competition and won another. I had narrowly escaped with my mother from behind the Iron Curtain and lived a hand-to-mouth existence in Paris, alternating between a cramped, smelly apartment and luxurious mansions and salons.

And then came the journey from war-torn Europe to the New World—and the conquest of that world.

In the midst of all this, there wasn't time for me to stop and reflect on how I felt; it was an amazing adventure where one thing led to another. But now things were different. There was nothing to do but walk around and soak up the sun. Instead, I collapsed.

I didn't feel well in my skin, even if the only thing that really hurt was my head. My head ached when I got up in the morning, and ached when I went to bed at night. Mother took me to a friendly Hungarian-American doctor who did a thorough check-up and found nothing wrong. As I was lying on the examination table, she chatted with my mother, and recounted that the great George Gershwin had also experienced headaches. In his case, however, they were caused by a brain tumor, which eventually led to the composer's death.

Oh yes, I said to myself, *now I know what's wrong with me. No wonder the reporter from* Life *called me "an earnest, intense boy"— I was mortally ill!*

Even though the doctor told me that I would be okay, I convinced myself that I had a brain tumor, which of course worried me and made my head ache even more. Mother realized that the situation was getting out of hand and something had to be done. The doctor said that I was overstressed and needed a distraction, and Mother thought that a dog would be just the right thing. And so we went to a pet shop on Broadway and bought the cute puppy we saw in the window. That was Goldie, formerly known as Lordie.

It wasn't enough. I walked with Goldie on the streets and walked with him in Central Park, and although he was a great companion, I couldn't stop thinking about my "terminal malady." I was sure that my headaches would continually worsen until it was time to take me to the hospital . . . and I would never get out again.

This thought was much worse than waiting for the Big Day a month earlier. Now I knew that the fateful day would arrive, but I also knew that when it did, there would be no other day to follow.

I explained my suspicions to Mother, but didn't dare make it sound serious so as not to worry her. She assured me that I had been thoroughly checked and there was nothing wrong with me, but *I* knew better. She even took me to a specialist who examined my eyes, and then patted my shoulder and smiled, saying, "You'll get over it. Just relax and take vitamins. Being a celebrity has its price, after all."

My manager had experience with child prodigies; he had been the impresario of the world-famous violinist Yehudi Menuhin since Menuhin was eight. After taking one look at me, he told Mother that we should spend some time in the country, among cows and chickens, and then I'd be as good as new. He called the renowned Austrian-born American pianist Rudolf Serkin, who agreed to take me under his wing. Serkin lived in the country, on a hill above Brattleboro, Vermont. I could visit him whenever I wished, playing the piano for him and playing in the garden with his children.

Mother and I went to Vermont and looked for lodgings in the area. We settled on a small cottage near the tiny hamlet of Green River. It was owned by the Van Waverens, a friendly farming family of Dutch origin. The cottage was small, and there was, of course, no piano in it. Nor was there space for one. Yet I needed a grand piano and the Steinway company offered to provide one for me.

When the Steinway people learned the size of the cottage, they wanted to send an upright piano, but Mother objected vigorously. Even baby grands had what was known as "accelerated action," which was fine for beginners and amateurs, but not for professional pianists. Such a keyboard felt very different from that of a concert grand. Practicing on anything less than a shorter version of a concert grand—a so-called Model B (full-size grands were marked with the letter *D*)—wouldn't help me prepare me for the concerts that awaited me in the fall.

We asked for a Model B grand and were told that this would take up most of the room: we would hardly have space to squeeze by. But no matter, I had to have it. Mother wired Mr. Greiner, the friendly manager at Steinway Hall, to send the grand piano in any case. A few hours later Mr. Greiner, who had a sense of humor, wired back: "Sending grand piano in piano case." It arrived two days later.

I started practicing, but something was wrong. The magic was gone—I couldn't live myself into the music. My playing, in addition to everything in my life, felt flat, lifeless. There were cows on the pastures and chickens at the Van Waveren farm, there was a picturesque covered bridge over a small stream, and there were many beautiful walks in the neighboring countryside . . . but to me, it was all like a vaguely threatening black-and-white movie. After all, what good were they for me, seeing that I was mortally ill. . . .

The weekly visits to the Serkin house lacked magic, too. Wisely, Serkin didn't insist on having me play; we just talked about music and performing, and then he would himself play something on the piano. Afterward, we'd go outside and play ball with his children. And I did my best to push thoughts about my fatal condition out of my mind.

That was how I passed my first summer in the New World. It was bad, but not hopelessly so. I had just turned sixteen, and the will to live and enjoy life seemed to slowly reassert itself. It helped when we moved back to the city and I had to start getting ready for my concert tours. I still had a morbid fear of hearing the words *brain tumor* and couldn't look at anything that had to do with doctors and hospitals, even if it was in a movie. But I began to practice seriously, and once in a while, the magic would happen. I could once again live myself into the music.

The "puppy cure" had to be given up, unfortunately. In the city, Goldie was even more depressed than I was. He had become a country dog. He hated hot, hard pavement and loud noises, and chipmunks in Central Park no longer held the same fascination. He became paranoid and feared the police cars and fire engines that would zoom down Central Park West with their wailing sirens and blazing horns. Goldie would hide under the bed and growl at anyone who came near him.

This was no life for a nice country dog, so Mother asked around and found a kind gentleman who lived on Long Island and was willing to adopt him. The last I saw of Goldie was him walking down the corridor with the leash held by the gentleman, looking up at him in astonishment, as if he were saying, "Who is this, now, taking me for a walk?"

♪♫♪♫♪♫

CHAPTER NINE

A SURPRISE MEETING IN WASHINGTON

Starting in the fall, I played all over the country and traveled with Mother, mostly by train. I became quite an expert at getting dressed and undressed in an upper berth, and was also good at shaking hands with admirers and hugging starry-eyed girls after concerts.

In the spring, I was scheduled to give a recital in Washington, D.C.'s Constitution Hall. That was to be my last concert in the U.S.; a week later, Mother and I were to return to Europe. We had no choice. We had come on a six months' visitor's visa, which could only be extended once, for an additional six months. We had already extended ours, and when the year was up, we had to

A fairly usual scene after a concert.

leave or risk being deported. A quick return was also out of the question: we couldn't obtain another visitor's visa, and a regular immigration visa on a Hungarian passport would require us to wait our turn for six years if not more.

But we didn't end up leaving . . . and neither were Mother and I deported. After the concert at Constitution Hall, an elegantly dressed gentleman with a friendly face and smiling eyes came to see me. He looked familiar. The young man at his side made the introductions: "Meet Senator Pepper." Of course! The memory of an amazing evening in Budapest in 1945 came flooding back.

The American embassy held a reception for visiting VIPs who came to meet the chiefs of the Red Army, which was occupying Hungary. One was General Keys and the other was the influential Senator Claude Pepper of Florida. The Cultural Affairs Officer wanted to have Hungarian musicians performing at the reception, but instead of the usual gypsy band, he decided to acquire "serious" artists. I had been recommended, together with the young tenor Miklós Vári-Weinstock, whose fabulous voice created a sensation the preceding week at the opera.

I was not yet thirteen at the time, and Senator Pepper wanted to know how I came to be an accomplished pianist at such an early age, where I studied, and what I had hoped to do now that the war was over. I was tremendously impressed by him and the general, and even more by the delicacies provided by the embassy. There were chocolate cakes, ice cream, and tropical fruit. Even candied tropical fruit, my old favorite! I had not seen such things for a long time.

Now in Washington, Senator Pepper remembered meeting me at the reception in Budapest, and having seen the announcement of my recital in Constitution Hall, he'd decided to visit. He came backstage after the concert and shook my hand. He was a thoroughly warm and kind gentleman. We chatted for a while, and then the senator was ready to leave and started walking toward the door. Fortunately, he turned around at the last moment.

"Is there anything that I can do for you?" he asked.

Mother replied in my stead: "We're leaving next week, returning to Paris."

"Why? Don't you like it here?"

Mother explained that we did, indeed, but that our visas were expiring.

"Would you like to stay?"

"Of course!" I said it with such fervor that the senator smiled.

"All right, then. Come to my office tomorrow morning."

On the following day the senator had his young aide draw up a so-called private bill that he would introduce into Congress. It requested full immigration status for me, issuing in citizenship on the basis of exceptional merit. The bill wouldn't come up for formal adoption for several months, but Senator Pepper explained that while it was pending, I (and also Mother, the closest relative of a future citizen) wouldn't face deportation.

"Now you can stay and play all the concerts you wish!"

♪♪♪

In the following years I toured all over the United States and performed in forty-seven of the forty-eight continental states (the "missing" state was Arkansas, but it wasn't skipped on purpose—it was just due to scheduling conflicts).

My tours were fun and rewarding. As soon as I'd arrive in a new town, I'd ask my local hosts to point me in the direction of interesting and picturesque sights. Leaving my suitcase at the hotel, I'd take off with my two cameras hanging around my neck. One was for 35mm color slides, and the other was my pride and joy: a prewar Rolleiflex camera with an original Zeiss Tessar lens, a gift from my grandfather who told my parents before he died that it should come into my possession when I turned twelve. I took black-and-white pictures with it and developed the film myself. I made artistic enlargements of my best shots and hung them on the walls of our apartment and gave them to my best friends. Sadly, my prized camera was later stolen outside New York's Grand Central Station when I'd left my car for a moment to pick up a friend at the Yale Club. The thief broke the glass of the small side window and discovered the camera in the glove compartment. This took place in less than a minute—a thoroughly professional job, but one that I've failed to appreciate.

I also collected articles and reviews of my performances, packed up the gifts people brought me backstage—I no longer received just candied fruit—and took home the rolls of film I exposed to develop. I had no other care or concern in the world. My manager handled the professional part of my existence, and Mother saw to the everyday aspects. The headaches that had vexed me began to diminish, and then they ceased entirely. It dawned on me that perhaps I wasn't fatally ill after all.

The program from my recital at Carnegie Hall. I took the photo of myself using the self-release of my Rolleiflex; I also developed the print in my improvised darkroom at home.

There were other "Big Days" in the course of my concert tours, even if none was as significant as my debut in New York City. Some performances were more critical than others; some could make or break a career in a single night. Giving a recital at Carnegie Hall, for instance, was one of those monumental events. Another was appearing with the Philadelphia Orchestra.

I recall the night when I was looking out the window of my hotel across the street from the Philadelphia Academy of Music, watching the elegantly dressed audience members gather by the entrance. To me, it looked as if they were coming to witness an execution . . . or perhaps to celebrate a triumph? Fortunately, that evening turned out to be the latter. On the suggestion of conductor Eugene Ormandy, the orchestra's manager booked me the very same night for a return engagement the following season.

Between tours I would return to the apartment I shared with Mother in Forest Hills on Long Island. Father joined us two years later; he stayed at first in Paris and then in Cuba, waiting for a visa so he could come to the U.S. When I received formal citizenship, he was allowed to enter the country, and he soon found work at a major insurance company downtown. Although Father's English wasn't perfect, he was at home with numbers. He thoroughly enjoyed his work and was good at it.

With our family reunited, my life seemed to have settled into a pleasant enduring pattern. But further adventures were just around the corner.

♪♫♪♫♪♫♪

CHAPTER TEN

THE HAZARDS OF TURNING EIGHTEEN

When I turned eighteen, my manager pulled me aside and said, "You are now a young man, Ervin, and your mother needn't do all this traveling with you." That was all right with me, and in the end Mother understood as well. But then Uncle Sam made the same discovery, and he was far less understanding. He said, "I want *you*"—for the U.S. Army.

I was subject to compulsory draft. The Korean War had started on June 25, 1950, and the young men who were drafted faced the prospect of being shipped to Korea and sent into the trenches. It wasn't a prospect that my mother—or any mother at the time—contemplated with joy. When the dreaded letter arrived— starting with "Greetings!" and ending with the order to show up at the nearest induction center—Mother ran to see the Baroness

Erzsébet. She was a successful psychoanalyst by then and would surely be able to advise us on what to do.

The baroness knew about my headaches and my "fatal illness," and suspected that they were linked with traumatic wartime experiences. She made an appointment for me to see a well-known psychoanalyst who would delve deeper into these events and their implications.

I had precisely two sessions with this renowned shrink—he said no more were needed. The first began with the usual questions about my early childhood and continued with queries regarding my current sex life. We passed over the latter quickly, as I didn't *have* a sex life (it was a year later that I would meet my first girlfriend, as well as a group of young people who became my best friends). During the second session, we discussed my wartime experiences. I told the doctor everything, from my fear of my family being discovered by the Nazis to the house next to ours being hit by a bomb. I also described the disturbing sights that Mother had tried to prevent me from seeing. Afterward, the doctor confirmed that my "fatal illness" was, without a doubt, related to these traumatic experiences.

The traumas that sparked my nervous collapse after the New York debut didn't disappear overnight. My headaches were nearly gone, but I still couldn't bear to hear about serious illnesses, especially brain tumors. Whenever I did, my head would start swimming, and if I didn't quickly bend down to increase the flow of blood to my brain, I would black out. I reacted almost as badly as Goldie did to the sound of sirens from passing fire engines—they triggered memories of the air-raid whistle that sounded when a bombing attack was about to start. The sight of the horrible bloodied shape on the staircase in Budapest continued to haunt my dreams, and I would often wake up trembling.

The analyst told me not to hide these complaints when the Army psychiatrist examined me, and so I didn't. The psychiatrist scribbled a note and told me to hand it to the chief induction officer. The officer looked at the note and then at me, and said, "Go home. You are rejected." I tried to look upset, but it wasn't easy. I wasn't all that dejected . . . and I can't say that Mother would have been either.

♪♪♪

Uncle Sam didn't release me entirely. I was deemed fit to join the USO, the Army's entertainment corps, which was made famous by the appearances of Bob Hope, Bing Crosby, and many other Hollywood stars. As a "serious" artist, I wasn't expected to entertain the frontline troops; rather, my job was to foster good relations with civilian populations in countries that hosted U.S. troops overseas. I was given the rank of captain, although I didn't have to wear a uniform; and in any case, the rank was valid only in the unlikely event that I was captured.

My first assignment was in Iceland. I was to give a series of concerts there, performing music by Aaron Copland and other American composers.

At the Air Force base just outside New York, I found that my travel companion was the young but already world-famous Russian-born American violinist Isaac Stern. We sat together on the backward-facing seats of the propeller-driven MATS (Military Air Transport Service) plane that took us to the U.S. base in Keflavík.

When we arrived, we were told that the local time was seven, but it wasn't clear whether it was seven in the morning or the evening—it was the month of December, and it would have been dark in either case. We were whisked away by an Army jeep that was waiting to drive us to comfortable quarters in the capital city of Reykjavík. But first we were taken to a reception in our honor.

The next few days seemed to be one reception after another, interspersed with short performances. We gave up trying to find out whether it was day or night—no one seemed to care anyway. If we were able to look out a window between eleven and three and saw a soft glow, then we knew it was daytime.

Formal concerts were scheduled first in Reykjavík, then in the Arctic Circle town of Akureyri. The people were gracious and appreciative; if this was Army life, I told Isaac, I certainly had no quarrel with it!

I had a few other "missions" to countries around the Mediterranean and in the Balkans, and then I was honorably discharged.

My service to Uncle Sam didn't end so soon, however. I'd received a call from the USIA (United States Information Agency, a part of the Department of State in Washington) asking if I would travel to conflict-prone regions as a "U.S. Goodwill Ambassador." I accepted and was dispatched to Israel and the Arab countries, where I would give concerts and speak about cultural life in America. These missions proved to be quite a bit more dangerous than the USO ones.

In the early 1950s, Arab countries wouldn't issue entry visas to anyone who had traveled to Israel. Since I had to visit both places, the Israeli embassy in Washington stamped my visa on a separate sheet so that I could remove it from my passport. With that taken care of, I was able to travel freely, flying in and out of Cyprus.

After my last engagement in Israel—speaking and playing at the frontier Ein Gev kibbutz below the Golan Heights—I was scheduled to proceed to Cairo, but there were no flights via Cyprus that would get me there in time. The USIA office in Jerusalem gave me a ticket for the daily flight to Cairo out of Amman. The only problem was that Amman is in Jordan, and I was in Israel. I was told not to worry and that I could cross by the Mandelbaum Gate, which served as a checkpoint between the Israeli and Jordanian sectors of Jerusalem.

The USIA car took me to the gate, and then I was told that I would have to go the rest of the way on foot. There were fortified military posts on both sides, with machine guns aimed at each other. In between was a cleared expanse: a no-man's-land. An Israeli soldier manning a machine gun told me to pick up my bag, walk calmly, and avoid making any sudden movements.

"Don't worry," the soldier added. "I'll cover you!"

That was certainly nice of him, but it didn't do much to soothe my nerves. What does being "covered" by a machine gun mean in practice? The prospect of being in the middle of a deadly crossfire was not reassuring. Would I survive?

I had to walk, and walk I did. After what felt like an eternity, I reached the Jordanian side. The soldiers were grinning at me there, too, and allowed me to pass. A USIA car flying an American flag was waiting to take me to the Amman airport. I ended up arriving in Cairo that evening in perfect time to start my lecture-performance, although I was hardly in a perfect state of mind.

Leaving Cairo was just as eventful as getting there, but in quite a different way. I was flying back to America and the first stop was Athens, Greece. I was on a "Connie," the nickname for TWA's Lockheed Constellation. Departure from Cairo was in the late evening, and half an hour after takeoff, we encountered an electrical storm over the Mediterranean. The sky was almost permanently lit by a series of lightning flashes, and the plane began to pitch and roll violently. The passengers were buckled up and gripping their seats tightly.

All of a sudden there was a tremendous bang, and a red floodlight lit up the right side of the plane. However, it wasn't a spotlight . . . it was a large flame, blowing behind the engine by the 200-mile-per-hour airstream under the wing. Like some malicious spirit, it was glowing and waving just outside my window. It illuminated the cabin eerily, making everything appear red. Looking out one of the oval windows, I saw that the number three engine—the one next to the fuselage on the right wing—had come to a stop. Its propeller blade was motionless. The plane was bucking ever more wildly and seemed out of control.

There was a single high-pitched scream from the front of the cabin, but it stopped abruptly. We all sat frozen in our seats, wondering how long we would remain in the air. The atmosphere inside shifted from a relaxing journey in a luxurious airliner to a terrifying experience in a flying coffin that was about to break apart and spew us into the stormy sea.

After an interminable period—which was probably not more than five minutes—the pitching began to subside and the lightning outside diminished. The flame went out, but kept reigniting.

It bathed the plane in an intermittent reddish glow, although this was less visible now, since the cabin lights were on again. The sense of being trapped in a flying coffin was no longer quite so overwhelming. Then the red glow went out and stayed out, and hope began to build in our hearts.

Four hours later (we were flying on three engines, and the captain was nursing them against overheating), dawn arrived and the sky began to lighten in the east.

We landed in Athens just as the sun emerged on the horizon. The cowling of the burned engine was black, but cheerful young mechanics placed ladders against the wing and began removing it. They worked on the engine for an hour, finally installing a brightly polished covering in place of the blackened one, and gave the pilot a thumbs-up. He announced that we were ready to continue our trip, and the next stop was Paris.

The nightmare was over, but the effect it had on me persists to this day. It's not necessarily negative—on the contrary, it elicits a joyful feeling, a sense of celebration. The sun is shining, the world is bright and warm, and I am alive. Absolutely, fully alive.

It was the same feeling I remembered having in Budapest, when in 1945 the city came back to life. It's a wonderful sensation. I draw on it whenever dark clouds gather on the horizon.

♪♫♪♫♫♪

PART II

THE
ROMANTIC
YEARS

CHAPTER ELEVEN

ROMANCES AND INITIATIONS

She gave me a warm hug, opened the door, and disappeared inside. I stood for a moment staring at the door, then turned around and ran down the stairs. I was elated yet composed, and felt utterly fulfilled. I was in love.

Earlier that day I had been taking pictures of Debbie* in Brooklyn's Prospect Park. I snapped photos of her posing in front of a fountain, sitting on a bench, holding flowers, and walking down a path . . . she was always smiling. Smiling at *me*. I could hardly wait to go home and develop the film.

During the following day, we would go walk somewhere else, and I would take more pictures of Debbie. We would hold hands,

---

*In this chapter—but only in this chapter—I have changed the names of the young people I was involved with in order to protect their privacy.

and when it came time to say good-bye, she would give me a big hug. It was a wonderful life.

I was living at the time in the comfortable apartment I first shared with Mother and then also with Father in Forest Hills on Long Island. I would practice the piano in the morning, and if I were so inclined, I'd drive around the city in the afternoon and explore. I obtained my driver's license when I turned seventeen and a year later I bought my first car, which was a two-door Oldsmobile with Hydra-Matic drive—the first series-produced car with a fully automatic transmission. I later exchanged it for a Packard Patrician, a sleek and beautiful car that I was very proud of. Even today, it would be considered chic and impressive.

The first year Mother and I lived in Manhattan I was enrolled in the Professional Children's School, where most of the students were musicians or young actors performing on Broadway and didn't have the time to go to school every day. Like the other students, I attended classes when I was in town, and the rest of the time I completed written assignments. I enjoyed attending the classes, but I wasn't crazy about the homework. Mother, as well as my manager, our friends, and my self-appointed mentors, told me not to worry about it. I already possessed the highest degree in music from Budapest and wasn't likely to need anything else. Whether or not there was another sheepskin on the wall over the piano made no difference. So I didn't bother to take the exams and left school without graduating.

Over the course of the next few years, the mental and physical effects of the war gradually faded, and my life brightened. Then it became really bright: In the spring of 1951, I met a group of young people who soon became my best friends. And I also met a girl—in fact, two girls. Debbie was one of them.

Debbie was my first love. This was a kind of puppy love, but it was sincere. And it was wonderful. Until then I didn't really know any girls and wasn't interested in meeting any. My life was full, giving fifty or sixty concerts a year, conquering new audiences, exploring new cities, and expressing my feelings through living myself into the music.

These young people were a brainy and artistic lot, deeply into art and literature. Robin, the leading spirit of the group, aspired to be a poet. His girlfriend, Sherry, was a fan of Virginia Woolf and an avid reader of the Romantic poets. Debbie was born in Belgium, loved music, and aspired to be a teacher. They all took classes at the New School for Social Research, and I audited the classes with them.

We had long discussions about life and literature. I recalled my walks with Uncle Pippa in Budapest: the questions he raised about the meaning of life, the harmony that reigns in nature but not in society, and the mistakes people (and sometimes entire countries) make when they are intolerant and attack each other. My friends listened avidly and suggested that I start writing my ideas down. I did—in the form of the short stories we all wrote and read to each other after our classes.

I remember one of my stories particularly well. It was about a snowball, a tiny speck of which detached itself on a steep slope high in the mountains. It grew and grew, picking up more snow that covered the slope. The snowball eventually became a brilliant ball that transformed everything it touched, lifting the entire landscape into a higher, loftier dimension. The people who saw it were awed and were themselves transformed. They sought to become as pure in their hearts as the snowball was.

Debbie was always ready to discuss my ideas. She was twenty-three—older than I was—and had a warm, caring, and almost motherly disposition. She seemed to like being with me. There were no boyfriends in sight, and one day I asked her to come out with me, just the two of us. She said yes. From then on, we would go out together almost every day, walking hand in hand. I would take pictures of her, and when it was time to say good-bye, she would give me a real kiss. Our friends in the group accepted that we belonged together.

♪♪♪

I was happier than I had ever been since coming to America. I was serious about Debbie and began to dream about spending the rest of my life with her. But those dreams came to an unexpected end.

After returning from a month-long concert tour, I missed Debbie terribly and rushed over to her apartment. Debbie's mother opened the door, although I could see Debbie, with red eyes, standing behind her. I was alarmed and asked what was wrong.

"Nothing is wrong," her mother replied. "Debbie just got married."

I couldn't believe my ears. Her mother explained that a young man who was the son of very close friends of the family was called up and given two weeks before being shipped to Korea. (This was during the Korean War, and many young men were being drafted into the Army.) His stint in the military would be two years, which was a long time and, of course, there was no guarantee that he would come home safe and sound.

This young man's mother and father were anxious to comfort him and decided to do what scores of other parents did at the time: match their sons with girls who would be waiting for them at home. This meant marriage. Many such quick weddings were arranged in the hopes of providing some solace to the young men who were going off to fight in a distant land.

Debbie had met the young man before and had no particular interest in him. But she also possessed a warm and generous nature. Her parents asked her to marry him, the boy's parents implored her, and the boy himself said that their life together would be wonderful. The day before he left, he and Debbie stood in front of a justice of the peace and exchanged vows.

I swallowed hard upon hearing the shocking news, but I still wanted to go out with Debbie just the same. So we did. She and I walked the streets and in the park, holding hands. Sobbing on my shoulder, she told me that she'd spent just one night with her new husband, and it was only me she kept thinking of. . . .

The next day I showed up on her doorstep as usual, and again her mother greeted me. But Debbie was nowhere to be seen.

"This cannot go on," her mother said. "Debbie is a married woman."

She was adamant, and I left, the world around me in shambles.

I continued hanging out with the group of friends I met at school, but Debbie stayed away. It was just as well because we probably wouldn't have been able to remain "just friends." The others knew what had happened and tried to console me. Sherry, Robin's girlfriend, was particularly sympathetic. She said that the two of us should go out to dinner to talk things over. Sherry was attractive and quite wonderful, and I started to look at her with new eyes. When we said good-bye after dinner, she kissed me and that astonished me. Wasn't she Robin's girlfriend?

I brought it up the next day when I saw her, and Sherry broke down. Robin said that he had tried, but he was not really interested in her "in that way." He wasn't interested in *any* girl in that way. He just wanted to be a poet and live the way he pleased. Robin's father—a successful businessman and a hearty, masculine man—was very upset, and Robin had quite a showdown with him. Now he wanted to make things clear to Sherry and hoped she would understand. She said she would try, but her world had fallen apart as well.

There we were—two dejected young people. Needless to say, we soon consoled each other. Sherry was the same age as I was, and just as naïve and innocent. In the months that followed, we explored, little by little, the mysteries of both emotional and physical love. The latter received a big boost when I came back from a weekend in the country.

I was a houseguest at the Long Island estate of a prominent Wall Street lawyer and Jeanie, his very young and attractive wife. They had a ten-month-old son who was climbing and crawling all over the place. Fortunately for Jeanie, who had ambitions in life other than taking care of a rowdy child, there was a nanny to look after the little fellow.

One Saturday morning, Jeanie's husband went out fishing on Long Island Sound but I elected not to go—I had no objection to sitting on a boat holding a fishing rod, but I was always worried that some stupid fish would swallow the hook and I'd have the unpleasant task of removing it. Jeanie had no interest in fishing at all, and instead, decided to spend the day with me.

She told me her life story. Jeanie had been a promising model before she met her husband, but he insisted that she give it up after they were married. She showed me pictures where she posed in various attires, even a few in bikinis. She had a fantastic figure. I told her about my own interest in photography, and Jeanie suggested that we look at her husband's collection of famous paintings —some originals, others full-sized museum reproductions.

We spent some time in front of Goya's celebrated *Naked Maja*— the work fascinated her, Jeanie said. Half joking, I remarked that she would be a more beautiful model than the Duchess of Alba, and that I could do almost as well with my Rolleiflex as Goya did with his brush. Jeanie turned quite red. This was a serious matter. She replied, "Perhaps you could," and then added, "Shall we try?"

Jeanie disappeared, and I went about setting up the camera, arranging the lights, and placing large pillows on the sofa roughly in the shape Goya had them in his painting. Jeanie reappeared appropriately attired—wearing nothing but a strand of curled hair over her left shoulder and the mysterious smile of the Maja on her face. She took her place on the sofa, and I used up a whole roll of film.

We went to the village to have the film developed. On the following day, before I left for home, we picked up the prints. Not all were perfect, but in some, at least in our modest but fully shared opinion, Jeanie was far lovelier than Goya's muse.

Later, I showed the pictures to Sherry. She was intrigued, but assumed that Jeanie and I had been "together," although we hadn't. Sherry wanted to enter the "competition" herself. She did, and then she and I *did* get together. It was a gentle and beautiful initiation for us both.

♪♪♪

We had been "going steady" for more than a year when things became difficult. Sherry's mother began to do what most mothers of young women tend to do: insist we declare that we were serious, which meant being ready for marriage. I asked myself if I was really ready to commit. I knew I was in love, but after my experience with Debbie, I wasn't sure whether I was in love with Sherry or just in love with being in love. Sherry was a wonderful person, but I realized that I had no desire to get married and settle down.

Sherry battled her mother for as long as she could, but in the end told me that it would be best if I gave her something that could pass for an engagement ring. It could be almost any ring as long as it had a diamond. I explained this to Mother, who gave me an antique ring that belonged to her mother, who got it from *her* mother. It had a small diamond in an elaborate gold setting. I told Sherry that it was hers, but it wasn't an engagement ring. However, Sherry's mother took a different view and insisted that we were engaged.

Sherry's father was a prominent executive in the New York entertainment world, and when his daughter got "engaged," *The New York Times* published the announcement along with her picture.

From there came endless dinners and parties at their home, attended by aunts, uncles, and cousins. There I was, not yet twenty years old, engaged to be married not just to a girl, but to an entire clan. I would have to fit in, and I wasn't ready.

Sherry knew that I wasn't happy, but there wasn't much she could do about it. Then the problem was suddenly resolved.

One evening we were out with a young couple a few years older than we were; they had been together for a number of years and knew that we were now "together," too. The night was warm, and we went out for dinner and to see a show. As we were leaving the theater, our friends suggested that we drive up to Bear Mountain in the Catskills. They said that we should get rooms and have breakfast on the terrace of the country inn.

I wasn't crazy about the idea. First, I wasn't comfortable about checking into an inn with Sherry because we would have to give assumed names. And second, I had a concert to prepare for and needed to get a good night's rest.

I said that I was tired and preferred to go home, which disappointed our friends. Sherry didn't say anything, but she was clearly furious. When we parted for the evening, instead of the warm kiss I'd been expecting, she took a step back, slipped the ring from her finger, and flung it at me.

"I never want to see you again!" she cried. She turned and slammed the door shut—for always, it seemed to me.

My initial reaction was much the same as when Debbie's mother told me that her daughter had gotten married: total devastation. But by the time I arrived home—it was a good 45-minute drive with my Packard to Forest Hills—I actually felt more relieved than upset. I knew our relationship had been special, and I wasn't sure if I would ever find anything so beautiful again. But there were also problems. Sherry's family was expecting me to settle down and start a life I wasn't ready to lead.

I was sad and disoriented for a while, but then I recovered. To my surprise, I found not just one, but half a dozen young women who were happy to step into Sherry's shoes, even if they were, perhaps with one exception, not as wonderful as Sherry or Debbie.

Sherry herself—someone from our group of friends reported— ended up going to a clinic in the mountains to help her overcome her depression. After that, I lost touch with her so I don't know how she did later in life. I sincerely hope that she found the right man who could fit her, and her family, better than I ever could.

♪♪♪

Other romances followed these youthful episodes, and they were definitely not as, in fact not at all, disappointing. One stands out in particular. For a year and a half, I traveled the world with a stunning girl named Ettie.

I was touring in South America when I first met her. I was in Buenos Aires, where I was especially popular, playing concert after concert. Many young men of my acquaintance had remarked, rather enviously, that a queue of girls would form after my concerts in the lobby of the Alvear Palace, the five-star hotel where my impresario reserved a suite for me. A queue of girls was surely an exaggeration . . . but it wasn't entirely off the mark.

Navarro, my manager, used this portrait
to publicize my appearances in Buenos Aires.

One morning I received a phone call from a young woman who said that she had been at my concert the night before and came backstage to see me but gave up—there were too many people. She was hoping to interview me for Air France's in-flight magazine.

I suggested we meet later that day at my hotel. She came up to my suite, asked her questions, and took studious notes. With the interview over, I asked if she would like to join me that evening to see the young Dutch conductor Edouard van Remoortel; I had known Edouard from before, and he had offered me two complimentary tickets to his concert. The young woman said she would like that very much, and so we went.

After the performance, we said good-bye, but she remembered she'd left her lighter, an engraved gold Dunhill, in my suite. I offered to get it for her, but she seemed anxious to recover it herself. We went up together and she did find her lighter . . . the next morning, when she remembered to look for it. As soon as the door closed behind us, we fell into each other's arms.

The young woman, it turned out, was indeed writing for the Latin American edition of the Air France magazine, but she wasn't a professional journalist. She was Marie-Etienne, a popular member of the French jet set. Born in Holland to a prominent shipbuilding family, she was sent to finishing school in Paris and decided to stay in the French capital after she graduated. Tall, blonde, and strikingly good-looking, Marie-Etienne—"Ettie" to her friends—was impeccably elegant and had a warm and spontaneous temperament. She knew all the best people and was adored by everyone. Ettie was soon asked by Air France to act as an informal agent for the airline: for every first-class passenger she would steer toward them, she would earn a commission and could have a passage on any flight that had an available first-class seat.

Ettie loved to explore and began to travel the world. She was visiting nearly every city served by Air France, which is how she happened to be in Buenos Aires when I was there.

When Ettie left the next morning, she mentioned that we would see each other again. I had no idea just when and how, but the same evening, she showed up with a suitcase. She got rid of the competition waiting in the lobby and moved in with me. With Ettie, it was always all or nothing, and no procrastination.

On the following day, I had a concert in Montevideo, Uruguay, on the other side of the wide estuary of the Río de la Plata. Ettie and I took a Pan Am "flying boat," a lumbering aircraft that had a belly much like a pelican, with a wide and deep fuselage that appeared to have been made of wood. Navarro, my efficient South American manager, was also with us. Born in Spain and bearing an impressive chain of given names but preferring to be called simply "Navarro," he was a smallish man with twinkling eyes, gold-rimmed glasses, and a fantastic sense of humor. He had a deep love of music and a thorough appreciation of the good things in life. He and Ettie got along famously.

We didn't see anything of Montevideo other than our room at the hotel and the concert hall (actually, I didn't even see much of the concert hall either). Ettie and I checked in before noon, and no matter how often the phone rang, we didn't answer it. At one point, there was an insistent banging on the door. Navarro was outside, and he was very agitated. The car was waiting downstairs, he nearly shouted, and I was to come right away. He was annoyed that I hadn't shown up for the cocktail reception given in my honor at the U.S. embassy that afternoon, which left the ambassador embarrassed and upset. I knew it would be an even greater insult if I were late for the performance itself.

Ettie helped me quickly locate the right shirt and socks and other items in the concert artist's traditional wardrobe of long tails and white tie. Having her there was fortunate, because I was in no condition to tie a bow tie by myself.

The concert passed in a fog, much like a deep, dreamless sleep. I must have done well, for Navarro was in a much better mood after the concert than he had been earlier in the evening. Ettie and I returned to our room as soon as we could, and picked up exactly where we had left off. The next time we heard banging on the door, it was noon the following day. We had to scramble once again to get dressed and take the flying boat back to Buenos Aires.

Ettie traveled with me wherever Air France flew, and that, it seemed, was almost everywhere. She had a romantic outlook and zest for life. And a lot of courage.

On one occasion, on a flight from the Argentine town of Rosario back to Buenos Aires, we had a rough ride in a very small plane. (I remember asking for two window seats at the check-in, only to be told that *all* of the seats were window seats.) Half an hour into the flight, we saw what looked like a funnel touching down in the distance. The pilot decided to make an unscheduled landing. All of the passengers disembarked, and we made our way to the terminal to wait for news. Some passengers promptly disappeared.

An hour later, the pilot said that the whirlwind was now sufficiently out of the way of our route, and we could safely continue to Buenos Aires. It seemed like most of the remaining passengers who didn't leave earlier elected to wait for the next flight in the morning. Not Ettie! Grabbing my hand, she said, "Let's go!" and marched off toward the plane. Navarro and I looked at each other—there was nothing to do but follow. The three of us got on the plane and made it in one piece, although the ride did nothing to quiet either our apprehensions or our stomachs.

Through Ettie, I learned to live and love spontaneously, with good spirits and an open heart. And I also learned to pay more attention to how I looked.

The first time we met outside of Latin America was when she joined me on my European tour in Madrid. She was coming from Buenos Aires via Paris, where she spent a few days at her old apartment. I went to the airport to greet her, looking forward to a joyous reunion. Ettie took one look at me, made a face, and gave me a very superficial hug. She didn't say a word on the way to town, and when we arrived at the hotel, she took a separate room and locked herself in. I couldn't imagine what was wrong.

The following day Ettie dragged me to a mirror. She pointed at my reflection and took a deep breath.

"Look at yourself," she said. I looked and didn't see anything amiss. I was wearing my usual slacks and travel jacket. The pants were perhaps a bit wide and the jacket somewhat loose (maybe a bit frayed around the sleeves, too), but they were comfortable.

"You look like a stable boy," Ettie stated matter-of-factly. "We're going to the tailor."

She got me outfitted, and when she was satisfied with the result, she came back to the hotel with me and gave up the second room.

We traveled all over Europe together. My hosts were often worried when they heard that I was arriving with a young lady in tow, but they were all smiles after a few minutes with Ettie. She could instantly win the heart of any man or woman.

Agnes, however, was the exception. This encounter took place in Vienna in 1955. Agnes was twenty-three, the same age I was. We had known each other in Budapest, and our parents were close friends. They had hoped we would grow fond of each over time and eventually marry. But in my early teens, I wasn't interested in girls. In fact, I was always embarrassed when boys from my class would see me walking down the street with Agnes, who would insist on holding hands.

And then our destinies diverged. I left the country soon after my fifteenth birthday, and Agnes remained in Budapest. But before I left, there was one occasion that had shocked our parents but also boosted their hopes.

We were fourteen years old at the time. After a day's hike in the hills of Buda, we returned early to Agnes's house because it started to rain. Our parents settled in the living room to discuss life and politics, and we were told to go to Agnes's room and amuse ourselves.

We did. First we played cards, but as I kept winning, Agnes accused me of cheating. I denied it, and when she insisted, I playfully told her that I'd have to spank her if she didn't stop accusing me.

Agnes stared me down, saying, "Don't you dare!"

I *did* dare, and a wild chase followed that ended on her bed. I tried to land a few smacks in the right spot, and Agnes resisted, but not very much.

Daylight faded and the room became dark, but we didn't notice. We were both still shrieking with laughter when the "old folks" came in to see what was going on. They took one look at the darkened room and us all heated up and disheveled on the bed, and drew the logical (but wrong) conclusion.

Mother swiftly grabbed me by the neck and wanted to know if I'd kissed Agnes. I told her that I hadn't, which was true. But our parents exchanged meaningful looks, and I was promptly taken home.

Now, nearly ten years later, we would have had other ideas about games to play. Agnes was attending a social-science seminar at the University of Vienna when she saw the billboard announcing my concert. She came to see me backstage and gave me a big hug. Ettie was next to me and smiled, as I quickly introduced Agnes as my old childhood friend.

I told Agnes where I was staying, and she came to visit the next day. Ettie was out exploring the city, and Agnes and I began to reminisce and catch up on our lives since we had last seen each other. She remembered our spanking episode and remarked that we could surely do better now. I was all for trying, but the door flew open and Ettie swept in. She'd heard from the porter that there was a young lady in my room, and she wasn't smiling anymore. Poor Agnes found herself on the street before she could identify the hurricane that had blown her out of my room.

Life with Ettie was exciting, joyous, and turbulent. It was an emotional roller coaster, shifting unexpectedly from the highest ecstasy to the deepest dejection, and back up again. It was exhilarating yet also quite exhausting.

A year passed, and Ettie turned thirty, which was very difficult for her and seemed more like a shock. She began to talk about planning a wedding. This was new and quite unexpected; until then, marriage was something she had scorned, calling it "bourgeois." I was twenty-four and still had no urge to settle down (my aspiration to share my life with a young Finnish girl whom I would meet a few months later was totally unforeseen). Ettie and

I didn't see eye to eye on the marriage issue, and our relationship became more and more strained.

In the summer of 1956, we spent a few weeks together in New York. The city was hot and muggy, which seemed to increase the tension between us. I realized that things couldn't continue as they were and knew it was time for a change. I explained my feelings to Ettie, and one morning in early September, I left for the airport without telling her where I was going. I was, in fact, beginning a concert tour that was to take me first to Italy and then Germany, Finland, and London.

I was deeply sorry and felt guilty about leaving her in this way, but I didn't see any other good alternative. Our "roller coaster" spent more time stalled at the bottom with fewer and fewer highs, and prospects for improvement were nearly nil. I consoled myself by thinking that with her looks, affluent family, and jet-set friends, she would have no problem finding her way—and her man—whenever she wanted to.

Ettie did indeed find her way (if not her man, at least at that point) when we had a surprise encounter in the VIP lounge of the World Expo in Brussels exactly one year later. But that is quite another story, as I will recount next.

♪♫♪♫♪♫

CHAPTER TWELVE

A True Love Story

The driver of the airport limousine was getting worried. I'd asked him to wait for the English-looking gentleman carrying an umbrella, but the gentleman hadn't emerged from the Fazer chocolate shop around the corner.

I was touring in Europe alone, feeling uneasy about having left Ettie without even saying good-bye, but was still convinced that it was for the best. Now I was in Finland, giving a recital in Helsinki, the capital city. It was a beautiful October day, and people were basking in the late autumn sun and strolling happily about. My recital the night before had gone particularly well; the reviews this morning were very favorable, and the gentleman I was waiting for had been delighted. But there was nothing I could do now because I had to get on a plane. The following evening I had a concert scheduled in London, and I was expected for rehearsals that very afternoon.

The gentleman understood my situation well. He was tall and thin, and didn't look Finnish at all—I later found out he was from a prominent Swedish family. He was a Renaissance man who loved music and culture, and who was fluent in many languages. His role was to manage visiting artists. He was my impresario and had taken excellent care of me from the moment I stepped off the plane a week earlier.

On my last day in Finland, he'd asked me for a favor. His daughter was studying in London, and since I was going there, he requested that I take a package for her—something small, he assured me. He had a gentle sense of humor and a romantic view of the world. Poets and artists were his heroes. I figured that if his daughter was anything like him, it might be quite pleasant to meet her. So I agreed, and he promptly disappeared into the chocolate shop.

Just as the driver was about to insist that I either get in the limousine or he'd leave without me, my impresario emerged, carrying a not very small but still manageable package. I took it, shook his hand, jumped in the backseat of the limo, and was off to the airport. Little did I know that this was the prelude to a meeting that would change my life.

♪♪♪

Shortly after arriving in London, I called the number that my Finnish impresario had given me. His daughter was not in, so I left a message: if she would come to Wigmore Hall tomorrow evening, she would find a ticket at the box office in her name; I could give her a package from her father if she would please come see me backstage after the concert.

The following day I almost forgot about the whole thing, but luckily I had placed the box of chocolates next to my briefcase when I unpacked to remind myself to take it to the concert hall. After my performance, among the usual group of friends and well-wishers, there was a pretty blonde who smiled nervously and said that she'd heard I had a package for her. We introduced ourselves, and I handed it over.

As she was thanking me and turning to leave, I asked, on the spur of the moment, "Why don't we have a cup of tea someplace?" I found myself drawn to this shy Finnish girl and thought it would be nice to chat with her for a bit.

"Okay," she replied, and we went over to the Lyons tea shop on Piccadilly.

We chatted over tea. Her name was Marjorie, and she was studying in London for a year as part of her language and literature major at the University of Helsinki. Time seemed to pass quickly, and by ten o'clock, I hailed a taxi for her and we said good night.

I thought she was charming, but now that she had the chocolates her father had sent and I was leaving England in a few days, we weren't likely to see each other again. But luck was on my side. . . .

The phone rang in my hotel room the next morning, and a young lady was asking for me. It was Marjorie. She had gotten my number from someone at the concert agency. She didn't have the package from her father and was wondering if I'd picked it up and taken it with me. No, I didn't have it either, I told her. Come to think of it, as she got into the taxi the night before, I didn't recall seeing anything in her hands. I didn't have anything with me except my briefcase, so we realized we must have left it at the tea shop.

There wasn't much chance of recovering a box of chocolates left the night before in a crowded tea shop, but I was willing to try anyway, and Marjorie offered to join me. We met there at five o'clock and asked if they'd found a box of Finnish Fazer chocolates. They hadn't, so we decided to walk to a nearby pub that looked friendly and very English.

We talked for hours. Little by little, Marjorie told me more about herself. She had a deep passion for languages and literature; and was an avid reader of Chaucer, Shakespeare, Byron, and other classic English writers and poets. She came from a family of Swedish origin, but her father was a great admirer of British culture and had insisted that his children have English names. So her given name was Barbro Carita Marjorie, her older brother was Georg Eric Reginald, and her younger brother was Carl Johan Dennis.

I talked a good deal about myself even though it was something I rarely did. I felt strangely buoyed and very happy in Marjorie's company. I called her the next day, and we met in the afternoon . . . and we met again the day after that. Two days later, I had to leave for Lisbon, the next stop on my concert tour.

I departed with a heavy heart—the past four days had been wonderful. Marjorie was an intelligent, sincere, and lovely young woman; and I was proud of myself for having spent several days in her company without having "tried" anything. I felt that it just wouldn't have been the right thing to do. Now our time together was over. She was to return to Helsinki at the end of the year, and I wasn't booked for concerts in Finland anytime soon. I didn't see how or where we could meet, and realized that I might never see her again.

♪♪♪

I gave several concerts in Portugal. I was in Lisbon first; then Porto; and last at Vila Viçosa, the former royal residence where I was assigned the queen's bedchamber as my dressing room. The stuffed mattress was hard and prickly. If that's what royals had to sleep on in the Middle Ages, I mused, I was glad to be a mere musician in the Modern Ages!

As I was leaving Portugal, the concierge of my hotel handed me a letter that had just arrived. It was from Marjorie! She continued our conversation as if we had never been apart. Her words were simple, and I thought they were simply beautiful. I was touched. I had a few minutes to spare before my flight departed, so I sat down to write a reply. It took longer than I thought, so I continued writing on the plane and mailed the letter in Vienna. I felt very good about it.

However, I arrived at my destination to a shocking scene. It was the end of October 1956, and the Hungarian uprising had just been crushed by Soviet tanks. There were thousands of Hungarian refugees, freedom fighters, and miscellaneous others crossing the border into Austria. I ran into several former friends and fellow musicians, and did my best to help them find accommodations and provide them with contacts so that they could start a new life outside of Hungary. The correspondence with the young girl from Finland seemed to belong to another day and age—one that was tranquil and sunny.

But then, to my surprise, another letter arrived at my hotel—I must have remembered to put my new return address on the envelope. Marjorie once again picked up our conversation, and I was delighted. I replied right away and ran to the post office to send it by express special delivery. I made sure the envelope had the return address for my next stop.

Sure enough, in Athens, too, a letter awaited me from Marjorie. That was the third one, and something clicked inside me. I saw what seemed like a vision while reading it, and the image stayed with me and reappeared whenever I thought about her: *I am walking in a meadow, a quiet clearing in the forest. A soft breeze rustles the leaves of the trees around me, but the meadow itself is bathed in a warm glow from the sun. I feel a sensation of purity, peace, and contentment. All is well with the world.*

The feel of this vision was not very different from the experience of living myself into a great piece of music. My next letter to Marjorie was a declaration of love. She felt the same way, she responded in her next letter. (We reread these letters years later, as Marjorie had saved all of our correspondence.)

So we continued writing. Marjorie wrote every day. She wrote while she was in London and then from her parents' house in Helsinki when she returned in December. This went on for almost a year. A day without a letter from her seemed bleak. But the occasional gap wasn't due to her not writing—it was just my traveling schedule. During that entire period, we had an almost perfect record.

It wasn't long before we began asking each other where and how we could meet again. My European tour was over in February, and I had returned to New York. That was much too far for her to travel—her parents would never agree to such a trip, but Marjorie had a brilliant idea. When she learned that my next European tour would have a three-week sojourn in Paris, she registered for a French language and literature seminar at her university and arranged for on-site study in Paris. This was to take place during October and November 1957, just a year after our encounter in London.

I could hardly wait until we would meet in Paris. As soon as my plane landed, I went to see Marjorie in nearby Versailles at the home of the family who was hosting her. I was suddenly very nervous, however. How would it feel to see each other again after our heartfelt correspondence? Surely, things would be different. Would we admit to each other in person the sentiments we had expressed in writing? How would we do it?

Now that we were finally together, not only did Marjorie act shy, but I did, too. It was one thing to make ardent declarations on paper and quite another to profess them face-to-face.

For the entire evening, we steered clear of "heavy" subjects. We talked about my concert tour and her language studies in France while we had dinner at a small restaurant in the student quarter near the Sorbonne. At ten o'clock, Marjorie looked at her watch and said that she had to leave—the family she was staying with had promised her father that she would be home at a decent time in the evenings.

There was no time to take the commuter train back to Versailles, so I hailed a taxi at the "Boul-Mich" (the popular Boulevard Saint-Michel) where life was in full swing. Marjorie jumped in the backseat, and we didn't have a chance for a proper goodbye. But no matter—we were planning to meet again the next day, and I hoped that there would be a perfect moment to talk about our feelings then.

We didn't do any better the second evening, and I was growing more nervous. When we were on our way back to Versailles, we sat in the commuter train across from each other and didn't dare look up. As we were about to pull into the last stop, Marjorie couldn't take it any longer and burst into tears.

"What's the matter with you?!" she sobbed.

I realized that there were tears in my eyes, too. *What kind of an idiot am I,* I thought, *to waste all this time?* Without another moment of hesitation, I took the plunge.

"Marjorie, I love you. Will you marry me?"

Starting the next morning, we had our hands full with lawyers, officials, and forms to fill out. It turned out that it is far from easy for foreigners to get married in France. Many people visiting Paris have romantic adventures and decide to elope on the spur of the moment . . . which often ends in disaster. The authorities require lawyers and witnesses, and the filing of a dozen complicated documents. We had several hearings at the courthouse—I remember that on one occasion, we were asked how many children we had. When I answered none, the official insisted that I admit them so that they would become "legitimate." Feeling rather inadequate, I had to insist that I was deficient in this regard.

On November 16, 1957, we had a brief but memorable civil wedding at the Mairie du 16e, the town hall of the 16th arrondissement of Paris. When our turn arrived, Marjorie and I stood before the mayor as the clerk read aloud our names and addresses. He hesitated for a fraction of a second when reading mine because it was the same as Marjorie's (couples were usually careful to give different addresses). But we had to have residency in this arrondissement to get married here, so this is the one we gave. The clerk need not have worried: while we both moved into the same family-style boardinghouse on Rue Nicolo, we only *inhabited* that house . . . we didn't *cohabit* it.

Then the mayor gave us a paternal smile and pronounced us man and wife. He offered his congratulations to "Madame," which duly impressed Marjorie—she had never been called that before.

This was taken minutes after the mayor of the 16th
arrondissement of Paris pronounced Marjorie and me man and wife.

Afterward our witnesses, Marjorie Ferguson, the cultural attaché of the U.S. embassy and her colleague John Evarts, took us to Foucault's at the Champs-Élysées for the traditional glass of champagne. Half an hour later we had to rush to the Gare de Lyon to catch the express train to Brussels, as I had to attend rehearsals that afternoon for a concert with the symphony orchestra the following day.

Once the rehearsals were over, the young conductor Edouard van Remoortel (whose concert I had attended when I had first met Ettie) invited me to his family's home for dinner. He said that I was welcome to bring the young lady who was with me. When I introduced her at the house as my wife, my shy spouse caused a happy sensation. My friend's father, the formidable white-bearded Senator van Remoortel, immediately took to Marjorie, and the ladies of the house descended upon her. They asked a thousand questions about where and how we met, and above all, just who she was—this young, sweet girl from a distant Nordic land. Marjorie replied in monosyllables and looked at me pleadingly. Mercifully, the ladies didn't insist, and it was up to me to provide the answers.

As soon as it was decently possible, we took our leave and checked in at the Hotel Le Plaza, where the honeymoon suite was waiting for us. We were exhausted . . . but, I thought, not *too* exhausted. Yet Marjorie was quite flushed and seemed a bit scared, so we spent the night just holding each other in our arms. There was no hurry: we had our whole life ahead of us.

We didn't have to wait the rest of our lives, though. My concert the next day was in the evening, and we didn't leave our room until it was time to get dressed for it. We shared a tender, relaxed, and joyous union.

A few days later, we received a copy of the wedding announcement sent out by my old friend the Finnish impresario, who was now my father-in-law. It was very formal and stated that Paul-Eric and Gunnel Jägerhorn af Spurila were pleased to announce the marriage of their daughter, Barbro Carita Marjorie, to concert artist Ervin Laszlo. It was beautifully embossed and had a four-pronged gold crown in the left corner. As tactfully as possible, I pointed out the faux pas to Marjorie: one can't use such a symbol as a decoration —it's only for those who have the right to use it.

Marjorie turned a pretty shade of crimson. "We do have the right," she confessed. The last part of her family name, *af Spurila,* she explained, meant "of Spurila," referring to the name of her family's estate that dated back to the early Middle Ages. It turned out that she came from one of the oldest aristocratic families in Finland. I was glad she hadn't revealed that to me earlier; I might have taken longer than two days to propose to a girl who traced her lineage to the royal house of Sweden!

♪♪♪

We had been married for a few months when I had a return engagement in Brussels. When we arrived in Belgium, the 1958 World Expo was in full swing. Thousands of people were visiting every day. We were among them, but despite the masses of people, the first person we ran into was Ettie.

Our Belgian friends took us to the VIP reception hall, and that's where I spotted her. Ettie was radiant as an official Expo hostess, greeting visiting VIPs in great style, while chatting alternately in French, English, Spanish, and Dutch. She saw me immediately and didn't miss the blonde Finnish girl at my side either. Smiling, she said something to the people she had been talking to and walked over to us. I performed the introduction: "This is my longtime friend Ettie, and this my wife, Marjorie."

I expected fireworks, but there weren't any. Ettie congratulated me and hugged both of us, and then excused herself for a moment. She was away for an inordinately long time, but when she reappeared, she was calm and composed, all sweetness and light. The three of us sat down together and chatted, catching up on what had happened since Ettie and I had last seen each other in New York. When it was time to leave, the ladies hugged each other again and promised to keep in touch. They did indeed exchange several letters in the months that followed, as well as Christmas and birthday greetings for many years after that. As far as the Brussels World Expo was concerned, we hadn't managed to see anything but the reception hall.

Later on I filled Marjorie in on my "travels with Ettie." My new wife was very understanding. She didn't think that I had lived in a monastery before we met and was glad that I'd had positive life experiences. Her only wish was that the good-bye to Ettie should really be a farewell.

For me it really was.

♪♫♪♫♪♫

CHAPTER THIRTEEN

PATERFAMILIAS

Following my concert in Brussels, we took a few days off, relaxing and thinking about nothing but each other. However, there were a few questions we could no longer put off: *What is next for us? Where shall we call home?*

Marjorie didn't want to go back to Finland, and I didn't want to return to Hungary. So our native countries were out, but that still left quite a bit of terrain to choose from. The decision wasn't really difficult, however. I was booked for concerts in Munich the following week, so we decided it would be convenient to see how we would like living in that friendly, music-loving Bavarian capital. We packed our bags—we each had just one suitcase—and boarded the train for Munich.

Upon our arrival, the first thing we did was visit the American consulate. We knew from our friends in Paris that the bulletin board at the French consulate was a veritable treasure trove of information, providing details on everything from where to find the best vintage wines to a list of luxury villas available for rent. Perhaps the Munich office could give us info on locating suitable housing.

As we were studying the notices on the board, a man wearing the dark blue garb of a diplomat passed by us. He headed down the corridor and disappeared behind a door marked "Vice-Consul." But a moment later, he stuck his head out and looked at me intently. He seemed familiar.

"Aren't you—"

"And aren't *you* . . . ?" I asked in turn.

We were. We had met before but had never seen each other dressed—at least, not fully dressed. During our first and only meeting we'd been in bathing trunks, snorkeling off the coral reef of Ocho Rios, on the north coast of Jamaica.

I introduced Marjorie. My snorkeling companion was Marion Baldwin, the U.S. vice-consul in Munich. He was as delighted to see me as I was to see him. He told Marjorie that she and his wife, Karen, who was Norwegian, would get along wonderfully and suggested we have dinner together.

The next day Marion took us to see Dr. Asbeck, who also worked for the consulate and happened to own a home he didn't use. It was located at the lake of Starnberg, just south of the city. This was, and is to this day, an area favored by actors, artists, and writers.

We decided to take the house and settled in. It even conveniently had an old but serviceable grand piano. We soon discovered that our next-door neighbors were Marianne Koch, the German movie star known for her heart-wrenching roles; and Hardy Krüger, the famous leading man, who usually played the "tough guy."

With the help of the consulate bulletin board, we also found a venerable diesel Mercedes that was "sure to last another hundred-thousand kilometers." It had red leather seats; a long, straight hood topped by the Mercedes star; large Rolls-Royce–style headlights over the fender; and a turn signal that popped out of the side, lit up, and waved up and down. We promptly named our new possession Jonathan, a name we both liked.

Three days after driving Jonathan back to our newfound cottage in Starnberg, I left for the U.S., as I was slated for concerts in Texas.

Marjorie bravely decided to remain in Starnberg, clutching the keys to the house and car along with a German conversation guide. Her French was good, and she spoke softly accented but nearly perfect British English—and of course, Finnish and Swedish —but she only knew a little German. She did just fine on her own, and Marion and Karen were also there to help. Karen, whose English wasn't much better than Marjorie's German, would ride with her in the car while Marjorie was preparing to get her driver's license. As Marjorie later told me, whenever she hesitated to cross an intersection, Karen would prompt her: "Go, go! You have the 'right away'!"

♪♪♪

I had many memorable experiences in Texas, playing first with the Dallas Symphony conducted by my old friend and fellow Hungarian Antal Doráti. He was the symphony's music director until 1948 and came back at this time as a guest conductor.

After the concert, I met a kind gray-haired gentleman who turned out to be a renowned portrait artist. He made paintings of all the Texas oil millionaires and introduced me to a few of his clients, who were happy to show me their portraits. They were large, beautiful works, with the subjects beaming benevolently from golden frames.

While I was in Texas, I toured many great mansions with stables, tennis courts, and swimming pools. For the most part, the splendid salons were hardly lived in—it seemed that the owners preferred small, comfortable dens furnished with big TVs and cozy armchairs. One house stood out because it had a living room and library where I felt surprisingly small. The reason, my hostess explained, was that she liked an intimate setting but also desired plenty of space around her. So the rooms were large with high ceilings; and all the furnishings, fireplace included, were scaled up and oversized. One almost disappeared while sitting in the giant sofa in front of the enormous fireplace.

The people I met in Texas were extraordinarily rich and also extraordinarily kind and easygoing. Spending time with them in their spectacular homes was an experience I couldn't imagine having anywhere else in the world.

My plane ride from Dallas landed in Frankfurt, and Marjorie offered to drive up from Starnberg to meet me. This was quite a long stretch and became even longer for her: she wasn't sure how to shift Jonathan into fourth gear and drove in third the entire way. But she was at the gate on time.

From then on, we traveled throughout Europe in our trusty vehicle, and Marjorie made sure to always have a fresh flower in a vase on the dashboard. Jonathan never let us down, and would even start up in the coldest weather without a hitch.

Marjorie and I were very happy: we had a romantic Bavarian cottage we could call home, and we were able to travel and see the world. I was doing splendidly on the concert stage in both Europe and America . . . *North* America, that is—for roughly six months later, my concert in Argentina was a disaster.

As any honest performer will tell you, life onstage is not all roses; it's certainly not an endless series of triumphs crowned with laurel wreaths. Unfortunately, there are also flops, occasions when the performer, to use the popular expression, "bombs." I'd already had experiences of this kind under my belt when I'd failed the preliminary auditions for the competition in Paris, and then at the competition itself. Now I had another flop—and it happened when I returned to Buenos Aires.

My previous visit had been a magnificent success both on and off the stage (it was where I met Ettie). My next visit was just the opposite.

When Navarro, my faithful impresario, wrote that he had arranged a fabulous new tour for me in South America, Marjorie and I were euphoric. But then we realized that she couldn't accompany me because it would be prohibitively expensive. Since we were eager to spend as much time together as possible, we pored over flight schedules to see how I could make the trip with the least amount of time away from her. The first stop on my tour was Buenos Aires: I was to play at the famous Teatro Colón with a visiting Brazilian symphony orchestra. The concert was already sold out.

Traveling from Germany to Argentina was a long distance, and flights were not as frequent as they are today. There was a direct flight from Frankfurt to Buenos Aires only three times a week. And on the four-engine propeller plane, the DC-7C (known as the "Seven Seas"), the trip took twenty hours, with refueling stops in Lisbon, Recife, and São Paulo. Air travel was also noisier than on today's wide-bodied jets, and because we couldn't fly at the altitude reached by planes today, it was also much more turbulent: planes flew right into bad weather instead of over it. And even during smooth fights, there was a noticeable vibration. This was not a relaxing experience.

My choice was between the flight that would land in Buenos Aires the very morning of the concert, and the preceding flight that would arrive three days earlier. With newlywed ardor and boosted by youthful overconfidence—I had just turned twenty-six—I chose to arrive the same morning. Then I could spend more time with Marjorie.

Navarro met me upon my arrival and took me straight to the Teatro Colón. The rehearsals were already under way. I shook hands with the conductor, and we played through the celebrated Tchaikovsky Piano Concerto in B-flat, a virtuoso piece calling for a high level of technical mastery. I noticed that my fingers were not working properly and feared that the long trip was taking its toll. I knew I had to do better that evening.

There was now another decision to make. I could either stay at the theater and practice, or go to the hotel and get some rest. (Navarro had booked the same suite I'd stayed in last time at the Alvear Palace.) I was again overly confident in my youthful endurance and decided to stay and practice right up until the performance.

It was the wrong decision. By the time the concert had started, my head was spinning and I had even less control of my fingers than earlier during rehearsal. But there was nothing I could do but go onstage and play.

I don't remember much of my performance—only that afterward the conductor refused to return onstage for the customary extra bow. Navarro patted my shoulder and told me not to worry. So I went to the hotel, unpacked, and fell into bed.

The reviews were a disaster. Navarro wrung his hands and paced up and down the room but couldn't do anything to fix it—except to change my return reservation to Germany to the first available flight. The tour had been cancelled.

I spent two miserable days waiting for my flight home. Having to stay in the same place where earlier I'd had such a joyous adventure made the situation even worse. This was a bitter lesson to learn . . . but an important one. Never again would I sacrifice proper rest before a performance.

Shortly after my return to our cottage in Starnberg, things took a decidedly positive turn. Marjorie announced the news: she was going to have a baby. Our union, I proudly announced to her and to my parents, was to be blessed with offspring.

Ultimately, our union was blessed with two. I became a veritable *paterfamilias*.

Marjorie and I lived a carefree and bohemian existence, but since we were expecting a child we decided to take life more seriously. The baby was due in six months. We packed up our reliable Jonathan and moved into the city. While waiting for "Christopher" to arrive (we didn't have the test done that determines an unborn baby's sex, but were sure it was a boy), we moved into a modern three-room apartment and between travels lived a regular city life.

One evening months later, we had our friends Marion and Karen over for dinner, and Marjorie began having labor pains. We decided to call the hospital and tell them we were on our way. Marion drove us—he thought he'd better do so, after I backed into a truck when pulling out of our parking space and then seemed unable to find first gear.

Marjorie was under the care of her obstetrician, who told us that we needn't remain at the hospital. I implored him and the night nurse to call the minute that Christopher decided to make his arrival. We dropped Karen off at home, and Marion and I retired to my apartment to await the happy news. We opened a bottle of vintage wine, swapped stories, and had a fine time.

The call finally came in the morning, but it was the nurse telling me that the baby wasn't ready to come yet, and I should pick up Marjorie. It wasn't time. Marion was in a huff. Here we were, celebrating all night—and now nothing.

However, five days later, it *was* time. I took great care to reverse out of the parking space, and Marjorie and I sped off to the hospital. I left her in the nurse's charge and told her to call me as soon as the baby was coming.

Once again, the call came early in the morning. I jumped into Jonathan and drove at a decidedly unsafe pace, but luckily without mishap. Still, I was too late. The delivery room door opened and there was the nurse with a big smile on her face, holding up the baby. She unwrapped the blanket so I could have a good look. I then uttered the famous words, which Marjorie has never let me forget: "It's a boy . . . *isn't it?*" It looked like a boy, but I had never seen a newborn before, and besides my eyes wouldn't focus properly. I thought it was best to get a professional opinion.

♪♪♪

The second offspring that blessed our union came into the world four years later in Fribourg, Switzerland. It was to be a girl named Alexandra. Her arrival was planned, not one left to chance. I'd broken my right ankle while skiing in Switzerland, and after I came out of the cast (it was a long process, during which, as I will recount later, I wrote one of my most important books), the doctor said it would do me good to walk barefoot in warm sand. Warm sand was available on the Adriatic coast of Italy—it was the end of April—and Marjorie and I took off for a week to have a "sand walking" vacation on the beach in Cesenatico.

Although my foot was still healing, there was nothing wrong with the rest of me, so we decided that this was a good time to "launch" Alexandra. We were successful, and nine months later on January 27, 1964, we welcomed our second child into the world.

Back in Fribourg when Marjorie's contractions started, I was to deliver her to the city's historic Hôpital Cantonal for the happy event.

We felt like old hands at the business of giving birth, so even though Marjorie was having some contractions, we both thought there was still plenty of time, and instead of going to the hospital, we went ice-skating on the frozen Sarine River. Our friends the Darbellays came with us. The husband was a professor of philosophy of law at the University of Fribourg, and his wife was a fine painter. They also brought along their teenage children, Etienne and Isabelle. Etienne, who was serious about becoming a professional musician, studied piano and took lessons with me. Isabelle, an extraordinarily pretty girl, was bright and affectionate. We all had a wonderful time playing tag, with Isabelle shrieking with laughter and Marjorie, twice her usual girth, gliding majestically across the ice.

That evening, Marjorie prepared supper and we settled down in front of the television: there was a famous detective show on. Even when her contractions starting coming more frequently, Marjorie insisted that we watch the program to the end. We did so, and then drove to the hospital.

A few hours later, I was called into the delivery room to be present at Alexandra's birth. I watched as the head, covered in dark hair, emerged and then the rest. But it appeared to be a *boy,* which surprised me, although this time I knew better than to ask for confirmation. My son was red faced and seemed quite upset. Soon he quieted down in his mother's arms, and I was told to go home.

On the drive back to our house, I passed the Darbellays' and saw their car parked in front. It was the middle of the night and I didn't want to wake them, but I wanted to let them know the happy news. I fished out a piece of paper from my pocket, found a pencil, and started to scribble the phrase *C'est un garçon!* (It's a boy!). It didn't look quite right, and I remembered that one of the letters has a funny squiggle under it, but I couldn't recall which one. So to be on the safe side, I wrote: *C'est un monsieur!* (We spoke French with the Darbellays, which was the dominant language in this part of Switzerland.)

Our friends found the note on their car's windshield in the morning and thought it was terribly funny. They rushed to the hospital, had a great visit with mother and baby, and inquired where the proud father was. He was at home—stretched out fully dressed on the bed and lost to the world until noon.

Marjorie and I would have loved to have had a daughter but found it just as wonderful to have another son. In fact, we were thrilled. But we had been so sure we were having a girl that when we were asked to register a name for the baby, we didn't know what to say. It's not that we didn't have dozens of perfectly good boys' names at our fingertips, but we wanted something that satisfied our quite particular requirements. The name had to have several syllables (to go with our two-syllable family name), have equivalents in other languages (or at least be familiar in other cultures), and go well with the name of our firstborn, Christopher.

Because of local regulations, Marjorie and I had to decide quickly. We came up with the same brilliant idea at the same exact time. Why not *Alexander?* It met all of our requirements and didn't even call for quite abandoning our treasured "Alexandra."

♪♫♪♫♪♫♪

PART III

THE
QUEST

CHAPTER FOURTEEN

RESOLVE AT BERCHTESGADEN

The event that marked the first of the many sudden shifts in my life occurred one night in the Bavarian Alps. It was New Year's Eve 1959, and I was twenty-seven years old. Christopher had been born in March of the previous year. Alexander wouldn't arrive until four years later.

To Marjorie, the birth of our son was a natural addition to our family, but for me he was a surprise—a wonderful surprise but, to be honest, also kind of a shock. I realized that I could no longer live as a happy-go-lucky concert pianist. I had a family to take care of.

Being constantly on tour was not the kind of occupation that befitted a responsible family man. I started asking myself who I was and what I wanted to do with my life. Success on the concert stage was no longer the be-all and end-all of my existence. It was gratifying, but I had become used to it. I was always in fierce competition not only with other brilliant concert artists, but with myself. It was a constant challenge.

But what other kind of life could I lead? Should I become a teacher? Teaching budding artists is worthwhile and rewarding only when one has brilliant pupils. So far, at least, I didn't stay long enough in one place to build up a group of promising young musicians under my tutelage.

I could not, or perhaps just didn't dare to, share these existential questions with others. Our best friends—Marion and Karen Baldwin of the U.S. consulate; and Dr. Klaus Bastian, a distinguished lawyer from Munich and his charming wife, Maria— thought of me as a musician. Philosophical speculations might have been a suitable hobby, but nothing more. There was no room in the life of a professional concert pianist for anything else. Yet I wanted to pursue the questions that intrigued me and moved me so deeply. My quest to uncover the answers began to dominate my life.

I started reading more and thinking about the questions that I was exposed to as a child and an adolescent. During the time I spent with the group of intellectuals in New York, I had developed a great admiration for many writers and poets. I'd tried my hand at writing "philosophical" short stories back then, and now I wondered if I could develop the ideas behind those stories in a straightforward, non-metaphorical way.

I recalled the walks I used to take in the park with Uncle Pippa. Those were real questions he'd raised, and they were well worth the time to contemplate. But I wasn't sure how I was supposed to go about seeking meaningful answers to fundamental questions. Public libraries made me shudder—there were so many books lining the walls, an entire lifetime still wasn't long enough to read them. Perhaps I could focus on the specific questions that interested me and select the books that dealt with those topics. This was certainly worth trying.

City life—after we'd relocated to Munich from Starnberg before Christopher's birth—was a welcome change. Munich was home to a renowned university and had wonderful resources. I still practiced the piano every morning but had plenty of time to visit the library and audit courses at the university in the afternoon.

My resolve to truly satisfy my thirst for understanding came to me on a moonlit night. A new decade—the 1960s—was approaching, and I had a feeling that it would mark a new phase in my life.

♪♪♪

To celebrate the New Year, Marjorie and I went to Berchtesgaden, a famous resort in the Bavarian Alps. Christopher was no longer an infant and could be entrusted to the care of Patricia, Marjorie's Finnish cousin who came to live with us so she could take classes at the university and help Marjorie with the baby.

On the last day of December, Marjorie and I did some hiking and in the evening went to an ice-hockey game, which is a New Year's Eve tradition in Berchtesgaden. Afterward, we returned to our room, and I went to the balcony to enjoy the view. The night was still, and the snow-covered valley lay glittering in the moonlight. I suddenly felt the sensation that I could not only look upon the valley below, but could also apprehend something about the purpose of my life.

As I stood gazing at the landscape and the snowcapped alpine peaks beyond, I realized that what I was feeling was similar to how I felt when I lived myself into a piece of music. There was meaning in the world and a purpose for my existence. But this time I felt quite different. There was the sense that I was here to do something other than give concerts. I didn't clearly understand what that something was, but it had to do with the questions raised by my philosopher-uncle. There were things to discover that weren't evident in the context of everyday life, yet they were real and important. I *had* to look for the answers.

The decision to alter my life path wasn't a rational one, made by a cool calculation of pros and cons—otherwise, such a resolve would have been presumptuous and unrealistic. What chance did

I have to join in the debate of the "big questions" with those who were far more qualified to discuss these topics than I was? Had I been truly rational, I would have enrolled in a university and started to study the history of science and philosophy.

Perhaps I was unwittingly unrealistic and presumptuous, but on that moonlit night in the mountains, I experienced a call that I couldn't ignore. I had to discover more about the world I lived in—the world we had ourselves created, filled with humanity's needs and wants—and how it fit into the larger realm of nature, the cosmos. I recalled the exclamation of Professor Székely when, as a ten-year-old, I played the *Appassionata* for him: "Simply genius!" I knew I had to follow my intuition.

So how does one start a new life? I decided that I would continue giving concerts—I couldn't think of doing anything else, at least as a profession, nor could I easily make a living doing anything else. But now I was sure that there was more to life than seeking success on the concert stage, and I was going to *pursue* that something more.

The next morning I talked to Marjorie about my intuition, and she was all for my following it. Although she'd married a concert pianist, she told me that she didn't expect her husband to be a one-track man. She wanted me to be fully alive and open to all aspects of life and living. We returned home full of plans, hope, and excitement.

As I embraced this new life mission, I began to search for the pertinent theories and insights, and started to jot down my own thoughts and ideas. As I'd never practiced the piano for more than three hours a day and my tours were intermittent, I had plenty of time to do so.

And so, while I continued living as a concert artist, I started a new life as a philosopher in the original sense of the word: a lover—and seeker—of wisdom.

That was my resolve during that night in the Bavarian Alps. I have never regretted it, nor have I ever wavered from it.

♪♫♪♫♪♫

CHAPTER FIFTEEN

ENCOUNTER IN THE HAGUE

The next stage in my quest brought the realization that the thoughts that I'd been jotting down just for my own interest might also be of interest to others. This dawned on me one morning while I was in the city of The Hague in Holland.

A year and a half had passed since my epiphany in the Alps, and since then my days had been filled with concentrated effort to follow up my quest. During that first year, we remained in Munich and I traveled alone on concert tours. Marjorie stayed home with Christopher.

But we didn't stay put in Munich for long. Marjorie and I felt a deep desire to live closer to nature, so we took out a map of Europe and once again asked ourselves: *Where shall we call home?* It had to be in a beautiful natural setting, and it also had to be centrally located so that I wouldn't have to travel great distances for my performances. The choice was clear: we would move to Switzerland.

During my next trip there, I started to look for a good place for us to settle. The lake around Zurich was enticing; it was a lovely area and in a convenient location. But my love for Lake Geneva prevailed in the end. I felt a deep connection to this beautiful spot the moment I caught sight of it in 1947, when Mother and I were on our way to the music competition in the city of Geneva. Seeing it once again revived that strong feeling. This, I felt, was home.

The *corniche*—the narrow high strip of land with a spectacular view of the lake around Geneva, Lausanne, and Montreux—is a vision. I found an apartment with this stupendous view in Lausanne, and I didn't waste any time signing the lease.

In the summer of 1961, Marjorie and I loaded up our Volkswagen Beetle—Jonathan, our stately Mercedes, had "passed away" by then. Our luggage and household items were in the backseat and Christopher's bed was perched precariously on top. Slowly and cautiously, we made our way to our new home. My Bechstein concert grand arrived a few days later.

Once we were settled in Lausanne, I spent the greater part of the day reading and writing on the terrace overlooking the lake. I wanted to take classes at the local university, but didn't find any that were of direct interest to me, and the professor with whom I spoke knew me as a pianist and didn't take my quest seriously. So I continued on my own, visiting libraries and ordering books, and filling up page after page with my thoughts and impressions. I carried these notes with me wherever I went, reviewing and revising them while in hotel rooms, on trains, and even backstage at concert halls.

I had taken my notes with me in the fall of 1961 when I traveled to Holland for a recital at the Diligentia concert hall in The Hague. Afterward we went with Mrs. Beek, my Dutch impresario, to join friends and well-wishers for a late dinner at the Parkhotel Den Haag nearby. That was also where I was staying; my notes were stashed safely in my room. I was in a relaxed, happy mood:

the audience had been receptive, and I expected the reviews to be good.

The people around the dinner table were of an intellectual propensity, and a philosophical discussion soon developed. I admitted to an interest in such matters, and when someone asked about the nature of my interest, I—somewhat to my own surprise—began to talk about my ideas and theories. The gentleman sitting across from me—I'd never seen him before and hadn't caught his name during the introductions—appeared particularly interested. He engaged me in a discussion that continued late into the night.

Before the gentleman took his leave, he asked if I'd committed my ideas to paper. I told him I had but that I had never shown my writing to anyone because most people thought it was odd for a concert artist to engage in something that had no real connection to music. He didn't think it was odd at all, he replied, and offered to read what I had written.

Emboldened, I ran up to my room and retrieved my notes. He thanked me and said he looked forward to reading about my theories. Then he left, with the large stack of paper under his arm.

Shortly after he had left, I began calling myself a series of fancy but decidedly uncomplimentary names for allowing him to leave with my notes. I realized that I didn't know who he was or how to reach him. And I didn't have a copy of what I'd written—the age of photocopying hadn't arrived yet, and duplicates at that time were made by a photographer in an expensive, lengthy process that produced black sheets of paper with white letters. In any case, copying my notes would have been quite futile, as I regularly tore up and rewrote most of the pages.

The following morning while I was having breakfast on the terrace, the gentleman showed up unexpectedly. He put my bulky stack of papers on the table and said, "We'll publish it!" I was amazed. Publish it for everyone to read? And who was this "we"?

It turned out that the gentleman was Mr. Priem, the chief philosophy editor of Martinus Nijhoff, the renowned Dutch publishing house. Their nonfiction titles, mainly of a philosophical and theological bent, were published in English and read by an international scholarly public.

Mr. Priem said that my ideas merited publication and translating my work into English wouldn't be a problem. But, he said, my notes had to be made into a proper manuscript, with clear chapter headings, an introduction and conclusion, and a full list of references. This was news to me, as I'd never thought of my notes as a book. Until that moment, it never occurred to me that my ideas and theories would be of interest to anyone other than myself.

I agreed to do what I could to put my notes into proper manuscript format, and Mr. Priem assured me that he would be happy to help. With that, he excused himself and left.

♪♪♪

Three months later I sent a package containing a sizable but somewhat-less-bulky manuscript to the philosophy editor of Martinus Nijhoff. I'd organized my notes, added major headings, and typed it all out on a Remington typewriter I'd bought for that very purpose.

After another nine months, Martinus Nijhoff published what was to be the first of my many—now over eighty—books. I titled it *Essential Society: An Ontological Reconstruction*. (I added the word *ontological* to indicate that this reconstruction was not merely a theoretical exercise; it was intended to reflect reality.) The premise of my book was that there is wholeness and meaning in the natural world, as well as in the world of society. I linked the great processes of evolution in the cosmos, living nature, and the human world, and showed that together they constitute an integral, dynamic, and harmonious whole.

This was an ambitious enterprise, well beyond the established science of the day. But it turned out to be a seminal work in the then dawning holistic philosophy of science. The interest it generated was a happy surprise to me, as well as to the publisher. It launched me on a life path that I'd never seriously thought I would—or even could—enter.

♪♫♪♫♪♫

CHAPTER SIXTEEN

THE INCIDENT IN BONN

The next happening that drove me along in the pursuit of my quest was neither an epiphany nor a happy chance encounter. It was a dramatic event—a near disaster. It occurred in April 1966 on the concert stage in Bonn.

I was giving a piano recital dedicated to the works of Ludwig van Beethoven. Contrary to popular belief, Beethoven wasn't born in Vienna, although he did live there for much of his life. He was actually born in Bonn, Germany. There, understandably, a profound devotion to his music developed, and performing his sonatas in that city was considered an honor and a privilege. I took it seriously, but, it seems, not seriously enough.

♪♪♪

Four years earlier, in the spring of 1962, we'd moved from Lausanne to Fribourg, a distance of about fifty miles, so I could pursue the answers to the "big questions" of life at the University of Fribourg. József Bochenski, a famous philosopher of Polish origin, was teaching there, and I went to see him with my soon-to-be-published manuscript under my arm. He was intrigued by a successful concert pianist who wished to devote his time and energy to philosophical questions. The professor told me that in his university such questions were studied in the framework of Thomistic philosophy (the philosophy of St. Thomas Aquinas), since Fribourg was a Catholic institution. I would be welcome to explore my ideas in this frame of reference, and if I wanted to move beyond it on my own, he would support me.

Being an astute academic, when Professor Bochenski learned that my native tongue was Hungarian, he asked me to join his Institute of East European Studies as a research associate. I would be assigned to research contemporary philosophy in Hungary, an assignment that was later extended to the Soviet Union. I agreed, elated by the notion of being an academic myself.

During this period I continued to earn a living by giving concerts, but I bundled my engagements in a way that allowed me to have extended blocks of time at home, affording me the opportunity to pursue my life's quest and conduct research for Professor Bochenski's Institute.

I led a curious life, and hardly anyone could really understand it. Friends thought of me either as a concert pianist with a curious but forgivable passion for philosophy, or as a young philosophy researcher who supplemented his income by giving concerts. I felt as if I were straddling two very different worlds.

My personal life didn't suffer. Marjorie fully supported my rather schizophrenic existence, and my daily routine didn't drastically change. I practiced the piano at home in the morning, then moved to my writing desk, which was next to the piano. Interestingly, the ideas that formed the substance of my theories flowed into my consciousness while I was playing music. Living myself into a piece liberated me from the here-and-now and allowed me to roam freely in the realm of concepts and ideas. Once I sat down at my desk, all I had to do was type out the thoughts that had spontaneously flown into my mind while playing the piano.

I saved the afternoons for my family. We made trips to the surrounding countryside, enjoying the beautiful alpine landscape. Marjorie and I flew model airplanes with Christopher, went on hikes, and explored local trails on our bicycles. Even at the age of four, Christopher was fast on skis and on his bike, and he was indefatigable. Marjorie accompanied us on our excursions with picnic baskets in the summer, and she waited for us at home with hot cocoa and cake in the winter.

I set aside time for private jaunts with Casimir, my new four-wheeled friend. Casimir was a worthy successor to Jonathan, with a powerful engine and a great road personality. He (I know I should say "she," but to me my cars were more like male companions) was a Porsche 356 Super B. He had a soft-cream exterior and a bright-red leather interior. I acquired him while living in Lausanne, with the generous help of a wealthy Swiss lawyer who was a great music lover. It was an exhilarating change from the aging Beetle, although that, too, stayed with us and served Marjorie as her city runabout.

Trips with Casimir were an extraordinary experience. I would choose less-traveled mountain roads where I could fly uphill with the throttle opened way up in third gear, and sometimes in second, for extra stability. Casimir and I were singing at the top of our lungs. On the few straight stretches of the curvy alpine roads, the speedometer would shoot up to a hundred miles per hour—the rpm gauge was nearly always just below the redline—and we would take the curves with full gas and a sensitive touch of the brake, all four wheels locked in a power slide. Casimir and I were one—free and powerful.

One day on the way from Lausanne to Fribourg I had Janet, Tom Blakeley's wife, in the car with me. (Tom, a young American political scientist, was Professor Bochenski's first assistant at the Institute.) We were driving happily on the single-lane road—there were no superhighways at the time—but when we came out of a curve, we were suddenly in the direct path of a semitrailer truck trying to make a U-turn. The truck was completely blocking the road. Janet gasped. I knew there was no way I could stop the car in time; acting on instinct, I pressed down on the accelerator and threw the steering wheel to one side. Casimir jumped off the road to the field on the right. A split second later, I threw the wheel to the left, and Casimir jumped right back onto the road—with the truck now safely behind us. It lasted a second. Janet didn't say anything; she just sat there, breathing deeply and staring straight ahead.

Back in Fribourg, I regularly went to the Institute to pursue my research, attend seminars, and report on my findings. There I wore my researcher hat, not mentioning that I had a musician hat, too; it would have just confused my colleagues' image of me.

An exception arrived one November, when the famous Orchestre de la Suisse Romande came to Fribourg. It was the same orchestra I had performed with when I was fifteen, during the finals of the international music competition in Geneva. On this occasion the conductor was the permanent music director, the legendary Ernest Ansermet, an impressive gentleman with white hair, a goatee, and crystal clear green eyes. I was engaged as the soloist, and we performed Beethoven's Piano Concerto no. 5, *The Emperor.*

This proved to be a historic occasion—not because my university colleagues finally got to see me play professionally, but also because of the news we received at intermission: Swiss radio reported an incident in Dallas, Texas, and the U.S. President was said to be involved. Then the shocking news quickly spread after the concert at the reception: President Kennedy had been assassinated. It was November 22, 1963. The tragic event took place at 12:30 P.M. Dallas time, which was 7:30 in the evening in Switzerland —just as the concert got under way.

My years in Fribourg were productive. In a matter of months, I'd written another treatise. This time I focused on a philosophical problem that had great current interest: the basic difference between the dominant worldview of the West and the Marxist ideology of Eastern Europe. Titled *Individualism, Collectivism, and*

Political Power, this was also published by Martinus Nijhoff, the prestigious Dutch publishing house.

Following its publication, I was thinking about taking some time off and busying myself only with music and my family, but then an accident in the Alps decided otherwise.

In Switzerland, most able-bodied men and women go skiing in the mountains. I'd been accompanying Christopher to the neighboring hills, but I wasn't a skier; I was a hockey player, the proud *kiskapus* ("little goalie") of Budapest's municipal ice rink near my parents' home. I was the youngest on the team and since being a goalie wasn't popular—one couldn't score from there—I was elected to the position. I soon proved my mettle, however, by being willing to throw myself onto fast pucks in a way few others dared. One day Tom and Janet Blakeley suggested that we go to a popular mountain slope so I could do some real skiing. We went to Les Diablerets, which should have given me pause—the mountain is named after the devil: *le diable*. Christopher couldn't wait to go, and at that time, "Alexandra" (who later turned out to be Alexander) was just a gleam in Marjorie's eyes. Marjorie, of course, was practically born on skis in her native Finland and was all for it. We decided to go for a week.

During the first two days, I practiced on the lower slopes reserved for beginners, and on the third day, I ventured higher. I accompanied the Blakeleys and Marjorie to the highest slope. I managed to make it down successfully, using the simple but inelegant "cross-ski" method of braking. I was in good spirits, and we had lunch in the alpine hut at the top of the slope.

Afterward, I thought I'd try parallel skiing. I kept my knees together and leaned forward. I soon realized that I was moving like an express train and kept picking up speed. I tried pointing my skis inward to brake but couldn't—I was going too fast. I knew I couldn't maintain that speed for long without crashing, so I threw myself into the soft powder snow to the left.

I started rolling, but then my skis abruptly stopped me. I felt a sharp pull on my right leg, but it wasn't painful. I promptly got up to continue downhill, but as soon as I was standing, I felt a massive jolt in my right leg that was like an electric shock. I looked down and saw that my right boot was at an odd angle. I tried straightening it, but this produced another shock of pain. I sat down.

A stream of skiers passed me, and I just remained where I was. Then an instructor happened by and, after taking one look at my leg, told me not to move.

Two young men with red crosses on the back of their jackets soon arrived, and they were towing a stretcher attached to a sled. They loaded me on it and skied me down to the emergency shelter at the bottom. There the chief medic asked if I'd like my leg put back into place, and I told him that I did. Two hefty young men then grasped my shoulders from behind, and another two took hold of my right leg. Someone put a clean towel into my mouth and said to bite down hard on it. They pulled and twisted, and my leg was straight once again. It only took a moment, and although it was far from pleasant, I survived.

Later on, I learned the reason why my right leg had fractured. We'd placed our skis against the back wall of the alpine hut where we had lunch, near the exhaust fan of the kitchen. Hot moist air warmed the bindings, and a layer of ice formed on them. The simple chain binding on my rental skis was frozen solid. So when I threw myself to the side of the slope, my skis didn't release on impact, but produced the sharp torsion that broke my ankle completely through.

On the car ride back home, my leg didn't stay in the proper position. The doctor at a hospital in Fribourg told me that I had two options: he could open up my ankle and insert screws to keep the bones together, or I could undergo the "natural method." I chose the latter. He gently raised my leg and picked up an instrument that looked like a power drill with a long, shiny bit. He placed it just below my ankle and started drilling. The bit slid smoothly through my foot and reappeared on the other side. I couldn't believe my eyes, but there was no pain. The doctor then pulled out the bit and inserted a stainless steel rod in its place. Wires were attached to its two ends and then hooked to a pulley, which was connected to a weight, at the foot of the bed.

For three whole weeks, I had to lie flat on my back with my leg attached to that pulley. I couldn't move, but I could sit up and read . . . and so I read and read.

Marjorie brought over the books that had been stacked on my desk, waiting for me to look at when I had the time. Now I did. Each day I consumed an entire book, and sometimes the better part of two, and took copious notes. I continued doing this throughout the six weeks of convalescence that followed my discharge from the hospital. I even gave concerts with my right leg in a plaster cast, using my left foot on the pedals. (Alas, that didn't work with Casimir, as I needed both feet for the pedals, so we had to spend some time apart.)

All of that reading and writing resulted in a new book called *Beyond Scepticism and Realism: An Exploration of Husserlian and Whiteheadian Methods of Inquiry*, published in 1966, again by Martinus Nijhoff. In it, I explored two seemingly opposing viewpoints: the skeptical and the realist, as exemplified in the works of German philosopher Edmund Husserl and English-born Harvard philosopher Alfred North Whitehead. I'd found that their approaches converged on key points, and these, I asserted, provided the most reliable avenue for understanding the world.

♪♪♪

I had just completed *Beyond Scepticism and Realism* when I went to Bonn for my Beethoven recital. I was already deep into my next book, based on the organic metaphysics of Whitehead. It was to be my principal work, a complete philosophy embracing the idea that all things in nature are dynamic, self-organizing systems, interacting and co-evolving to higher and higher levels of coherence and complexity. It took me five years to research and write this book, and it was published in 1972 in New York under the title *Introduction to Systems Philosophy: Toward a New Paradigm of Contemporary Thought*.

On the way to Bonn, my head was full of these dynamic and evolutionary concepts. I remember looking out the train window as we followed the Rhine on the stretch made famous by the legend of Lorelei. The rock where she was said to have sat overlooking the river was on one side, and picturesque medieval castles topped the hills on both sides as far as the eye could see.

I looked at this breathtaking sight, but I didn't really see it—at least, not in the way one normally does. I didn't see trees, rivers, castles, and clouds; rather, I saw dynamic shapes interacting, fusing, differentiating, and evolving. There were no trees and clouds . . . only things "treeing" and "clouding." Nouns were no longer applicable—only verbs were. I later learned that this was also how some Native American cultures viewed the world, including the Hopi.

I asked myself: *How could all of this active "be-ing" have started? And where would it lead?* I was so deep into these questions that I almost forgot to get off the train. We'd already been in the station in Bonn for a minute or two when I realized that the conductor was whistling for the train to depart. *No harm done,* I thought to myself, but more serious harm was nearly done the following day on the concert stage.

The next day I caught myself deep in thought over these questions when I suddenly realized that I was onstage, playing the second movement of Beethoven's *Waldstein* sonata, Opus 53. This piece, like most second movements, is slow and lyrical and doesn't require much attention to the physical aspect of the performance. My fingers were touching the right keys, but my mind could be, and was, elsewhere.

But just how far was I into the second movement? As always in the classical sonata form, the main theme starts, develops, returns, and then takes a different direction toward the coda. This follows a basic A-B-A-C pattern. I was playing the main theme A, but was I playing it for the first time or the second? I started to panic, wondering, *Should I continue with the middle part B, or go to the ending C?*

I had no idea, and making the wrong choice would be disastrous. I'd risk repeating the entire middle part or skipping it altogether—a scandal either way. I took a deep breath and decided that I was playing the theme for the second time. I went on to the coda and launched right into the lyrical, but much more vigorous, third movement. I listened with bated breath for gasps from the public. Nothing. I relaxed and turned off my metaphysical concerns, and committed myself to what I should always have been doing during a performance: living myself into the music.

After the concert, I went for a long walk. I was lucky this time, I told myself, but this couldn't go on. I had to make a choice: either remain a concert pianist and concentrate on my playing, or give up my musical career and devote myself to my intellectual quest.

Both options were open. A week earlier I'd received a letter from Professor John Schrader, the head of the philosophy department at Yale. He'd read my books and invited me to pursue my research in his department. This was late spring, and if I agreed, I would start in September for the fall term. I needed to make a decision as soon as possible.

I was gratified and deeply flattered to receive an invitation from Yale but initially didn't take the offer seriously. My concert engagements were already set for the year, and I had to respect them. But now, after this near disaster onstage, I saw things differently. I realized this was a major opportunity, and I had a serious decision to make.

When I returned to my room at midnight, my mind was made up. In the morning I wrote a letter to Professor Schrader and went to the post office to mail it. The letter said: "It is my pleasure to accept your invitation. I will be at the Yale campus in New Haven as of the beginning of September to join your department."

♪♫♪♫♪♫

CHAPTER SEVENTEEN

THE LIFE OF AN ACADEMIC IN AMERICA

With the decision to go to Yale, an entirely new phase of my life had started. Not only was I moving from Europe to America, I was shifting from the life of an itinerant concert pianist to that of a stable university professor. I was becoming an academic in America.

In the fall of 1966, I went to New Haven alone, and Marjorie stayed in Switzerland with the boys. I became a Fellow of Silliman College and was given lodging and meals in the college. I participated in the seminars of the philosophy department and attended a variety of lectures, ranging from quantum physics and astrophysics all the way to evolutionary biology, aesthetics, and mathematical logic.

I made friends with some of the great scholars I had studied and had always hoped to meet: the philosopher F.S.C. Northrop, an eminent disciple and close friend of Whitehead; Henry Margenau, the quantum physicist who was also a leading-edge thinker; Norwood Russell Hanson, the renowned philosopher of science who, not long after I met him, died in a plane crash; and Paul Weiss, the maverick thinker who wrote dozens of treatises, including *The Philosophy of Sport,* although he never engaged in any sport himself. (He told me that he was only interested in things he knew little about.) Upon their suggestion, I studied the work of Ludwig von Bertalanffy, the Austrian biologist who founded general system theory, and exchanged letters and papers with him. We met a year later, and remained close friends and collaborators until he died in 1972.

I also met Raymond Polin, the French philosopher who was then a visiting professor from the University of Paris. He attended one of my research seminars and asked if I would be prepared to submit a doctoral thesis on my topic at the Sorbonne. I was happy to accept. Even though no one had insisted on my having a "sheepskin" that testified to my work in the theory and philosophy of science, it was certainly a welcome addition. I wrote the thesis in French (the choice was between French, Sanskrit, Greek, or Latin) and defended it at the Sorbonne's historic Amphitheatre Richelieu. My thesis, titled *La Metaphysique de Whitehead: Recherche sur les Prolongements Anthropologiques* ("The Metaphysics of Whitehead: Research on the Anthropological Extension"), was published by Martinus Nijhoff in 1970.

While I was at Yale, I received invitations from several American universities. James Wilbur, who had just been named chairman of the philosophy department at the University of Akron, was among those who came to see me in New Haven. This marked the beginning of a long-lasting friendship. Jim invited me to join him in Akron, where the university had become part of the Ohio State system. He had been charged with building the faculty in the philosophy department and thought I would be someone who could give it the needed breadth of interest and vision.

I liked Jim and I liked the offer, so in the following fall, I joined the Akron faculty. Marjorie and the boys and I spent an enjoyable winter in Ohio, living in the tranquil suburb of Tallmadge.

♪♪♪

We didn't get to Akron right away. First there was an adventurous trip across the Atlantic and then a memorable summer in Bloomington, Indiana. Wilfred C. Bain, dean of the renowned School of Music at Indiana University, wanted me to join his school's faculty on a permanent basis. As a musician active in philosophy, I would be teaching both a master class in piano and a seminar on the philosophy of music. I finally agreed to give a philosophy of music seminar during the summer semester, but then I would be going on to teach philosophy at Akron.

Back in Switzerland, Marjorie and I said good-bye to our friends, Professor Bochenski, and my colleagues at the Institute of East European Studies. I performed one last concert in Le Locle, near the French border where I took leave of my Bechstein concert grand that had accompanied me first from Munich to Lausanne, and then from Lausanne to Fribourg. I donated the lovely instrument to the local concert society to ensure that it would be kept in mint condition.

Marjorie and I acquired a VW station wagon to transport our belongings, which consisted mostly of boxes of books. Casimir, my two-seater sports car, came along, but he wasn't much help in this regard. We drove to the Italian Riviera for a last family vacation on the Mediterranean, and then boarded the SS *Independence* in Genoa bound for New York.

I was an old hand at ocean crossings, having traveled between Europe and the U.S. dozens of times by sea in the 1950s. I would always take either the *Independence* or the *Constitution,* the twin flagships of the American Export Lines. The ships would spend four to five days in the Mediterranean, calling at Naples, Genoa,

Barcelona, and Lisbon before embarking on the five-day crossing to New York. On every voyage, I would give a concert during the trip and in return receive first-class passage and an invitation to sit at the captain's table.

The trips were enlivened by innocent and mostly soon-forgotten shipboard romances, but there was one particularly memorable occasion. The captain introduced me to a striking young woman with flowing red hair who seemed strangely familiar. I soon realized that she was Rita Hayworth, the glamorous Hollywood movie star. After dinner I asked her to dance, wondering how it would feel to have a world-famous sex symbol in my arms. But instead of snuggling close and concentrating on me and the dancing, she talked about her next film role. Even so, I could later remark in a suitably offhanded way that I'd danced with Rita Hayworth. Sherry, who was my near-fiancée at the time, was much impressed.

Now in 1967, I had a wife, two children, two cars, and several boxes of books and other belongings in tow. All went well until Marjorie developed a very bad cold with a high fever, probably owing to sudden changes from the hot upper deck to the air-conditioned stateroom. The ship's doctor, anxious to ensure that all passengers walked off the ship on two legs, shot her full of antibiotics. The result was that Marjorie's fever ceased, but she was quite nauseated. When that problem had been treated, she could finally sleep—and sleep she did. She was out most of the time, barely managing to keep her eyes open at mealtimes.

At the end of the journey, we arrived majestically in New York Harbor, with tugboats shooting streams of water into the air, as first the Statue of Liberty and then the Manhattan skyline impressively came into view. I had been looking forward to showing this fantastic sight to Marjorie, who had never been to the United States. But she didn't see it—she was sleeping.

Marjorie tried to shake off her drowsiness when it was time to disembark, as we were headed to Yale for the weekend, and since I was driving Casimir, she had to drive the station wagon. She managed to keep herself alert during the trip by concentrating on Casimir's taillights. She didn't see anything of New York either.

Once we were installed in the guest suite at Silliman College, Marjorie continued sleeping, and a doctor from Yale Medical School came to examine her. He found nothing amiss, saying that she just needed to rest, eat well, and wait for her body to heal.

In the meantime, we still had to drive nearly a thousand miles from New Haven to Bloomington, Indiana. Marjorie was driving the station wagon behind me, trying desperately to stay alert and not lose sight of Casimir's taillights. Christopher was with me and sat facing the back in the rear jump seat, reporting on whether his mother's car was still in sight—and still on the road.

In Bloomington, we found the house Dean Bain had rented for us; it belonged to a faculty member who was out of town for the summer. It was large and comfortable. After a week or two, Marjorie was fully recovered, neither nauseated nor drowsy. We had a wonderful time. We reconnected with many Hungarian musicians who had left the country at about the time I did and had become well-known artists in their own right, including pianist György Sebök and cellist János Starker.

That summer semester also marked my first attempt to teach a regular college class. At Yale I had a research assignment, and the seminars I gave were for interested students and faculty members; they were informal presentations followed by in-depth discussions. Now I had the responsibility of teaching students who were enrolled in a degree program.

Since I personally had never taken a university class for credit, I never had to take exams and wasn't quite sure how to conduct them. I couldn't ask anyone for help, as my colleagues took it for granted that I had a bona fide university background. I was comfortable with lectures because I could prepare in advance, writing out all of the material by hand, but I had to invent the exams as I went along. At the end, nobody found anything amiss, but I was relieved when it was over. I wasn't quite sure that I would be able to pull it off without embarrassing hitches.

Starting in the fall, as I was teaching philosophy at the University of Akron, I steadily grew more confident in my abilities. And by the end of that year, I felt like a veteran college professor.

♪♫♪♫♪♫

CHAPTER EIGHTEEN

THE CALL FROM PRINCETON

A few years later, the next stage of my quest was ignited. It was centered on applying, in a practical way, what I was beginning to understand in theoretical terms about the world—in particular, the world we had created for ourselves on this planet.

The phone call that triggered this shift from theory to practice came out of the blue. Professor Richard ("Dick") Falk, whom I'd never met and knew only by reputation, called to invite me to conduct a series of seminars at the Center of International Studies at Princeton. The topic to be discussed was the world system.

I told him that I knew next to nothing about the "world system," but he said not to worry and explained that he just wanted me to discuss my theory of the evolutionary dynamics of complex systems. Surely, he said, not only were individuals and particular societies complex systems, but the entire human world was a complex system as well. Therefore, my concept of how such systems evolve could be applied to the "world system." I couldn't argue with this and agreed to apply for a leave of absence and come to Princeton.

By this time, which was in the fall of 1972, I was a professor at the State University of New York (SUNY) at Geneseo. The invitation to join the faculty at SUNY came while I was still in Akron. The offer was excellent: I would be free to teach the courses I wanted to and was also able to bring Jim Wilbur aboard to assume the chairmanship of the department. (Jim was adept as a department head, while I detested all types of administrative duties and avoided them as much as possible.) Dr. Robert MacVittie, the president at Geneseo, granted all of my wishes.

So back in June of 1968, after a year in Ohio, Marjorie and I packed up our two cars once again. This time we drove from Akron to the beautiful Finger Lakes district of upstate New York so that I could assume my new position at SUNY.

Our move, however, was marred by a freak accident on the New York State Thruway. It was due to a defective front tire on the VW station wagon that Marjorie was driving. The tire was brand new, but it had simply exploded on the road. I was driving Casimir, following behind Marjorie, and experienced the worst moments of my life.

As we were driving, there was a sudden loud bang, and I saw that one of Marjorie's front tires had blown out as the heavily loaded station wagon swerved sharply. Apparently, some of the boxes had shifted, and one hit Marjorie on the head, knocking her out. The station wagon spun out violently and actually flipped over—not once but twice, and then landed on four wheels just inches from where Marjorie was now lying unconscious in the middle of the Thruway. She'd been thrown from the car moments before. Alexander, who was sitting next to her on the front seat, had also been launched out of the car and was lying in a daze not too far from where Marjorie was. Miraculously, he was shaken but unhurt, having survived nearly unscathed.

Traffic came to a screeching halt, of course, and people gathered around the inert figures on the road. An ambulance arrived and whisked Marjorie and Alexander to the nearest hospital. I managed to follow the ambulance, with Christopher next to me in Casimir.

I have no idea how much time we spent in the middle of the Thruway, and I don't have any recollection of the accident itself. The last thing I can clearly remember is the station wagon swinging from one side of the road to the other and then starting to turn over. The next thing I remember is seeing Marjorie lying motionless on the ground. Christopher later said that as I brought our car to a halt, a strange sound came from my throat.

Marjorie spent the first night in the hospital hovering between life and death. I held her hand throughout the night. She regained consciousness the following day and told me that she saw herself lying on the bed, as if she were suspended just below the ceiling. Then she was somehow floating higher and higher, seeing first the hospital and then the whole town in the moonlit night. When dawn started to break, she floated back down and saw me dozing in the chair next to her bed, still holding her hand. She knew she had to come back. The next morning, the doctor told me that she was out of danger and would fully recover.

A week later we rented a car and continued on our way to Geneseo, where we met wonderful colleagues who did everything to help us and make us feel at home.

We settled into a well-built house that was surrounded by fields and a forest, six miles from the campus. I taught classes three days a week and thoroughly enjoyed the drive to school. The rural road crossed a beautiful countryside and had little traffic, allowing me to fly with Casimir without having to fear immediate arrest. I had an eight-track tape player installed in the dashboard and listened to the mystical, nature-inspired compositions of Brahms, Grieg, and Sibelius—music I chose to fit the setting, and my mood.

It was in the course of this ordered life that I'd completed my major work: *Introduction to Systems Philosophy*. Then, almost immediately, I wrote a shorter book called *The Systems View of the World,* which eventually led to the invitation to Princeton.

To my happy surprise (and my publisher's), *Systems View*—although mainly intended for philosophers and philosophy students—caught the interest of natural scientists, especially biologists and ecologists; it was also picked up by schools of management, institutes and departments of psychology, and schools and departments of public affairs. Dick Falk had come across it and thought that the ideas I'd presented could provide useful input to the World Order Models Project (known as "WOMP") he headed with Professor Saul Mendlovitz of Rutgers University.

Writing *Systems View* wasn't something I had planned; it just happened. In 1972, after five years of reading, writing, and rewriting, *Introduction to Systems Philosophy* was published in New York, first by Gordon & Breach Science Publishers and then as a Harper Torchbook. I was just going to sit back and spend a few weeks decompressing, until something occurred at a faculty party that Marjorie and I had attended. Everyone was having a good time dancing, sipping martinis, and carrying on spirited conversations. I was chatting with the wife of a colleague who remarked that she'd just finished reading my new book. Then with a laugh, she said, "When will you write something that ordinary mortals can understand?"

Her question got me thinking. True, my books were mainly geared for philosophers, but I'd hoped that my style of writing was clear enough that anyone interested in the topic would understand my work. Evidently, on that score I needed to do better.

The following week there was a snowstorm, which was not unusual in upstate New York, and the campus was shut down. I had the day to myself and was wondering what project to get into next, when the young woman's remark came to mind. *All right,* I said to myself, *I'll explain what this book is all about.*

I sat down at the typewriter and started. It took longer than I had anticipated: by the evening, I was only a third of the way through, yet I had already filled two dozen pages. Classes were again cancelled the next day so I continued. The day after that I took the stack of about a hundred pages and went to the den to read through it. I needed to polish some parts, but on the whole it read well. I gave it to the faculty wife who made the comment at the party, and she returned it the following day with some questions. I clarified some sections and worked the answers to her queries into the text, and gave it back to her again. The next time I saw her, she told me that she now understood what I had in mind.

On an impulse, I stuffed the pages into an envelope and sent it to George Braziller, the New York publisher who—having published Ludwig von Bertalanffy's groundbreaking *General System Theory* a few years earlier—had just asked me if I would edit a series of books on systems thinking. He said that my manuscript would fit the series beautifully, but he wanted a proper title for it—I was originally calling it "Systems Philosophy Explained." We settled on *The Systems View of the World,* and George Braziller published it in record time; it was released in the late fall of 1972, the same year as *Systems Philosophy.*

One book took five years to write and the other, one week. In the years that followed, the "one-week book" was reprinted several times, translated into seven languages, and outsold the other by ten to one. And it was also the book that sparked the phone call that led to the invitation to Princeton—and to the practice-oriented phase of my quest for a deeper understanding of the world. Of *our* world.

♪♪♪

When Marjorie and I went to Princeton, the quiet life of upstate New York came to an end. Giving seminars in the great lecture hall of the Woodrow Wilson School was a fascinating experience. Not only would Princeton faculty members attend, but students from various departments would also sit in. I could invite scientists from other universities as guest lecturers, and I took full advantage of this option. I prepared thoroughly for each seminar and noted the main ideas that cropped up in the discussions. These notes became the basis for my next book: *A Strategy for the*

Future: The Systems Approach to World Order. It was published two years later by George Braziller in New York.

Strategy wound up on the desk of Aurelio Peccei, the founder and president of the global think tank known as the Club of Rome. I had been in touch with him for some time regarding the Club's much-discussed report *The Limits to Growth.* Published in 1972, *Limits* was based on a series of computer runs on MIT's supercomputer. Although using computer projections to simulate trends is commonplace today (and most laptops now have as much computing power as MIT's giant machine had then), at the time this was a sensational innovation. It was the first time that this type of technology was employed in order to examine humankind's prospects for the future.

The results showed that if the kind of growth we were having since the middle of the twentieth century would continue unchanged, the world system would collapse in less than a hundred years. Aurelio Peccei, an international businessman who was also head of the South American branch of the Italian automaker Fiat, turned to me because he wanted to take the next step. Now we have an idea of the "outer" limits to growth, he said, but what about the "inner" limits? Having read *Systems View,* he asked if I would write a book on the limits to growth that are innate to people and societies.

I agreed that the question of inner limits surely merited serious attention but told him that writing a book or report on it would call for more than armchair theorizing. Firsthand research in various regions of the world would be necessary, and this, in turn, would require an international research team.

Since Aurelio was traveling through New York on his way to Rome, we decided to talk this over in person. When I met with him at his hotel on Park Avenue a week later, I put a proposal for an international research project on the table.

He looked at it and said, "This is good, but you can't oversee this international project from your college campus—you need an office equipped for global communication." He told me that he needed to discuss this with his friend Dr. Davidson Nicol, the head of the United Nations Institute for Training and Research (UNITAR).

A world-class manager, Aurelio didn't waste a moment, and Dr. Nicol was soon on the line. Aurelio outlined the project and then handed me the phone. Ten minutes later, Dr. Nicol appointed me as Special Fellow at UNITAR and offered me an office at the institute's UN headquarters. There I would have access to telephone, telex, telegraph, and postal services through the UN's diplomatic pouch. These were unique resources at the time, as it was before the global telecommunications revolution.

The chance to work from UN headquarters couldn't be passed up, yet I couldn't just leave my position at SUNY either; I had already been away long enough doing seminars at Princeton. In any event, I needed to assemble a core team. I stayed on in Geneseo and assembled a group of bright young researchers from various parts of the country to work with me. One of them, Skip Fedanzo, stayed with me for many years. We held meetings at major international research institutes, including the Aspen Institute in Colorado and the International Institute for Applied Systems Analysis (IIASA) outside Vienna.

By fall 1977, the time had come for me to begin full-time international research, which meant that I needed to operate out of the UN office made available by Dr. Nicol. So once again, Marjorie and I packed up our belongings and moved from the Upstate campus of my university to the center of Manhattan. I shifted from lofty if rather isolated "halls of ivy" to the halls where all the nation-states of the world attempt to come together to tackle the common problems they face.

♪♫♪♫♪♫

CHAPTER NINETEEN

ASSIGNMENT AT THE UNITED NATIONS

My office at UNITAR was in the old IBM building, directly across from the famous "glass palace" of the Secretariat. It was spacious and had an impressive view of the rest of the UN and the East River beyond. The staff, which included two professional assistants, a multilingual secretary, and two interns, was given nearly unlimited telecommunication facilities. A grant by the State University of New York's Research Foundation took care of travel costs and provided us with a monthly stipend.

I exchanged my academic slacks and sweaters for the white shirt and dark suit of a diplomat. I became an international civil servant but had the kind of freedom and autonomy that few civil servants could enjoy, whether at the United Nations or elsewhere.

Marjorie and I had the good luck to be offered Dr. Nicol's apartment when he moved to larger quarters in the East 80s. It was next to UN headquarters, with windows facing Dag Hammarskjöld Plaza. This location had the advantage of being only a five-minute walk to my office, and I could come home for lunch every day. (The disadvantage, Marjorie would point out, was that I would sometimes show up with a colleague or two in tow without warning.)

Dag Hammarskjöld Plaza was a quiet location, except when demonstrations at the UN were taking place. Protesters would set up before daybreak, and by morning thousands would assemble . . . right below our window. Until the processions moved across the street toward the Secretariat, we had the "benefit" of listening to slogans shouted a thousand times and amplified by powerful loudspeakers.

At the office there were the usual intrigues and jealousies, and endless administrative red tape—but there were compensations. Working at the world's only universal organization was a heady experience. Here all of the nations of the world came together. Although those assembled were there to officially represent their government, they also, in many ways, represented the habits, cultures, and even the hopes and expectations of their home countries. This was the human family meeting face-to-face.

I went to the office each morning with the joyous expectancy of a child entering a candy store. If I managed to get things done it was owing in no small measure to Nina, my secretary. When my first secretary, Tessa, who was from the Philippines, decided to leave the United Nations, I called my good friend Sally, who was the head of the UN's NGO office. Sally knew everyone in the system and said that she had the perfect replacement: Nina, a super-efficient German woman. She had been experiencing problems with insistent advances by her current boss and was looking for a new assignment.

Nina came to my office for an interview, and after taking one look at her, I could understand why she was having difficulty with her boss. She was tall, with long blonde hair and blue eyes, and had the kind of magnetism that I thought only movie stars possessed. When she walked down a hall, all heads would turn.

As she and I chatted, she told me her story: when she was nineteen, she met a young English journalist in her native East Berlin. They fell in love and escaped to England together. They got married and eventually came to New York. Nina gave birth to their daughter, but her journalist husband soon developed other "interests" and disappeared. Nina only had a temporary visa, but working for the UN Secretariat allowed her to stay in the country.

That had transpired nearly ten years ago. Since then, she'd been forced to change assignments several times, always for the same reason: unwanted attention from her boss.

I hired Nina on the spot and never regretted it. She spoke English with a soft German accent and could speak some French in addition to her native German. When she typed, it sounded like a small machine gun, and she was always on time. She knew all of the other secretaries, which was an invaluable asset. (As insiders know, it's the secretaries who run the United Nations—no wonder some say that the headquarters is called the "Secretariat.") If I needed to see someone way up in the hierarchy, Nina would say, "Leave it to me—I know his secretary." She would conduct a long conversation on the phone. Then a few minutes later, her phone would ring and she would stick her head in my door, asking, "Tomorrow noon—is good?"

Nina also considered it her duty to protect me from scheming females. At one time an attractive young Hungarian woman asked for an interview. She'd recently finished her master's in international relations at Columbia University and was seeking a job at the UN. She thought that my program at UNITAR was just what she was looking for. She came to see me and was full of ideas about how I should be running it. She spoke at length, entirely in Hungarian. Nina didn't like it at all.

A few days later, I invited the young lady to lunch at the Delegates Dining Room in the Secretariat building, and was planning to offer her a job. No sooner had we finished our appetizers when Nina showed up, carrying an official-looking file. How she'd managed to get into the dining room, I don't know—executive secretaries could enter only if a crisis erupted somewhere in the world and the Secretary-General or one of his associates had to be notified. But Nina could gain access anywhere.

She came to our table and said that I needed to sign an urgent document. I opened the file she placed before me and scanned the paper: indeed, it was a letter I needed to sign, but it wasn't urgent. Attached to it was a handwritten note from her: "Attention: sure this is good idea?" I signed the letter and scribbled on the note: "Don't worry." Nina nodded, had a last look at my guest, and left. I thought twice before offering the job to the young lady—and in the end, I didn't.

♪♪♪

While working at the United Nations, my former life as a professor didn't cease; in fact, I kept receiving invitations from all over the country for guest lectures and seminars. One such invitation from the University of Houston at Clear Lake City intrigued me in particular. Clear Lake was a new campus at the time and was located close to the Houston manned-spaceflight center, which is where astronauts on space missions would contact when they needed to "talk to Earth." The college administrators were looking for ways to collaborate with their world-famous neighbor, so they created a program in "Futures Studies." They asked me to come down from New York and consider running it.

The campus was in the beautiful bayou region near the Gulf of Mexico, and the classrooms were in a large ultramodern building where all of the rooms faced inward toward a central court. The structure was high-tech and stood apart from its surroundings—it looked like it belonged on the moon. The students enrolled in the program were mostly mature individuals who had a passion for space exploration and the future of humanity, which they believed were closely linked.

The invitation to head the Futures Studies Program at Clear Lake was enticing, but my own projects at the UN couldn't be abandoned. In the end I arrived at a compromise, at least for a while. I decided to combine the two assignments and responsibilities, which meant lecturing at Clear Lake two days per week and carrying out my tasks at the UN the other three. Every Sunday, I would take the Delta flight from LaGuardia to Houston Intercontinental, drive a rental car the considerable distance to Clear Lake, check into a motel, and be at the campus on Monday morning. After my last class on Tuesday, I would drive back to the airport in Houston and take the return flight to New York. I did this for an entire semester.

When the semester was over, I knew that I couldn't maintain this routine and had to decide which way to go. After talking it over with Marjorie, I elected to stay in New York and pursue my research for the Club of Rome at UNITAR.

My first objective was to establish criteria for the required global-level survey. With the help of Dr. Nicol and other high-level UN officials, I managed to create a network of more than ninety research institutes in different parts of the world. We investigated what I determined were the main questions: *What is it that people and states really want? What are their basic goals and objectives? Could all these goals and objectives be achieved on a finite planet with finite resources?*

After a year of intense work based on mountains of research, we came up with an integrated report. Aurelio Peccei liked it and insisted that we title it *Goals for Mankind*. I would have much preferred giving it a more down-to-earth title, such as "A Survey of the Goals of Mankind," but Aurelio said that it wasn't time to be modest; the report must offer a clear vision and direction. This was my report to the Club of Rome, published in the original English version in 1977 and in several other languages soon after. The full title was *Goals for Mankind: A Report to the Club of Rome on the New Horizons of Global Community.* (Had it been published today,

159

I would have insisted on using the word *Humankind* rather than *Mankind*.)

Once the report to the Club of Rome was completed, I thanked Dr. Nicol for hosting me at UNITAR and was getting ready to return to the SUNY campus at Geneseo. A few days later, however, Dr. Nicol called me. The General Assembly decided to establish a United Nations University and accepted Japan's offer to host it, he told me. Would I be willing to represent UNITAR, an ex officio member of the board, at the UNU's founding conference in Tokyo?

I went to Tokyo, presented my findings, and then returned to Geneseo. But again, I was not there for long. Dr. Nicol's next surprise call was to ask if I would head UNITAR's research on the New International Economic Order, known as the NIEO. The General Assembly approved the NIEO as an objective to take into consideration and requested that the Secretary-General write up an evaluation. Kurt Waldheim, the Secretary-General at the time, requested UNITAR to take on the project, and the head of UNITAR asked me to head it.

This was not something I felt I could turn down, so I said yes. Soon I was back at my office at UNITAR, this time not as a Special Fellow, but as the director of the official UNITAR Programme on the NIEO.

I was now an integral part of the system, which meant that I was also subjected to the office politics that went with the position, but I did gain new privileges and opportunities. I met with foreign ministers and other dignitaries in many parts of the world, hosted international meetings, and made frequent trips to Kuwait, given that the Kuwait Fund for Arab Economic Development had provided much of the financing for the project.

I experienced a lot of frustration and setbacks. International politics combined with internal UN politics was a heavy load to bear—it called for a great deal of fortitude and patience. I was not known for my unceasing patience, and the situation often unnerved me. But thanks to Dr. Nicol's support (he was the Under-

Secretary-General in charge of all research and training at the United Nations), I was able to make surprisingly good progress.

♪♪♪

Robert "Bob" Maxwell, the world famous (and later infamous) media tycoon, was a thoroughly likable man, larger than life in every way. He was tall and broad, and had made and lost enormous fortunes several times in his life. He lived in a castle overlooking Oxford, and his ambition was to displace Rupert Murdoch as the world's top media magnate. He died tragically in 1991 under mysterious circumstances: he had either fallen, jumped, or been pushed overboard from his yacht while sailing near the Canary Islands.

Bob visited me at the UN and became a dedicated supporter of my program. Pergamon Press, a company he co-founded, published our research reports in the form of a beautifully produced set of volumes known as "The NIEO Library." He provided enough extra copies so we could pass them out to all of the ambassadors and delegates in the UN system. Most of them responded favorably, and we expected that the project would become an international economic reality before long.

The future of the NIEO in the world was to be decided at the Special Session of the General Assembly called "Global Dialogue." The Session was to take place in the fall of 1980 and vote on the adoption of the comprehensive package of measures that would constitute the new international economic order. The plan was to shift additional financial and decision-making power into the hands of the developing countries so that they could determine and manage their own future. The industrialized nations needed to agree to this shift for it to work.

I sat by the Under-Secretary-General during the preparatory negotiations. The developing countries were getting organized, and some of the industrialized countries were with them—Canada, the Nordic countries, and Holland among them. We were hopeful that the General Assembly would launch the global negotiations, and the program we had researched and elaborated would be adopted.

When the time came for the Special Session, Dr. Nicol and I were in the General Assembly Hall, anxiously waiting for the voting to start. But before it could even begin, three delegations announced that they are "not participating": the U.S., the U.K., and the FRG (the Federal Republic of Germany—West Germany, prior to its unification with Communist East Germany). Since they represented the major economic powers of the world, the other countries could vote all they wished but nothing meaningful would come of it. As a result, the vote didn't take place.

The much-heralded Global Dialogue never even got off the ground. The NIEO was dead.

What now? New ideas were needed. Secretary-General Kurt Waldheim consulted Under-Secretary-General Davidson Nicol, who consulted the head of the now-defunct research program on the NIEO. I did have a proposal to suggest: there was a good way to overcome the stalemate in the negotiations. We had to avoid letting this turn into a purely "North-South issue" (rich vs. poor), a "dialogue of the deaf" as former Chancellor of West Berlin Willy Brandt dubbed it. We must create a more differentiated and globally realistic process. How to achieve that can be discovered, I explained, on the basis of modern systems theory.

When you have an overall system with as many highly unequal members as the UN, making decisions that are acceptable to everyone is extremely difficult. Some members have great wealth and a large population, others have great wealth and a small population, and some have no wealth at all, only a substantial population. It doesn't help to assemble the poor countries on one side and the rich countries on the other. The wealthy countries perceive the negotiations as a "zero-sum game" where the number of "chips" remains the same—they only get redistributed. So if the poor countries are given more chips, the rich countries assume that they will have to do with less. Any program with this type of foundation would never even get off the ground—as the collapse of the Special Session had just illustrated.

I argued that we needed to start a "game" that is positive sum, where the gain of one is a gain for the others. This means pooling the complementary resources of the poor players and strengthening them through *regional cooperation.*

All countries in Asia, Latin America, and Africa would benefit from a system of regional cooperation. The cooperative groups in the various regions could then develop relations among themselves; this could be the second tier of the systemic global reconstruction process called "*inter*regional cooperation."

I argued that the system of regional and interregional cooperation is bound to produce results. The cooperating developing countries would come to the global negotiating table when their efforts had started to bear fruit. They would then have more going for them than just a power lobby—the so-called Group of 77 in the General Assembly—instead, they would carry real economic weight. And as they would then bring more chips to the table, the "game" between developing countries and industrialized nations could take off. It would no longer be a dialogue of the deaf.

This was the crux of the scheme I proposed through UNITAR to the Secretary-General. It was to be implemented by creating a "Programme on Regional and Interregional Cooperation among Developing Countries" (RCDC for short). The program received the green light, and I was put in charge of it.

Implementing the RCDC was an even bigger challenge than preparing the NIEO, because this was now a UNITAR project that, while it had the blessing of the Secretary-General, was not formally adopted by the General Assembly. This meant no direct access to UN financing. I was forced to raise the funds myself.

Some of the wealthy Arab supporters came through with funds, and I could assemble another research network topped by what we called following UN usage the "Panel of Eminent Persons." The members of the panel were foreign ministers and ambassadors from Kuwait, Algeria, Venezuela, and Sri Lanka, among others. The Panel met in various places in the world and produced resolutions and decisions that were incorporated into the final proposal. Bob Maxwell once again published the principal reports, and we placed another set of handsomely bound volumes ("The RCDC Series") on the desks of the UN ambassadors.

After four years of painstaking work, made difficult by the growing financial penury of the United Nations, the fully elaborated and frequently reviewed and revised "Declaration on Regional Cooperation among Developing Countries" was ready to be transmitted to the Secretary-General. As it happened, Dr. Nicol's tenure as Under-Secretary-General was up, and another African diplomat (whom I shall not name here) succeeded him. As protocol required, I was to hand him the declaration for official transmission to the Secretary-General.

I submitted our precious document, and the new Under-Secretary acknowledged that he had received it. But despite frequent and increasingly insistent inquiries, nothing happened. I inquired week after week, and then my lack of patience got the better of my diplomatic tact. I transgressed UN protocol and went to see the new Secretary-General, Javier Perez de Cuellar, myself (Perez succeeded Kurt Waldheim in 1982). I asked him "off the record" to tell me what the problem was.

Perez de Cuellar explained that he had *seen* the RCDC Declaration but couldn't *recognize* it. Did I hear him right? Yes I did. In regard to research, the Secretary-General can only "recognize" documents transmitted to him by the Under-Secretary-General in charge of research, who was the head of UNITAR. If that official didn't transmit the declaration, there was nothing the Secretary-General could do. He couldn't act on it.

So why didn't Dr. Nicol's successor submit the declaration on RCDC to the Secretary-General? Insiders have told me that they thought the answer was obvious. Incoming heads of a UN body are eager to put their own stamp on their organization and want to start with a clean slate—"clearing the deck." This means discontinuing or burying projects and activities that were initiated and implemented by their predecessors. The project on the RCDC was my brainchild, created largely through my own efforts, but it was launched and carried out under the aegis of Dr. Nicol. That became its downfall.

Earlier, three years of intense work had come to naught for the failure of the General Assembly to launch the Global Negotiations. Now, four years of equally intensive and even more difficult and frustrating work went down the drain because of institutional power politics. I remarked to myself that getting things done at the UN required the obstinacy of a bulldog and the patience of a saint.

But despite many setbacks and frequent frustrations, my work at the United Nations did not fail to produce results. Since the mid 1980s, when I left the United Nations, a number of "cooperation agreements" have been signed by states in Latin America, Africa, and Asia. Many of them reflected the recommendations we had put forward in the RCDC Programme. The way this salutary process unfolded was surely slower than if the Secretary-General had "recognized" the RCDC Declaration: then the UN system would have put its weight behind the cooperation initiatives and facilitated their implementation through such specialized agencies as the UN Development Programme and the Economic Committees for Asia, Africa, and Latin America.

But the RCDC Programme, unlike the project on the NIEO, didn't really become a victim of international and institutional power politics. It seems that when the time for an idea has come, not even shortsighted national and personal power politics can prevent it from making its mark in the world.

♪♫♪♫♪♫♪

PART IV

THE
THREE
CAPSTONE
PROJECTS

CHANGE THE WORLD! THE CLUB OF BUDAPEST AND THE GIORDANO BRUNO GLOBALSHIFT UNIVERSITY

The life shifts that took me from concert halls to the halls of academe, and then to the conference halls of the international community didn't come to an end when I left the UN. My involvement with world affairs continued, albeit in a different key. How it continued is a story—indeed it is several stories—in itself.

♪♪♪

It was late, but the night in Rome was balmy and the sky was clear. We didn't feel like calling it a day. The three of us— Aurelio Peccei, the founder and president of the Club of Rome; Victor Urquidi, the head of El Colegio de México and a leading economist of the day; and I—were walking through the Campidoglio, the famous landmark where the city hall of Rome and the Michelangelo-designed center court are located. We walked silently, deep in thought, and then, out of the blue, all three of us asked out loud the same question: "What next?"

This was during the early fall of 1978, and we'd just concluded the tenth anniversary meeting of the Club of Rome. It had taken place at the historic Accademia Nazionale dei Lincei and was attended by several hundred specially invited individuals. There was Giulio Andreotti in the first row and next to him was Amintore Fanfani—at the time, they were the most respected politicians in Italy. Aurelio described the key objectives of the Club, based on the discussions we'd conducted during the closed-door members' meeting the day before. The assembled VIPs congratulated the Club members and assured us that they would take to heart the important objectives we had presented. Afterward, we dined at the luxurious residence of the Bulgari family, one of the world's leading jewelers. All of us members should have been feeling optimistic, but we were not.

We questioned whether the objectives we had just outlined would make a real difference. Would anything *really* change? The published reports of the Club attempted to demonstrate the ways in which humans are destroying the environment and show that we are quickly running out of adequate food, drinkable water, and other essentials of life. The first report, *Limits to Growth* by Donella Meadows, Jorgen Randers, and Dennis Meadows; the second report, *Mankind at the Turning Point* by Mihajlo Mesarovic and Eduard Pestel; and the third, *Goals for Mankind*, of which I was the lead author, have all insisted that real change must happen—and soon.

We had hoped that political and business leaders would take the necessary steps, yet both Aurelio and Victor confessed that they very much doubted this would happen. When the compliments had been delivered before the media and lip service to the proposed changes had been paid, the top men and women would return to their desks and carry on much the same as before. But what could *we* do?

Victor suggested that we had to find a way to reach the heart of the *people* to effect real change. Aurelio concurred, and I was also in agreement. We must speak directly to the people; our approach was too limited. We had been addressing the select few, and they wouldn't make changes unless they were pushed by a critical mass. But where could we begin? The nearly one hundred members of the Club of Rome were political and business leaders, with a sprinkling of physicists and social scientists—intellectuals who were at their best when communicating with their fellow colleagues, rather than with the average man or woman on the street.

"How about getting some artists on board?" I asked.

"Good idea," said Aurelio, "but since our membership is limited to one hundred, we only have room for three new members, and the few artists who could join us wouldn't be able to set the tone. We need many artists, writers, singers, and spiritual leaders."

Victor had an idea. He turned to me, saying, "Ervin, you were a musician. You must have many friends and contacts in the music world and other creative fields. Could you bring at least a dozen of them together to advise the Club?"

"That still wouldn't be enough," Aurelio remarked. "We must have a true counterweight made up of 'right-hemisphere' people who balance the 'left-hemisphere' dominance of our current membership." (It is common knowledge that artists, writers, and other creative people rely more on the intuitive, holistically perceiving right hemisphere of their brain than on the rational, verbally, and linearly oriented left hemisphere.)

Victor agreed.

"Then we must create a sister club," I said.

Aurelio looked at me. "Can you make that happen, Ervin?"

I told them that I would try. And so my commitment to creating a kind of artists' and writers' club was born. This, however, proved much more difficult than I had imagined.

♪♪♪

I resolved to speak about the need for an artists' and writers' club whenever and wherever I could. I was met with understanding and even enthusiasm—but not with money. I knew that I wouldn't be able to establish an effective think tank without a working secretariat for contacting prospective members, ensuring ongoing communication between them, and bringing the ideas and conclusions to the attention of the public—all of which requires financing and presupposes having a sponsor: a state, a company, or a group of well-endowed individuals.

For years, nothing came to fruition. In the meantime, Marjorie and I had moved to Tuscany; Aurelio had met with a tragic, untimely end; and Victor was busy tending to his duties at El Colegio de México. None of the other Club of Rome members made a determined effort to create the sister club we had in mind. I had almost given up. But then I received an invitation from the World Federation of Hungarians to give a keynote speech at their forthcoming World Congress in Budapest. I decided to use this forum to give the project one more try.

In June 1993, three years after the end of the Communist era, the Third World Congress of Hungarians was convened, with the goal of bringing together Hungarians dispersed throughout the world to deliberate on the future of Hungary and the role of its citizens. There are nearly ten million Hungarians within Hungary, and some four million living elsewhere, many just beyond the country's borders where they live as disadvantaged minorities. But there are also large Hungarian colonies in other parts of the world, especially in the U.S. Cleveland is said to have the second-largest population of Hungarians in the world, even more than Szeged, the second-largest city in Hungary.

The World Congress was to be the third such event, the first since the mid-century. During the Communist era, such a meeting could not have been free of political constraints and would have been subject to ideological propaganda. It was not even attempted.

The discussion centered on the future of Hungary, a future that was more open since the Iron Curtain had been lifted. American (but Hungarian-born) physicist Edward Teller, considered the father of the atomic bomb, was also a keynote speaker. Teller proposed that the government should adopt a plan to build a nuclear power plant using the latest and, according to Teller, now quite safe, reactor technology. My own agenda was more modest. I came forth with the proposal of an artists' and writers' club to be hosted by Hungary. I explained that it would work hand in hand with the Club of Rome, addressing basic human needs and aspirations.

I didn't expect anything more than the usual acknowledgement that this was a good idea, but on the following day, I was invited to visit the president of the World Federation, together with the head of the newly formed Hungarian Culture Foundation. They informed me that the minister of culture, on the suggestion of the prime minister, was willing to help establish the club I had spoken about. The Hungarian Culture Foundation would be the official host, and provide office facilities, means of communication, and seed money.

The Culture Foundation had just received a wonderful property from the government: a building that took up a full city block in the Castle district, across from the landmark St. Matthias Church. It was the largest single real-estate property in Hungary and potentially the most valuable. The problem was that much of it had burned down at the end of World War II, during the siege of Budapest; and although it had been rebuilt, a great deal was still needed to make it into a functional office building and conference center. The government proposed that the Culture Foundation complete the restoration, manage the building, and use the income from renting offices and meeting halls to pursue its objectives.

This proposal was now expanded to include the hosting of a club of artists and writers.

This was fantastic news! Right then and there, I decided to create this enterprise in Budapest and to name it after the city.

"But let's be clear," I said. "It's not a city club and not even a Hungarian club. It's a global club, carrying the name of the city where it was founded, much as the Club of Rome does."

Everyone agreed. The available office facilities were inspected, and a working budget was allocated. I didn't ask for, nor did I receive, compensation for myself—I have never taken anything for working for the Club of Budapest. We had a wonderful start-up team, made up of my old friend Ivan Vitányi and his two closest collaborators, the social psychologist and musical creativity researcher Maria Sági and the polyglot dance and culture historian Gedeon Dienes. A business manager was engaged, and we were off to the races.

As a native of Budapest, I was delighted that the long-sought-after artists' and writers' club would be born in this city. However, a club without any dedicated and able members is just a name. An effective global think tank needs globally thinking, globally credible members. Who would they be, and how would I get them to join?

The first person I asked was Árpád Göncz, who was the president of the Republic of Hungary at the time. "Uncle Árpád," as he was affectionately called, was not a typical politician: he was a distinguished literary figure and a prized translator of Shakespeare and other classics. He accepted my invitation immediately, and we called him our "Honorary Member No. 1." By *honorary,* we meant not merely a member in name, but an honored active member.

We also knew that we needed members from outside the country. As it happened, the renowned violinist Yehudi Menuhin was in town for a concert, and I had a chance to speak with him at a reception given in his honor by the British embassy. I'd met Yehudi—now "The Lord Menuhin"—in my teens in New York, when we had the same concert manager. He remembered me as the Hungarian piano prodigy, and we had a warm reunion. He listened to me describe the objectives of the Club of Budapest and agreed to join on the spot.

Together, we contacted the celebrated actor-playwright Peter Ustinov, and Sir Peter joined us as well. Then came Mikhail Gorbachev, Václav Havel, Elie Wiesel, Liv Ullman . . . and the Dalai Lama.

In a matter of months, we had the basis for a global-thinking membership. We also knew what we wanted to achieve: timely and fundamental change in the world through timely and fundamental change in people's consciousness. But we lacked a document that would spell out this objective. On the insistence of my colleagues, I sat down to draft what I hoped would turn into the Club of Budapest's "Manifesto on Planetary Consciousness."

I had a draft with me in February of 1995, when I attended the annual meeting of the Auroville Foundation in India; I was then serving as chairman of the foundation's international advisory board. My Auroville colleagues told me that the Dalai Lama was visiting the country, and I asked them to arrange a meeting.

His Holiness had a schedule that was more than full, but his secretary said that he could squeeze me in if I wouldn't take up too much of his time. Five minutes would be good, I was instructed, and ten was the maximum.

And so it was that on the following day, I sat across from the Dalai Lama, wearing the white silk scarf he had ceremonially placed on my shoulders, and described the mission of the Club of Budapest. I said that I had with me a manifesto I had written on the new consciousness we need if we are to live in peace and dignity on the planet.

His Holiness said, "Let me see it."

I produced the six-page document and placed it before him. As he read, he made comments, such as: "You should make this quite clear here . . ." and "You might want to add this over there. . . ."

We went back to the first sentence and ended up revising the entire document. This took more than ten minutes—it took over three hours. His Holiness cancelled all of his appointments for the rest of the day, and we sat side by side, engrossed in the project.

His secretary, a Buddhist monk with a perfect command of English, jotted down every change and addition we came up with.

That is how the Club of Budapest's "Manifesto on Planetary Consciousness" was born. I sent it to all of our honorary members and received many important suggestions that we incorporated. The final document was signed by the Dalai Lama, Peter Ustinov, Yehudi Menuhin, and a dozen other eminent members at a ceremony held at the Hungarian Academy of Sciences on October 26, 1996.

The manifesto clearly stated:

> The challenge we now face is the challenge of choosing our destiny. Our generation, of all the thousands of generations before us, is called upon to decide the fate of life on this planet. The processes we have initiated within our lifetimes and the lifetimes of our parents and grandparents cannot continue in the lifetimes of our children and grandchildren. Whatever we do will either create the framework for reaching a peaceful and cooperative global society and thus continuing the grand adventure of life, spirit, and consciousness on Earth, or set the stage for the termination of humanity's tenure on this planet.

We ended the document with a call for a planetary consciousness, defined as "the knowing as well as the feeling of the vital interdependence and essential oneness of humankind, and the conscious adoption of the ethics and the ethos that this entails." And we said it loud and clear: "The evolution of this consciousness is the basic imperative of human survival on this planet."

The Club of Budapest has been dedicated to this proposition ever since. With the help of a small but efficient secretariat headed by Maria Sági, we have had many notable achievements. We have created the Club of Budapest Planetary Consciousness Prize and have awarded it to globally thinking individuals of honesty and integrity, among them Václav Havel, Mikhail Gorbachev, Archbishop Tutu, and Paulo Coelho. We have organized Planetary Consciousness World Days. The biggest took place on March 21, 2001, and brought together people in twenty-nine countries to celebrate the rise of the first spring sun of the twenty-first century. People had congregated at scenic or significant sites at dawn to sing, dance, play music, pray, or meditate in order to facilitate the flow of new energies into our planetary home. The celebrations started with the first sunrise of the day in New Zealand, circled the planet following the rising sun, and ended at dawn in Samoa, the last sunrise of the day.

The celebration in Budapest started on the mystic hill called "Dobogó Kő" where, according to tradition, the Earth's heart is beating. A traditionally vested horseman brought a flame kindled there at dawn to the Gellért Hill in the capital, where he shot it with a bow and arrow to light a bonfire. Hundreds sang and danced, and a several young people entered into a kind of trance. The celebrations concluded with a festive evening at the Károlyi Palace where Jane Goodall, Peter Ustinov, Lady Fiona Montagu, the city's deputy mayor, and other personalities spoke about the meaning of a new planetary consciousness.

We have also created and co-hosted with the World Peace Prayer Society the annual Global Peace Meditation and Prayer Day. On appointed days, up to a million people have joined together to pray and meditate for peace in the world.

We had then added a major element to our network of activities aimed at promoting a real worldshift: the "WS20," the twenty-member WorldShift Council. The Council brings together eminent individuals from diverse parts of the world to form a "shadow cabinet" of the group of industrialized countries, the G20. The members of the WorldShift Council review the statements and declarations of the G20 and offer their own views on the topics discussed by the national leaders. The WS20 Declarations contrast the G20's predominantly economic and nation-state oriented statements with the Club's humanistic, holistic, and global philosophy. The WorldShift Council's mission is to "give urgent attention to the new condition of the world emerging today and provide essential orientation so that an informed and determined movement toward a peaceful and sustainable planetary civilization could be brought into being."

In addition to events, councils, and celebrations, the Club of Budapest has published a number of "handbooks to change the world." First came the *Third Millennium: The Challenge and the Vision,* published in English in 1997 and then in ten other languages. That was followed by *You Can Change the World: Action Handbook for the 21st Century* in 2002. The most recent title, published in September 2009, is *WorldShift 2012: Making Green Business, New Politics & Higher Consciousness Work Together.* Several of the Club's honorary members have contributed to these books, including Deepak Chopra, Mikhail Gorbachev, and Paulo Coelho.

On September 9, 2009—the auspicious date of 09/09/09—the Club launched the WorldShift 2012 Movement at the British Museum in London. This initiative brought together like-minded organizations and forward-thinking individuals from all parts of the world. They came together to catalyze the critical mass needed to shift the world. The WorldShift Movement is "a movement for the People and it is the People who will remain its main focus in terms of campaigns, events, and activities." It is to empower the collective voice of humanity in the historic task of substantially shifting current global trends that threaten human well-being and even survival. The WorldShift Movment is complemented and supported by "WorldShift Media," which is a kind of encyclopedia of holistically change-oriented individuals and organizations the world over. All these initiatives make up the membership of what we call the "WorldShift Community" brought together on a special page of my website: **ervinlaszlo.com**.

At the same time, the Club has given birth to a highly focused operative arm: the Club of Budapest International ("COBI"). The COBI Board was constituted in December of 2010, made up of top executives in the information, education, and global transformation fields. It coordinates and oversees the activities of the various national Clubs that bear the name "Club of Budapest" (for example, Club of Budapest France, Club of Budapest Japan, and so on), and develops global-reach projects that all chapters of the Club can pursue together.

This is still not all. In the spring of 2010, something entirely unexpected happened: the Club acquired a powerful new partner: an online world university dedicated to the mission of changing young people's consciousness so they could change the world.

♪♪♪

I have always maintained that to change the world, we need to change the consciousness of a critical mass of people in society. I founded the Club of Budapest to contribute to this task through projects, events, and publications that are meaningful to everyone and open fresh vistas for constructive action.

This, however, is only part of the task: it is the part addressed to the present generation by means of information and communication. There is also another part: it is to address the next generation, the young people, the "movers and shakers" of the world of tomorrow. This is a task for education. Not education in the classical sense, which instructs students on what they should get into their head, but in the timely sense of helping young people wake up, look around, and ask themselves what needs to be done—and what they themselves can do to get it done.

To fulfill this task we need to address the problems we face and show that they not only are urgently in need of being solved, but also that they *can* be solved. We must offer fresh perspectives on what's wrong and create new vistas for how people themselves can make it right. This is education in the service of changing the world. The Club of Budapest is now better able to respond to this challenge thanks to an unexpected visitor from Mexico who showed up one fine spring day at my house in Tuscany.

A week before he came, I received a message forwarded from the Club of Budapest's website. A gentleman whom I had not known before had read my writings and heard of my ideas, and wanted very much to speak with me. Such messages are not uncommon, and due to my busy schedule, I can't always respond to them. This time, however, I felt that I should respond, although I didn't know why. I said to my friends of the Club of Budapest to tell the gentleman that I would be pleased to meet him, but could not do so at present, as I was traveling. I would be home in ten days' time, however, and I could meet with him then at my house in Tuscany. The response came back immediately: the gentleman—whose name was Francisco de Paula León—had planned to return to Mexico the week before then, but he would postpone his return to come and see me.

Francisco arrived in the early spring of 2009 the day after I got home. He was a soft-spoken, silver-haired gentleman with dreamy eyes and a simple, unassuming manner. It was only later that I learned that he had been a successful entrepreneur since his late teens, having made a fortune in his twenties, and then left his business activities to devote himself to composing classical music and writing books about the future of humankind. In his late forties, he interviewed Václav Havel for Mexican television. Havel was president of the Czech Republic at the time. In the course of their in-depth conversation, Francisco realized that the best chances of surmounting the world's problems and creating a more humane and sustainable civilization lies in education; more precisely, in education aimed at helping to evolve the consciousness of young people by waking them up and prompting them to question the way human affairs are run on this planet. In Francisco's view, they were run by a small minority that used its wealth and power to subordinate the great bulk of the people to serve its own narrow and egoistic interests. This kind of subordination-based order had to be changed, and the sooner the better.

From then on, Francisco devoted nearly all his time and energy to designing an educational system that could respond to this paramount challenge. This, he said, must be a system of higher education that is both physically and financially accessible to young people in every part of the world. It must deliver high-quality learning at an affordable cost. This meant creating an online world university.

In the history of thought, Francisco's hero and ideal was Giordano Bruno, the great scientific pioneer who was burned at the stake in Rome in the year 1600 for refusing to retract his views on an infinite universe infused with the spirit of a god that is omnipresent in space as well as in time. This, Francisco asserted, is the kind of "heretical" wisdom we needed today, to enable young men and women to question the dominant system and seek alternatives. He intended to call his online world classroom the Giordano Bruno University.

But what exactly is the substance of the heretical knowledge that the university is supposed to deliver? Being familiar with my writings and the work of the Club of Budapest, Francisco was convinced that the answer lay in the ideas that I'd written about—ideas to which the Club of Budapest is fully dedicated.

The purpose of Francisco's meeting with me was to make a simple request: Would the Club of Budapest and I join forces with him and the Giordano Bruno University? I listened to his plea and was convinced as much by his reasoning as by his sincerity and dedication. I said yes. On my suggestion, he rebaptized the online world university as the Giordano Bruno *GlobalShift* University.

♪♪♪

The need to establish a kind of "worldshift university" has been clear to me for some time. I did try to create such a forum, but without success. In the late 1990s with the help of some colleagues, I outlined a fairly detailed educational plan, and I spoke about it everywhere I lectured in the world. Although I found that people generally agreed that there was an urgent need for a widely accessible, high-quality program of higher education, no one came forth with the practical means—the start-up capital and the organizational infrastructure—to get it launched.

I had then met the Indian businessman Vinay Rai. He devoted much of his considerable fortune to Rai University with campuses all over India. These are principally business schools, but

Vinay felt that they needed to be expanded to bring students more substantive content in addition to necessary technical skills.

I went to see him in New Delhi in the company of my friend, literary agent, and Club of Budapest trustee, Bill Gladstone. Vinay was enthusiastic about the idea of a "worldshift university" and willing to adopt the proposed curriculum into Rai University, but he wasn't interested in extending the project beyond India. We, however, were looking for an online world university, an educational body that would operate throughout the six continents. Bill and I came to the conclusion that the association with Rai University had to be postponed until we could achieve this more ambitious aim.

During the following year, Bill and I, together with some like-minded friends, tried our best to create the "WorldShift University." We engaged an experienced educator as CEO, met with prospective faculty members, and courted possible sponsors. Our CEO insisted that the first task is to come up with proper financing, since an undertaking of this kind couldn't be launched on a shoestring. But in the difficult climate following the financial crisis of 2007, we didn't succeed in raising the necessary funds. I had to put the idea of the WorldShift University on the back burner, and that is where it remained—until Francisco came into the picture.

The Giordano Bruno University and the Club of Budapest were a perfect match. The Club had the content but not the means to put it to work, and the GBU had the means, and also much of the operational structure, but not the content. We didn't waste any time: on June 12, 2010, we signed the basic agreement under which the Club of Budapest became the major partner of the Giordano Bruno GlobalShift University: the GBU rechristened as the GBG-U.

On Francisco and his colleagues' request, I assumed responsibility for the intellectual orientation of the GBG-U. This meant acting as the University's Chancellor and creating the academic body that could carry out this challenging task. Evidently, I couldn't do this alone, nor could I draw only on the existing structures of the

Club of Budapest. I had to create an academic center for the University, and have trusted collaborators with whom I could run it. I came up with the project to create the "Giordano Bruno Center for Advanced Study," and my closest collaborator showed up all by herself.

About three years before this I had received another request for a meeting. This one came from a beautiful young woman who was pursuing her master's and wanted to enroll in a Ph.D. program. She was convinced that my theories and ideas were essential for her work. Accompanied by her English husband, Gyorgyi Szabo (then Mrs. Byworth), who was born in Budapest like I, had traveled and lived in many parts of the world, the same as I. She had the kind of values and aspirations I did.

I advised Gyorgyi (rhymes with "worthy") on her thesis work, and before leaving, she had spontaneously asked if there was anything she could do for me—could she help me with my own work in any way? I said that indeed she could. I was badly in need of a bright multilingual executive assistant who could take from my shoulders the burden of a correspondence that had grown unmanageably large and complex. Gyorgyi accepted on the spur of the moment and became my personal assistant. And three years later, when the Giordano Bruno GlobalShift University started its activities, she continued to work for me as Assistant to the Chancellor.

Where to locate the Giordano Bruno Center for Advanced Study was never in question. Francisco had always dreamed of founding an academic research center in Tuscany, the heartland of the Italian Renaissance. Soon we were on the lookout for a suitable property, preferably a historic site in the Tuscan hills. Thanks to an amazing coincidence, we found what we were looking for practically next door to my house.

The historic Palazzo Marchionneschi at the edge of "my" village, the village of Montescudaio, has been standing unused for decades, as the noble family that had built it and owned it through the centuries had moved away. The last member of the family now lived in Bologna, and was happy to make available the historic palazzo to an institution of higher education. It proved to be the perfect home for our Center for Advanced Study.

The three-hundred-year-old Palazzo Marchionneschi in Montescudaio, the home of the Giordano Bruno GlobalShift University's Center for Advanced Study, in its original state at the end of 2010.

The Center is the academic heart of the university—more exactly, its heart *and* brain. The arms and legs, and all the muscles the university needs, are at its administrative and executive center in Washington, D.C., headed by Louis Goodman, who for many years has been the distinguished dean of American University's School of International Service. At the Washington center, a multidisciplinary faculty has been hired to teach four master's programs through the university's four incorporated schools: The Erasmus of Rotterdam School of Theology, Philosophy, Consciousness, and Spirituality; The Thomas More School of Government, Communication, Political Science, and International Relations; The Buckminster Fuller School of Economics, International Trade, Administration, and Sustainable Development; and The Leonardo da Vinci School of Art, Aesthetic Science, and Cultural Resources.

The Center for Advanced Study advises and coaches the teaching faculty, and brings together leading-edge thinkers and scientists to develop relevant new knowledge to bring to our students.

♪♪♪

Let me add now a word on just what it is that I consider the gist of the relevant new knowledge.

In my introduction to the curriculum of the university, I pointed out that in the course of history, the structures of society and the forms of consciousness prevalent in society have interacted. The kind of consciousness possessed by a critical mass of the people tended to shape the social structures that arose in a given society, and in turn these structures shaped the dominant forms of consciousness.

The problem is that the social structures shaped by the consciousness that dominates the modern world are flawed. They are hierarchical, domination-based structures that subordinate the bulk of society to the self-interests of a power elite not only in the political sphere, but also in the economy and even in religious and spiritual domains. A vicious cycle had developed: the domination-seeking mind-set of the modern world gave rise to social structures that serve the aspirations of the power elites, and the presence of these structures reinforces the domination-seeking mind-set.

This cycle needs to be broken. Breaking it calls for the transformation either of today's social structures, or of today's dominant forms of consciousness.

The holders of power resist the transformation of the social structures, for these structures are the basis of their own wealth and power. As a result, at least for now, the option of a timely transformation of the structures of society "from above" is foreclosed. On the other hand, breaking through the vicious cycle "from below," by evolving the consciousness that legitimizes the social structures, appears feasible. Even if they don't necessarily act on it, all people are capable of changing their apprehensions, values, and aspirations. Education can be a crucial factor in motivating this change and opening positive perspectives for a new consciousness.

In my "Open Letter to the Youth of the World," I wrote:

You, the young people of today, are the most privileged people who have ever lived on this Earth. For the first time in history, one generation—your generation—holds the key to the greatest challenge our species has faced since it proudly named itself Homo sapiens. This is the challenge of change—of profound and timely change.

And I concluded:

There was chaos in the human world in the past as well. But it was local. And the opportunity to change was likewise local. Today's chaos is global, and the opportunity it brings is also global. Failing to seize it would be not just the height of ignorance, it would also be a crime against humanity.

I believe that today's young people will not commit a crime against humanity. They will live up to the challenge of changing their consciousness—and with a new consciousness, they will change the world.

The call of the Club of Budapest and the Giordano Bruno GlobalShift University must be loud and clear: *Change your consciousness.* This call is revolutionary, but it's not a call for revolution. It's a call for *evolution*—so as to enable us to create a better world for you and for me, for our children and grandchildren, and all the people who share our precious planet.

♪♫♪♫♪♫♪

CHAPTER TWENTY-ONE

EXPLORING THE AKASHIC FIELD

The problems of our world and of our future are basic concerns of mine, but they are not exclusive, all-encompassing concerns. They do not replace my perennial quest of finding out all I can about the nature of the world. Even as I was engaged in creating the Club of Budapest and providing an orientation for the Giordano Bruno GlobalShift University, I continued to read and to reflect, to give talks and seminars, and to ask myself how I could deepen my understanding of who I really am, and what the world truly is.

This philosophical and scientific concern of mine is constant in time, but it's not constant in the way it evolves: it evolves in leaps and bounds. The greatest leap with the largest bound came seemingly of its own accord: I neither planned it, nor was I prepared for it. But at least I was smart enough to seize the window it opened for me when it came my way.

♪♪♪

It happened one summer evening on the Adriatic shores of the Mediterranean. A telegram was handed to me that told me that a scientist whom I viewed as both a spiritual and intellectual guide had, as he would have put it, "left his body."

The year was 1986, and I was at a summer seminar on the Adriatic Sea. Earlier, I'd mentioned to my wise friend that if he needed to speak with me, he could find me here. He had kept my note on his desk, and when his secretary looked for friends to notify about his sudden passing, she found it and called me. I had to put the news aside until I had a quiet moment to come to grips with it.

It was September, and the bulk of the tourist stream had left; the hotels were given over to conventions and conferences. Our seminar was in one of them.

After dinner that day, I went for a walk on the beach with three longtime colleagues who were also close friends. We found a secluded spot and looked out over the moonlit sea. I felt great sadness for having lost a dear, valued teacher. I realized that I'd never be able to read the book he'd been working on. I had been looking forward to it, for I was sure that it held many new insights.

We sat together speaking quietly on the moonlit beach. I brought up the loss but didn't mention his name—a modest and retiring man, he wouldn't have approved of me talking about my respect for him and my admiration for his work. For a while, nobody said anything—there wasn't anything to say. Then, surprisingly, Maria Sági, the scientific secretary of the Club of Budapest, spoke up.

"Are you sure?" she inquired.

"Sure of what?" I asked. "He died—of that I am sure. His secretary certainly wasn't trying to pull my leg."

"Not that. I meant that are you sure you could never know what he had in mind. Are you quite sure that he really took his insights with him to the grave?"

Without realizing why I said it, I replied, "No, of that I am not sure."

There was a long silence—we sat looking at the sea, pondering. Could it be possible to access the thoughts of someone who was no longer with us? To believe this was to believe in the survival of the soul—a spiritual tenet that could not be substantiated by science. As a scientist and philosopher, I couldn't hold such a view.

Then I spoke again. With a conviction that surprised me as much as it did my three friends, I said that the experience and wisdom of my friend had not vanished from this world—in fact, its "trace" still existed, the same as the trace of all things that ever took place in the universe.

We fell into silent contemplation once more. The truth of this assertion, bold as it was, had hit us. After a few moments, Maria said that she, too, believed this to be so, but how could I be so certain? I responded by drawing on a store of ideas and concepts that I didn't know I possessed. Let me cite here the passage I wrote shortly after this incident. (It's included in my book *The Creative Cosmos*, published in 1993.)

Although we do not know much about the mystery of life and perhaps never will, we do know a few things. For example, we know that life is the most remarkable adventure of molecular matter in the universe, but it's not above or beyond nature, it's a part, a manifestation, of it. Life could not be an exception to the law of preservation of all things and events in the cosmos. The wealth of impressions and insights of a person's life cannot disappear without a trace; it's bound to remain registered at the very heart of reality. This is like the ray of light that comes to our eyes from one of the myriad stars in the domed sky far above us. At that very moment light from all parts of the universe is entering our eyes, bringing to us signals that stretched out across the whole history of the cosmos. Nothing in this world is ever lost without a trace, neither a single photon from a star in Gamma

Centauri nor a cell in the network of neurons in the brain of a departed friend. The thoughts, the ideas, the very consciousness of a person do not disappear with his or her body. Their traces are conserved and remain accessible for all times to come.

During a break in the following morning's session, Maria asked me if I still believed that the thoughts, ideas, and consciousness of my friend were conserved in the universe and remained accessible to me and other living people. My first impulse was to shake my head—the whole idea was just poetical fantasy. But I couldn't dismiss the intuition I felt the night before. The concept held me in its thrall; it felt right. This was, I realized, something I had always known.

But how did I . . . how *could* I have known this? Was it the same kind of "knowledge" that came to me at the piano whenever I lived myself into the music? That was an intuitive certainty of how to interpret a given piece—it wasn't anything verbal and conceptual. This, too, was an intuitive certainty but about a different thing: about access to the ideas of someone who was no longer flesh and blood.

Was the intuition of the night before something real and true—and worth looking into? I began to think seriously about this possibility.

♪♪♪

I soon realized that quite apart from stories of spirits and ghosts visiting the living, and of mediums channeling disembodied intelligences, there is an impressive record of spontaneous intuitions that come to highly credible people—even scientists. Einstein himself spoke about the importance of intuition in his work, and so did many other researchers. Even the great inventor Thomas Edison made a surprising comment about the role that it played in his life. In a little-known interview (published in *The Indiana Gazette* in 1911), he declared: "People say I have created things. I have never created anything. I get impressions from the Universe at large and work them out, but I am only a plate on a record or a receiving apparatus—what you will. Thoughts are really impressions that we get from outside."

But if something like this is true, how does it actually take place? Is there a scientific explanation for it?

All forms of intuition, I reflected, whether true or imaginary, have one thing in common: they are some form of information. Would the information produced by a person remain available even after death?

There is more to this than is commonly assumed. Leading-edge scientists know that "information" is not only what we produce when we speak or write—it's objectively present in us and in the world. The human organism, as all living things, is a dynamic system that contains, and is vitally dependent on, information.

But could one's brain capture the information present in the brain of another human being, or in nature for that matter, in a direct and spontaneous way? The evidence from veridical intuitions, anecdotal as it is, points in this direction. And if this were the case, it would be a mistake to dismiss as mere delusion the intuitions of artists and scientists, and even of otherwise quite ordinary people.

Until the advent of contemporary quantum physics, scientists would have been obliged to dismiss the possibility that information could be accessed by our brain beyond the range of the eye and ear. But quantum theory opened a whole new perspective. Among "quanta," the smallest discernible units of the physical world, a direct form of "information-transmission" has come to light, known as "entanglement." In their pristine state—in the absence of measurements or another form of interaction—quanta are "entangled" with each other. Every quantum in the world is entangled with every other quantum. The physical universe is connected beyond the ordinary limits of space and time. In the terminology of the renowned physicist David Bohm, all things throughout the world are connected by "in-formation"—all things "in-form" each other. This is a revolutionary concept, a discovery of mind-boggling magnitude.

Could these "nonlocal" entanglements persist over time? Evidence indicates that they do. But if so, then the information present in the world must be encoded somehow in the universe. The simplest scientific explanation is that it is encoded in a universal *field*.

Fields occupy a privileged position in the panoply of scientific concepts. Things that were thought to be separate, independent entities are now known to be part of, or connected by, fields. Light, for example, which consists of a stream of photons, is carried and conveyed by the electromagnetic field. The attraction and repulsion among quanta is carried by nuclear and quantum fields. The attraction of massive objects to one another—the familiar fact of gravitation (which on Earth is due to the attraction of ordinary-sized objects to the far greater mass of the planet)—is likewise carried and conveyed by a universal field: the gravitational field. Fields make up the "betweenness" of things—of *all* things.

Evidently, the "in-formation" that "entangles" every quantum with every other quantum must be carried by a field—more exactly, by a universal nonlocal in-formation field.

The fact that we don't see this "in-formation field" is not an indication that it doesn't exist. We don't see the gravitational field either, only objects falling to the ground; and we also don't see the electromagnetic field, only an energetically excited stream of photons that appears to our eyes as light. Fields are like fishing lines: so subtle that their strands are invisible. We only see the things that are caught in them.

Gathering evidence for the ubiquity and the preservation of "in-formation" in nature was an exciting and an unexpectedly fruitful task. Theories that spoke to this hypothesis have been considered pure speculation a decade or two ago, but in recent years they have been receiving more and more support in quantum physics and its wider applications.

The evidence coming to light about nonlocal connections among the parts of living organisms is particularly impressive. It's common knowledge that the human body is a constant flux of thousands and thousands of chemical and biological reactions and processes. These interface and interconnect molecules, cells, and organs throughout the brain and body. Until recently, scientists believed that these interactions work in a linear sequence, with information passing from one molecule, cell, or organ to the others. But then they discovered that information is present in all parts of the organism simultaneously; it penetrates every molecule, every cell, and every organ.

The simultaneous presence of information throughout the body cannot be explained by classical biochemical theories: it calls for quantum processes. Studies in neuroscience, quantum biology, and quantum physics revealed that the living organism is not a classical biochemical system; it's a "resonating macroscopic quantum system."

I had the opportunity to meet and exchange ideas with biophysicist Mae-Wan Ho, a pioneer of the new quantum biophysics. She discovered that the communication of every part of an organism with every other part is through a nonlocal medium permeated by quantum waves. The living organism is not a solid, discrete, classical system. It's the place where the "wave function" of this nonlocal medium is the densest.

The new concepts apply to the biosphere as a whole. Invisible quantum waves spread not only from one part of the organism to its other parts, but also from one organism to other organisms. The flow of in-formation embraces every living thing within a nonlocal quantum field that permeates the entire biosphere. Our bodies are decoders and transmitters within this embracing information field.

♪♪♪

These were the concepts and discoveries that I came across following my unexpected intuition on the shore of the Adriatic. I thought about the implications and began to write up my findings. The initial intuition occurred in September 1986, and I had the first book-sized manuscript in hand a little over a year later. I showed it to my friends the Italian philosophers Mauro Ceruti and

Gianluca Bocchi. Mauro immediately said that he would like to include it in the book series he was editing, and Gianluca began to translate it into Italian. And so in July 1987, a slim volume of 113 pages saw the light of day. It was titled *L'Ipotesi del Campo* Ψ: *Fisica e Metafisica dell'Evoluzione* ("The Hypothesis of the Ψ [*Psi*] Field: The Physics and Metaphysics of Evolution").

In this book, and for some years later, I denoted the nonlocal in-formation field present in nature with the Greek letter psi: Ψ. This indicated that entanglement among individual quanta complete the wave function—the so-called Ψ function—of their quantum state.

For modern science, the hypothesis of a nonlocal in-formation field that is part and parcel of the physical universe was a revolutionary proposition, and I half expected that it would be attacked by the scientific community. But it wasn't. I was asked to explain my Ψ-field hypothesis in a number of lectures and interviews; and various articles were published about it in newspapers, journals, and magazines. Encouraged by this reception, between 1993 and 2003, I wrote four full-sized Ψ-field books: *The Creative Cosmos, The Interconnected Universe, The Whispering Pond,* and *The Connectivity Hypothesis.*

Although the mainstream of the science community didn't attack my hypothesis, it didn't endorse it either. I could understand why. The English biologist Rupert Sheldrake, who suggested that an invisible field shapes all development in the biosphere, had by then published his *New Science of Life* and he had suffered a veritable shock wave of rejection, even ridicule. My hypothesis concerned the concept of an information conserving and conveying "morpho*phoretic*" field (rather than Sheldrake's form-generating but physically unexplained "morpho*genetic*" field), and it demonstrated that the theory of this field meshes with established theories in the physical sciences. Consequently, my hypothesis couldn't be easily rejected, nor could it be readily ridiculed. But it could be ignored.

Even though the mainstream science establishment ignored my Ψ-field hypothesis, I wasn't discouraged. I remembered

Gandhi's teachings: When you innovate, you will first be ignored, and then attacked. If your innovation is sound, it will then be accepted as something we had known all along.

If my theory was to make an impact on the mainstream science community, I needed to produce solid, repeatable evidence to show that a nonlocal field captures and conserves in-formation in nature. I managed to come up with evidence for this in a surprisingly short amount of time.

An old friend, Dr. Nitamo Montecucco, who later became the head of the Italian chapter of the Club of Budapest, was also a medical doctor who had a great interest in meditation. He'd spent years studying it in India. Nitamo had a device for measuring the electrical activity of the brain and displaying the resulting wave patterns on a computer, and he used it to measure and record the brain waves that come about during meditation.

The electroencephalograph (EEG) waves produced by the two hemispheres of the brain are normally uncoordinated with each other; each hemisphere works nearly independent of the other. However, during meditation, Nitamo found that the left and right hemispheres become coordinated; and in deep meditation, they become amazingly synchronized: up to 98 percent.

I suggested that we measure the EEG patterns of two people at the same time to find out if the left and right hemispheres become coordinated between different individuals. If they do, this would be evidence that some form of information has been transmitted between them. And what if some level of coordination is found among meditators who are not in any evident form of contact and communication with each other?

We conducted experiment after experiment and found that the synchronized left and right hemispheres of people in deep meditation would become synchronized with each other. The EEG display of the meditators showed a high level of coordination —nearly identical patterns—even when the meditators didn't see, hear, smell, or touch each other.

We measured the EEG patterns of as many people as the system could accommodate simultaneously, which was twelve. When all twelve test subjects entered a deeply meditative state, all twelve EEG patterns became highly synchronized.

I wanted to go still further. Let us have two groups of meditators, I proposed, at two different locations without sensory contact among them. Each group is to be tested, and the results are to be recorded so that we could observe the level of synchronization of their EEG waves on the monitors. Since we could record the exact time the measurements were taken (the system could be linked to the atomic clock in Frankfurt), we could make sure that the patterns we observed had occurred at exactly the same time.

We found that the level of synchronization between groups hundreds of miles away was weaker than among people meditating at the same location, but it was still significant: the statistical probability that it would have come about by chance was negligible.

What explanation is there for individuals influencing each other's brain waves without any ordinary form of contact among them? I didn't want to resort to the esoteric principles usually invoked to explain extrasensory perception. The explanation must be, I asserted, that the meditators entered a state of consciousness in which they tapped into a nonlocal in-formation field around them. They communicated through this field much as we communicate with our computers and cell phones through the electromagnetic field.

Is there further evidence for the transmission of this subtle form of "in-formation" between people who are not in any ordinary form of contact with each other? It occurred to me that the experience of natural healers who diagnose and heal their patients from a distance could be relevant. Could "remote healing" be based on nonlocal in-formation transmission between healer and patient?

I was fortunate in finding a remote healer with whom I could test this hypothesis. My friend and Club of Budapest colleague Maria Sági had remote healing abilities. Years ago, she had met a priest in Hungary who had practiced remote healing for decades. She became his apprentice and learned how to use a pendulum to prescribe herbal remedies for people with health complaints, even when they were far away from her.

Maria practiced this method of healing for years, treating friends and others who would turn to her for help. Then she met the Viennese scientist Erich Körbler and became first his disciple, then his collaborator, and when Körbler died in 1994, his successor.

Körbler devised a one-arm dowsing rod and a sophisticated system for interpreting its movements. Maria learned to hold the sensitive "Körbler rod" in her right hand and use her left as an "antenna" to pick up information on the condition of her patients. After Körbler's passing, she continued to teach this method of healing. Then she attempted something that Körbler himself didn't: to practice the method remotely. Much to her surprise, she found that both diagnosis and treatment functioned just the same whether the patient was next to her or in another part of town— or even in another country.

For the typical modern person remote healing seems like magic. But Maria showed that it works. It proved effective for adults, small children, babies, and even dogs and cats. And it works over any distance. Maria had also treated me, and it didn't matter if I was in Italy, New York, or Tokyo at the time. She would concentrate on me and observe the behavior of her dowsing rod. Then we would speak on the phone and she would tell me what she had found and what I should do about it. No matter how much physical distance there was between us, the rod would indicate whether something was wrong with me (a chill, a backache, an upset stomach), and what kind of herbal or homeopathic remedies I should take for it. Her diagnosis was invariably correct, and the prescribed treatment was always effective.

The evidence for the nonlocal transmission of in-formation furnished by these experiences was meaningful, but it was not scientific. I wanted controlled experiments, and I knew that Professor Günter Haffelder of the Institute for Communication and Brain Research in Stuttgart, Germany, had the know-how and the instruments to carry them out.

I had known of Dr. Haffelder's work from a meeting in Italy when he displayed the EEG wave patterns of volunteers on a monitor. I wondered whether he could display two different people's EEG waves at the same time so that they could be compared.

Maria and I went to see Dr. Haffelder at a conference in southern Germany and explained what we had in mind. Right then and there he placed electrodes on both Maria's and a young volunteer's head, and hooked them up to his computer system. They were in separate rooms, and they couldn't see or hear each other. He and I then watched the display of Maria's and the young man's EEG on a large monitor in the meeting hall. What we saw was frankly amazing.

While Maria was engaged in healing, the left hemisphere of her brain was emitting waves in the deep delta range (below three hertz), even though brain activity in this region normally occurs only during deep sleep. Yet she was awake, in a relaxed, altered state of consciousness. And then, about two seconds later, the young man's brain reproduced Maria's EEG pattern almost without variation.

These results were witnessed by more than 120 people at the meeting in Germany, and Dr. Haffelder recorded them so that they could be reviewed by anyone who wished to delve into this phenomenon. The results of further experiments confirmed the initial findings. I reported on them in *Science and the Akashic Field*, and Maria wrote a detailed description of her part in the experiments in a chapter of *The Akashic Experience*. I believe that these experiments offer clear-cut evidence that information can be transmitted from the brain of one person to the brain of another without passing through the senses.

♪♪♪

In the spring of 2007, I encountered something that opened up a truly mind-boggling feature of nature's nonlocal in-formation field: it appears to conserve some elements of a person's consciousness even when that person has died.

I spoke to the dead. I can say this without hesitation, for there is no doubt in my mind that this was the case. (In light of a report I read later I should qualify this statement. The report, coming apparently from a group of deceased persons, specified, "We *are* the dead, but *we are not dead.*") What explanation is there for what I had experienced?

At first I didn't find any explanation that would satisfy me. Not that explanations hadn't been attempted: research in the disciplines known as ADC (after-death communication), EVP (electronic voice phenomena) and within it ITC (instrumental transcommunication) and DRV (direct radio voice) is booming. Scores of researchers describe highly documented and prima facie cases of communication and contact that extend beyond the brain—and even beyond the grave.

The wave of evidence suggests that consciousness doesn't cease with the cessation of brain function. If that is the case, the explanation must involve the Ψ field. Nature's nonlocal in-formation field must be capable not only of conserving the trace of all that happened, but also of allowing the autonomous development of some of the traces that it conserves.

In my explorations of these remarkable phenomena, I couldn't resist asking a personal question. Would a nonlocal field that transmits in-formation beyond the range of the senses explain my own life experiences as well?

The experiences I wanted to shed light on were highly intuitive, and they played a major role in my life—for example, the intuition on that moonlit night in the Bavarian Alps shifted me from being a professional concert pianist to a full-time academic. These experiences were not some kind of "channeling"—I didn't hear voices or see disembodied spirits, although I sometimes wished I had since they must be fascinating. In a more subtle way, these moments led me to new ways of approaching the problems that occupied my mind. When my principal concern was how to interpret a given piece of music, the intuition I gleaned suggested a particular kind of interpretation. And when my problem was to understand the deeper nature of reality, my intuition oriented me toward ideas that I could then fruitfully explore.

This was beginning to make sense to me. If nature's nonlocal in-formation field conserves the trace of all that happens, it also conserves how composers envisaged the music they had created—and also how philosophers and scientists posed and perhaps resolved their problems. The logical explanation was surprisingly simple. The conceptions of great philosophers and scientists, and the interpretations of great artists and composers, are encoded in the Ψ field. In an altered state of consciousness, typical of deep aesthetic and meditative experiences, one can gain access to that field.

As I've mentioned, when I first began to explore nature's nonlocal in-formation field, I thought that the best way to identify it was with the Greek symbol Ψ. Then I had another idea. I came across an even more appropriate name while studying traditional Eastern cosmologies.

♪♪♪

In the East the universe is seen as part of a cosmic cycle in which universe follows universe. The notion of a cyclic universe is thousands of years old. It's often likened to the breathing of Brahma. As Brahma breathes in, the universe expands and brings forth the many things that include us and all the things around us. As Brahma breathes out, the universe re-collapses and we, and all things in it, return to our cosmic origins to reemerge again in the next cycle of the universe, effectively in the next universe.

In Sanskrit and Hindu cosmology, the element from which our universe arises and into which it ultimately descends is known as the *Akasha,* the most fundamental of the five elements. The others are *Vata* (air), *Agni* (fire), *Ap* (water), and *Prithivi* (earth). *Akasha* is the womb of all the things that exist in space and time. And in the form of the Akashic Record, it conserves the trace of all things that emerge and evolve in the universe.

Contemporary cosmologists in the West have come up with a strikingly similar conception. They no longer view the universe as a one-shot affair, and the big bang as a singularity that constitutes a kind of virgin birth, a creation out of nothing. In current theories what was previously considered empty space—the "vacuum"—is now seen as the grand unified field. This field is the matrix of the particles that furnish cosmic space, and it is the source of the laws and constants of the universe. When at the end of their evolution stars and entire galaxies become black holes, their super-compressed mass dies back into this field. The gigantic forces unleashed by the super-compacted mass of a super-galactic black hole create a cosmic explosion that catalyzes the particles that furnish the next universe—a baby universe, born in the womb of our own universe.

This means that the big bang was in fact a *big bounce*—not the birth of *the* universe, but the rebirth of a *local* universe within a larger and perhaps infinite "meta-universe" (or "metaverse"). The new universe arises in the same cosmic space into which the previous universe had died back.

Why is this concept so important? Because it clarifies a puzzle that has vexed cosmologists for decades. It does so by pointing to the formative role of information in the birth of a universe. The puzzle is to try to understand how our universe was born with its current, extremely improbable physical characteristics. According to a branch of contemporary physics, so-called string theory, as many as 10^{500} universes are physically possible, but only a dozen or so among them have properties that would allow complex systems to emerge. Only this tiny fraction could harbor life. Evidently, our universe is one of this privileged few. Is this mere serendipity? Or is it evidence for divine purpose—for intelligent design?

In their professional capacity, scientists refuse to resort to forces and events that transcend the natural world. If the universe is truly the product of conscious design, then science must retreat before theology. But what if there is a "natural" explanation for the astonishing serendipity that our universe can bring forth life—that we are here and can wonder how this could have come about?

The natural explanation is that the "vacuum" in which our universe was born was not empty space. It was a nonlocal field that "in-formed" the birth of our universe. Our universe inherited the in-formation that defines its laws and constants from a conceivably long (and perhaps infinite) line of parent universes, much as the zygotes that became what we are today inherited the information that had governed their development from a long line of progenitors.

The concept of a cyclic, informed universe is familiar in traditional conceptions of the world. The "vacuum" of Western science is the "Akasha" of traditional cosmologies. Akasha, it turns out, is the functional equivalent of science's unified field, the ultimate source and sink of all things. And because Akasha preserves the trace of all that happens in space and time, it's also the memory of the universe: it's the much discussed Akashic Record.

Here, ancient intuition finds fresh confirmation. The nonlocal in-formation field that pervades space and time is an Akashic field. So why not call it that? I promptly renamed the Ψ field the *Akashic field* (or A-field for short).

Since 2004 I have produced several books on the A-field, including *Science and the Akashic Field, Science and the Reenchantment of the Cosmos, Quantum Shift in the Global Brain,* and *The Akashic Experience.*

There is no longer any doubt in my mind: Ours is a highly informed universe. It had arisen from, and is constantly interconnected by, a cosmic in-formation field: the rediscovered Akashic field of the wisdom traditions.

I have come to believe that it is this Akashic in-formation field that I have been accessing since I was a child. It is the same field that artists, poets, prophets, and scientists access in their moments of creativity, enlightenment, and inspiration. It is the same field that we all access when we experience profound awe, elation, empathy, and joy. And our prophets and poets tell us that we access it when we feel the love that binds all things in heaven and earth.

Come,
sail with me on a quiet pond.
The shores are shrouded,
the surface smooth.
We are vessels on the pond
and we are one with the pond.
A fine wake spreads out behind us,
traveling throughout the misty waters.
Its subtle waves register our passage.
Your wake and mine coalesce,
they form a pattern that mirrors
your movement as well as mine.
As other vessels, who are also us,
sail the pond that is us as well,
their waves intersect with both of ours.
The pond's surface comes alive
with wave upon wave, ripple upon ripple.
They are the memory of our movement;
the traces of our being.
The waters whisper from you to me and from me to you,
and from both of us to all the others who sail the pond:
Our separateness is an illusion;
we are interconnected parts of the whole—
we are a pond with movement and memory.
Our reality is larger than you and me,
and all the vessels that sail the waters,
and all the waters on which they sail.

♪♫♪♫♪♫♪

---

*I first published this poem in 2004 in *Science and the Akashic Field*.

CHAPTER TWENTY-TWO

GROWING
ON IN TUSCANY

My third capstone project was just as important to me as the other two, and it arrived just as suddenly—and seemingly just as serendipitously. The Change the World project of the Club of Budapest came my way through an unexpected offer by the prime minister of Hungary to host its secretariat in Budapest, and the Akashic field phase of my long-standing quest for a deeper understanding of the world happened through a likewise unexpected intuition, flowing spontaneously into my mind on the shores of the Adriatic.

The third capstone project came about thanks to another kind of intuition, and it had another kind of consequence, but it was just as sudden and life-transforming as the other two. But it was neither a research project, nor an action project: it was an existential project. It brought me to the latest, and at present still current, phase of my life.

♪♪♪

While I worked at the UN, I would gaze at the painting of our Italian farmhouse on the wall of my office. I'd tell myself that the time will come when I would go there to collect my thoughts. When it became clear that there was no future for me at the UN's research institute unless I served the ambitions of the new Under-Secretary-General, I realized that the time had finally come. I decided to leave, but all I wanted was a quiet sabbatical year—thinking, reading, writing—before returning to my university in upstate New York. I never thought that my twelve-month sabbatical would uproot my existence and transform my whole life.

It was in the winter of 1973 that I had acquired a farmhouse in Tuscany. We were on a brief vacation in our favorite part of Italy. Christopher was fourteen and Alexander was nine. Father and Mother were also with us; they lived in Switzerland at the time and were happy to spend a brief holiday with the family.

We had driven up a hill on the spur of the moment. We were on the way to the coast from the historic town of Volterra, the center of the Etruscan civilization that had already thrived there over five thousand years ago. I spotted the house from the road: it was on top of a hill on the opposite side of the river, and I wanted to see it up close. We were looking in this area for property we could buy for our summer vacations and chose this part of Tuscany because it hadn't yet been "discovered" by tourists and tour operators. For the most part, it was the same as it had been for centuries.

We had been spending our summers in this region for a number of years, and now we came during the winter break. We went first to Zurich to pick up my parents, and then the whole family came down to look. We checked out some of the farmhouses advertised in the Swiss papers, but most of them turned out to be in ruins or hastily restored, and all were exorbitantly priced. We didn't find anything we liked, and the next day we had to head home; our winter break was drawing to a close.

That is when I spotted the house. We soon found ourselves standing in shoulder-high wild grass on a hilltop not far from the sea, trying to push our way through to the broken-down wooden doors of an old and apparently abandoned farmhouse. It was large and square, built out of enormous blocks of stone. The front door gave when pulled open and revealed a dark chamber that appeared to have been used to house cows, sheep, and other animals. It had a vaulted ceiling and a large wooden trough.

"This is where I want to live," I announced.

Mother was too polite to say what she really thought of the idea; she only went back and sat in the car. Christopher and Alexander started to explore the surroundings, and Marjorie, always supportive, looked for the positive aspects.

"It's not far from the sea. We could easily go down to the beach, and with these thick stone walls, it probably wouldn't be too hot in the summer, so we could sleep at night," she said.

Father struck a pragmatic note. "Well, we don't know who owns it, and it might not even be for sale. In any event, it would take a lot of work to make it livable, even during the summertime."

The view from the hilltop was stunning, but that alone didn't explain the feeling I had. I felt at peace, in harmony with everything. I knew that I could live and work there. I would have liked to have just lain on the grass, except that it was far too high . . . and besides, it was getting late and we had to head back to town for dinner.

I had to admit that the idea of purchasing an abandoned stone house on an overgrown solitary hill was preposterous. Yet, for some reason, I truly wanted this house—most of all, I wanted to live on this hill.

"There's no harm in finding out who owns the property and whether he is willing to sell it," I remarked. I knew we wouldn't have any problem ascertaining this information, for all we had to do was go to the village "bar" in Montescudaio and inquire. Bars in

Italy are not places for "serious" drinking; they are for socializing and relaxation, while enjoying an espresso or sipping a *digestivo*.

I spoke to the barkeeper who told me to wait for a moment, and when he returned, he was accompanied by a dapper middle-aged man. Signor D'Antilio, the major local winegrower, was the owner of extensive vineyards on the hills between the village and river. He was also the owner of the hill on which "our" house was located, but he didn't use the property or the vineyard that surrounded it, mainly because the area was too steep for his tractors. The family who had previously lived there used to harvest the grapes by hand, but they had moved away long ago, and no one showed any interest in moving in. Only hunters during the season would spend a night in the stone house while passing through the area. The villagers hunted pheasant, wild boar, and occasionally rabbit, porcupine, and deer, but our friends told us to be careful as they'd shoot at anything that moved.

Signor D'Antilio and the barman were amazed that I was interested in acquiring the abandoned house on its steep hill. They must have thought that the Swiss, like most foreigners, were a curious people, and if they wanted the house, there was no harm in selling it to them. (We had Swiss plates on the car we'd rented in Switzerland. Casimir was in America, and it wouldn't have accommodated the whole family anyway.)

"How much?" I asked Signor D'Antilio. He thought for a moment and then named a figure. It sounded like a great deal in lira, the Italian currency at the time, but converted into dollars it was an almost ridiculously modest sum. I quickly accepted, and we agreed to meet next morning with the notary who would draw up the sales agreement.

When we met the next morning, the price had gone up overnight by about half. But it was still very reasonable, and since my family and I were leaving on that day, I didn't argue. We signed the papers and then talked to a builder who was recommended as the best person to quickly make the house habitable. Part of the roof had fallen in, there was no bathroom, and the toilet was a cubicle jutting out precariously from the back wall with a hole in the floor. All of the windows and doors needed work, and there was no electricity or water, not to mention heating or a phone line. The previous tenants used the large fireplace on the upper floor for heating and cooking. Animals were kept on the ground floor to help keep the house warm during the winter.

With the sales document in my pocket, a check for the full amount of the property in Signor D'Antilio's pocket, and another check in the hands of the builder, my family and I got into the car and drove back to Zurich. The following day, Marjorie and the boys and I flew back to New York.

♪♪♪

During the next ten years, we would vacation on our Tuscan hilltop. The house was known as the "Podere Franatoni," a name that dated back centuries. (*Podere* means country cottage or farmhouse.) Down by the river there was another podere, known as the "Franatoni Sotto" (the "lower Franatoni"), and Signor D'Antilio had originally offered it to me as well. But I had no interest—the "upper" Franatoni was quite large enough.

In later years, our house was renamed as "Villa Franatoni." The transformation from *podere* to *villa* took quite a long time. It received a boost in 1982 and 1983. We were then living in Rome; I was running the UNITAR Programme on Regional and Interregional Cooperation from an office that Emilio Colombo, the Italian foreign minister, had put at our disposal. Marjorie and the boys and I would make the 300-kilometer journey from Rome to Montescudaio almost every weekend.

Our two-year stay in Rome proved to be a typically Italian experience, beginning with our search for an apartment. It was very difficult to find housing in the historical center—most people would normally look in the "third Rome," the series of ultramodern satellite developments at the city's periphery. If one worked in the center of town, this meant commuting. Public transportation during rush hour was slow and crowded, and if one elected to drive, the trip could take hours moving at a snail's pace on jammed roads. Furthermore, it was practically impossible to find a parking space in the center.

Fortunately, we didn't need to go house hunting: as we did years ago in Munich, Marjorie and I consulted the UN bulletin board. The one in Rome was in the Food and Agriculture Organization (FAO) building, the principal UN body in town.

Just like it did before, the board supplied quick results. As international civil servants, we had more housings options than ordinary mortals. The reason, we discovered, was that locals who were renting out property often charged more than the maximum they were authorized to charge, yet people working for international organizations would normally be willing to pay the extra amount—they received housing subsidies in addition to generous salaries. Above all, they weren't likely to dispute the rent and would be leaving sooner or later. Many local residents, on the other hand, would first agree to a figure, but once they found out how much they *should* be paying, they would refuse to pay the agreed fee. They couldn't be evicted for not paying the full rent or, indeed, for not paying rent at all. Court proceedings would typically take years to resolve, and the law often favored the *inquilinos*—the tenants—over the landlords.

The apartment we decided to take was conveniently located, close to the offices that the Italian foreign minister had put at my disposal. The offices were on the famous Via Giulia, and our apartment was just below the Campidoglio, the city hall of Rome. The street, called Via dei Foraggi (the "street of fodders"), had initially housed the stables of the Roman aristocracy, but as Rome grew, the stables were torn down and two- and three-story houses sprung up in their stead. For centuries, they housed the concealed families of Rome's powerful elite, the mistresses of political leaders, and undeclared families of bishops and cardinals.

The apartment had marble bathrooms and hand-carved doors and closets. The plumbing was noisy, the heating hardly ever worked, and the small elevator was so slow that I seldom had the patience to wait for it . . . but this was a fantastic location, with amazing, historic surroundings.

It would take twenty minutes for me to walk to Via Giulia, half an hour to go there by city bus, and about an hour by car: fifteen minutes to get there and forty-five to find parking. But it took less than ten minutes to go by bicycle. I bought a small folding bike and used it to travel back and forth from the office. This was a fast and surprisingly safe way to travel. Roman drivers have a supreme disregard for pedestrians but great respect for cyclists. Hitting a cyclist would be considered clumsy and a serious offense to boot.

Running an office in Rome was quite an adventure. I had a small staff consisting of a co-director, two assistants, and a secretary. Adriana, one of the assistants, appeared to do nothing but sit at her desk all day and talk on the phone while chain-smoking. Despite how it looked, though, she wasn't wasting anyone's time. The daughter of Ambassador Venturini, she knew everyone in the Italian Foreign Ministry. When strings needed to be pulled, Adriana would know which ones to pull successfully. Dr. Basurto, my co-director, was an old foreign-office hand and knew what we could reasonably hope to achieve and how to go about doing so. Elvira, my other assistant, was the one who actually worked on the program with me, together with Liliana, my secretary. Although Kafkaesque on first sight, this arrangement proved to be surprisingly efficient.

The Roman Forum, the central square of ancient Rome, was just down the street from our apartment. Its world-famous structures, now in ruins, included the Regia, the royal residency, as well as the living quarters of the vestal virgins. The Forum was the central hub where the citizens of Rome came to seek justice, celebrate holidays, and perform sacred rituals. It was also the economic center of the city, the heart of the Roman Republic, and later of the Empire. Now it was the place to which I would retire in the evening to sit and read.

Nearly all of the historic landmarks were within walking distance of our apartment. We roamed the small streets around Piazza Navona, gazed at the designers' shop windows near the Spanish Steps, and visited the myriad famous sites of the Eternal City.

On Friday afternoons, we would get into our car and shoot up to Montescudaio for a spell of country living. (I had diplomatic plates on my car and was immune to speeding tickets.) Marjorie would often stay on to supervise the plumbers, electricians, and stonemasons entrusted with upgrading the house. We quickly learned that our hired help were excellent craftsmen, but they didn't make much progress if we, the owners, weren't around. They wanted to consult with us on particulars and looked forward to getting praise for good work. Remarking "Sei un artista!" ("You are an artist!") worked wonders.

The builder we'd first hired didn't do a very good job, but we couldn't blame him since we just instructed him to make the house habitable. Plus, at the time we were still living far away in upstate New York and weren't there to supervise. There was a new roof and the house was wired for electricity, but the roof was already leaking and sagging, and the electric lines were a fire hazard, running along the walls without proper insulation.

There was no connection to a power grid, so we bought a generator typically used for boats. It had to be hand cranked, and then it produced power at 16 volts until the fuel ran out. But the house was cool in the summer, and kerosene stoves, although smelly, could provide enough heat in the winter.

We had the ceiling of the ground floor sandblasted, and to our delight beautiful bricks forming double arches appeared. The arches were entirely self-supporting, and our stonemasons said that they wouldn't know how to build such intricate and precise structures today. Another fascinating discovery was that the lower part of the house, which was about four hundred years old, was originally a chapel. This must have been an ancient, sacred location, topping a hill at the entrance of the valley leading to Volterra, the center of the Etruscan civilization. It felt replete with the presence of the thousands who must have worshipped here over the centuries.

When we had moved in, many of the locals would visit to have a look at us and at the house. The first man to drop by, who must have been in his eighties, asked if he could come in for a closer look because he had been born in this house. The next person to show up said the same thing—and then the one after that, too. It seemed that half the village had come into the world at the Podere Franatoni. Regardless of what they claimed, the first thing that almost every one of them would say was: "Ah, che pace!" ("Ah, such peace!") And I could certainly agree with that.

Life on the Tuscan hilltop is very different from life in Manhattan. There my lifestyle was like that of the typical New Yorker: intensely centered on work, always short on time, and with little concern for emotional and personal well-being. Every morning I would eat a quick breakfast and rush to the office. At midday I would either have a working lunch at the Delegates Dining Room or a nearby restaurant, or bring a colleague home, using (and sometimes abusing) Marjorie's patience and hospitality. But often I would just run down to the corner deli for a chicken-liver or egg-salad sandwich. Or, even worse, I'd ask Nina to pick something up for me so I could eat while I worked at my desk.

Catharina Roland

A recent photo taken in the garden at Villa Franatoni with my best friend Tykie.

Around Villa Franatoni, there are no delis or fast-food chains. Weather permitting—and weather *is* permitting nine months out of the year—Marjorie and I enjoy our meals on the terrace. We use olive oil that comes from our own olive trees, and drink organic wine made from the Sangiovese grapes from our vineyard. We eat fresh vegetables and fruit from our garden during the growing season.

My daily routine is simple: when my reading and writing is done for the day, we go down to the Cecina River below the house, walk to the village of Montescudaio (about a mile away), or stroll around the seashore at Cecina Mare.

Over time, I developed a veritable craving for the sea, and from the beginning of June to early October, I have an urgent need to throw myself into the water. We take the car to the beach, because bicycling downhill to the coast is fine, but uphill back to the house is less so. We keep our bikes in Cecina Mare and ride in the pine forest that lines the coast for miles.

I have no real roots anywhere in the world, but Villa Franatoni comes as close to being my home as any place on Earth. It has double-vaulted sacred rooms on the ground floor, and living quarters on the upper floor. It houses my collection of books and records in a high-ceilinged room with a large fireplace. From its windows and terraces, we have a clear view of the winding Cecina River with its podere-dotted valleys and hills. We've added an enclosed pool heated by solar panels for year-round swimming. The panels also provide energy to heat the house and water for cooking and washing. The latest addition is a photovoltaic panel mounted on a massive pillar on the hillside. It tracks the sun from morning till evening.

Catharina Roland

In my study at the Villa Franatoni.

♪♪♪

This Tuscan hilltop is a wonderful place to think, read, and write. Since I moved here I became engaged in one project after another. First I joined the UN University's European Identity Project to head its European Perspectives section. Then Alfred, the young prince of Liechtenstein, called to tell me about his dream of creating an academy in Vienna that was dedicated to the problems and opportunities humanity is likely to encounter in the near future. This, of course, was of great interest to me, and we decided on the spot to join forces in establishing what was soon to become the Wiener Akademie für Zukunftsforschung (The Vienna Academy for the Study of the Future). Alfred was its president, and I was the founding rector.

For nearly three years, I went for a week each month to Vienna to run the Academy's programs. We offered seminars for media and business leaders, and a series of lectures for the interested public by eminent thinkers and scientists.

All went well until the principal sponsor, attached to the city administration in Vienna, felt threatened by the opposition party and decided to place its own man as manager of the Academy to make sure that we served its agenda. As I was opposed to catering to local politics (or any politics at all), I resigned. Prince Alfred left a year later and the Academy collapsed.

Shortly afterward, to everyone's surprise, Spanish biochemist Federico Mayor Zaragoza—my old friend and Club of Rome colleague—was elected Director General of UNESCO. He promptly asked me to join him as his science advisor. I was happy to oblige, and from then on, my trips from Tuscany had Paris instead of Vienna as the destination.

Delivering the Inaugural Lecture at the Hungarian Academy
of Sciences in Budapest on October 12, 2010.

In the years that followed I gained more and more recognition from the international community as well as from the academic world. Since 1989 I have received four honorary doctoral degrees (from the U.S., Canada, Finland, and Hungary) and in 2001 was given the Goi Award (the Japan Peace Prize). In 2004 and again in 2005 I was nominated for the Nobel Peace Prize. I received the Assisi Mandir of Peace Prize in 2005, and the World Complexity Science Academy's Medal for Systemic Research in 2010. And in the same year I was elected Member of the Hungarian Academy of Sciences in Budapest.

This hilltop in Tuscany is where I write and research, and pursue my plans and projects for a global shift. It's where I intend to grow on, for as long as I have before me in my current lifetime.

♪♫♪♫♪♫

POSTSCRIPT

BUDAPEST, MON AMOUR— MY ROMANCE WITH MY ROOTS

Over the years I've developed a kind of love affair with Budapest. I left my homeland at the age of fifteen, and since then I've lived in many places throughout Europe and the U.S. but have never settled in one area for long. My periodic visits to my native city have been nourished by a deep desire within me to rediscover where I came from and reconnect with my roots.

♪♪♪

The first time I returned to Budapest was in 1963, as part of my research assignment for the Institute of East European Studies at the University of Fribourg in Switzerland. My research centered on the work of the leading Hungarian philosophers of the time, and I was eager to meet them. The Iron Curtain separating Eastern and Western Europe was still in place, but there was a simple way to pass through it: to come as a visiting artist. My concert manager made contact with the Hungarian state concert agency, and the officials were pleased to invite me for a recital—especially since I didn't ask for a fee.

I gave a piano recital at the Academy of Music, which had remained unchanged since my student days. Friends and relatives I didn't even know I had attended my performance, and we spent hours reminiscing afterward. For them, my having become a "Westerner" seemed like a fabulous accomplishment. Aside from achieving renown in the "free world," the money that Westerners had in their pockets was considered a small fortune. I remember trying, and not succeeding, to spend more than a dollar and a half on dinner in the best restaurant in town, Tokay wine included. The Socialist state supported the price of everyday goods and services, and that was another reason why everything had cost so little.

The impression of my affluence wasn't reinforced by my car, however. We had arrived in Casimir, our Porsche. I drove and Marjorie sat beside me, and we'd placed a mattress on the folded-down jump seat in the back so that Christopher, who was four, could nap and play to his heart's content. In the Soviet world, the Chaika, a long black limousine, was the height of luxury and favored by Soviet and East European dignitaries. A Volga was for less exalted dignitaries, and a Zhiguli was geared for the few who could afford—and had the permission—to own a vehicle. The appeal of a sports car was entirely lacking; in fact, a small car meant that one couldn't afford (or didn't qualify for) a bigger one.

Although Casimir was seen as nothing more than a scaled-down Beetle, we enjoyed riding around town. We could drive from one corner of the city to another easily and surprisingly fast. Aside from heavy trucks, some taxis, and a few official cars, there was hardly any traffic on the roads. To me, houses and trees that once loomed large seemed to have become smaller, and distances had shrunk miraculously. I could hardly get over being able to cover in less than ten minutes the stretch from the Városliget (the park where I'd played soccer in the summer and ice hockey in the winter, and also where I had my memorable walks with Uncle

Pippa) to the shores of the Danube where our hotel was located. It used to take me the better part of an hour to make this excursion, walking several blocks and then changing streetcars.

I loved every minute of my visit. I went to concerts, the opera, and the theater—there was a profusion of offerings and the price of even the best ticket was negligible. I spent time with friends and laughed at the political satires where things were said about government officials that would entail a prison sentence if spoken in public. I visited my old haunts and wandered the hills of Buda just as I used to as a boy. I was back in my childhood but with a grown-up body and mind. It was a remarkable experience.

Yet upon closer inspection, I knew that this was not the world of my childhood—it was a very different place. The appearance of the city remained much the same. At the time hardly any new buildings had been erected, and only the worst reminders of the war had been cleared up. But this was a Communist state. Shops and factories were owned by the state, not by individuals. The government supported all forms of culture but was poor in regard to everyday items. The factories produced primitive products and advertised them in a clumsy imitation of free enterprise.

Everything was regulated. The ironic saying, "In a Communist dictatorship everything is forbidden except what is permitted —and that, too, is forbidden," was an apt description. I was at home in the familiar city, but not in the world that greeted the visitor.

It was not long that I realized, however, that although the Soviet-bloc dictatorship had changed how people were *living*, it didn't change how they were *thinking*. The ideology of Marxism-Leninism had never taken root in the consciousness of Hungarians. Of course, there were the opportunists and the climbers who would kowtow to the powers that be and join them if they could, but the great majority preserved their cultural heritage and remained a liberal European people. Those whom I met were not changed by the regime; they were simply enduring it.

I was eager to meet the philosophers whose works I'd read and written about, and I found, to my happy surprise, that they in turn were eager to meet me. I spoke to the head of the university, the director of the library, and the chairman of various faculties. I sat down with the legendary Georg Lukács, the top Marxist scholar at the time. He was 78 and had an entire library of philosophical treatises to his credit. When I asked if he had plans for another book, he pointed to a mountain of paper on his desk and said that he was almost finished writing his ontology (theory of reality).

Interestingly, while I was in Budapest, the editors of a journal that I frequently quoted in my research approached me with a surprising request: they asked me if I would contribute to their publication. Theirs was a fiercely independent monthly journal called *Valóság* (*Reality*). The authorities had evidently known about it but allowed it to pursue its aims, at least within limits. This was wise, for debates and discussions of this kind had let off steam and relieved pressure that could otherwise have built to major frustration and outright conflict.

I agreed to contribute, and have published several articles in that journal over the years. One of my first was particularly daring: titled "Roundhead and Flatheads," it was a thinly disguised allegory that made fun of the ideological conflicts that dominated the politics of the Communist system.

♪♪♪

My next visit to Budapest was in the summer of 1968. During this trip, which was primarily a family vacation with Marjorie, Christopher, and Alexander, we stayed outside of the city by permission of the state tourist agency. We met once again with friends old and new, toured the city and the surrounding countryside, and enjoyed the traditional home cooking that took me back to my childhood.

One morning—it was the 20th of August—our landlady rushed in looking agitated and told us to listen to the reports coming from the BBC. (She apparently did listen to this radio station, although it was prohibited; the BBC was considered a subversive capitalist institution.)

We went behind the house and tuned in to the BBC World Service on the car radio. The news broadcast reported that Soviet tanks were moving toward Prague, the capital of Czechoslovakia (now the Czech Republic). The Soviets were squashing the liberal movement there known as the "Prague Spring." Armed forces from the neighboring countries—Hungary included—were converging on the Czech capital.

The broadcast by the Voice of America confirmed the story and added that U.S. citizens in Hungary should take precautions. Marjorie and I knew we had to be ready to leave on short notice.

In a secluded place, I met with a group of young scientists and philosophers, and after intense debate, they decided to issue a proclamation condemning the violent suppression of the liberal movement in Czechoslovakia. I added my signature to it, and a young man rushed off to have it reproduced and distributed. We were very aware that these were not only illegal but also downright dangerous activities.

On the following day, Marjorie and I took the Voice of America warning to heart. We packed the car and headed west to the Austrian border. We were held up on the way by a convoy of military vehicles, including heavy Soviet-made tanks, going north, presumably to Czechoslovakia.

When we at last reached the frontier with Austria, the Hungarian border guard looked at our passports and checked our visas, which were in order. But after a moment, he handed my passport to another guard. Then he pointed to a parking lot behind the guardhouse and told us to wait there.

It was nearly three hours before the guard returned with my passport. We were told that we were free to leave, and Marjorie and I heaved great sighs of relief. The time waiting in the parking lot had felt like an eternity. Having signed the protest letter, I could have been considered a *persona non grata* and perhaps even a spy.

There was an occasion, however, when we crossed into Hungary with the feeling that we were coming *into* the land of freedom, rather than *leaving* it. This was in 1972, when Marjorie and I came from the east, after a visit to the Soviet Union. The occasion was the Second International Conference on the History of Science, held at the University of Moscow. There was a section on systems theory, and I had been invited to address it.

This was during the Brezhnev era. Soviet communism was rampant and dogmatic. While most of the common people enjoyed the company of the rare visitors who came from the West, the regime didn't welcome Westerners with open arms. We were capitalists, considered to be exploiters of the proletariat and enemies of the Soviet state.

Not surprisingly, our trip was quite adventurous. We presented ourselves as individual visitors, rather than in a standard group hosted by Intourist, the official tour operator. As invited conference participants this was permitted, but it was by no means facilitated. Practically every step we took had to be submitted in advance for approval, and our progress along the approved itinerary was rigorously monitored.

We'd rented a VW Beetle in Helsinki and drove to Leningrad (now St. Petersburg), a wonderful city that had maintained its cosmopolitan atmosphere and tradition of hospitality despite the official ideology. In the afternoon we walked down Nevsky Prospekt, the "main drag," and chatted with the locals. I was happy to try out my Russian. In the evening we dined at a small restaurant that wasn't on the list of approved places, but we were welcomed warmly. While we were eating, a waiter brought us a bottle of champagne that we hadn't ordered. The waiter pointed to a table in the corner, where a group of Russians, who were grinning broadly, waved at us. We raised our glasses to their health, and by the time the bottle was finished, we had sworn eternal friendship.

The next day we set forth on our drive to Moscow. We followed the approved itinerary after being told that this was for our own safety. We soon understood exactly what they meant by this. When we turned off to a smaller road that promised to lead to a beautiful nearby lake, a guard jumped out of the bushes and blocked our way. He didn't speak English, and I didn't understand what he shouted at us in Russian, but there was no need for verbal communication. The way in which he waved his Kalashnikov at us left no doubt about his meaning. I promptly turned the car around and didn't veer off the designated route again.

We had no difficulty locating our accommodations in Moscow. The Ukraina Hotel was a landmark, one of the giant Stalinist "sugar cake" buildings that was the pride, and later the embarrassment, of the Muscovites. (Moscow University was another.)

Our reception was frosty and slow, but at last we were assigned rooms on the 25th floor. Getting up to that floor wasn't difficult—elevator doors would open regularly on the ground floor—but getting back down was another matter. During the day the elevators going up were soon filled on the lower floors with people wanting to get down, and when an elevator was full, it was unceremoniously turned around. This stranded the people on the higher floors. With luck, an elevator would eventually make it to the 25th floor, but it was quicker to walk down the stairs than to wait for it.

The conference was well organized and filled to capacity with eager students and professors. The systems-science section was a popular attraction. I enjoyed making contact with the Russian systems scientists and their bright and eager students, and I met with them in their homes as well.

One evening just before leaving the country, over a glass of superb Russian vodka, I rashly promised to help a biologist, whom I'd met at the conference, publish his book in the West, since he couldn't do so in the Soviet Union. (He'd refused to abide by the official interpretation of evolution, which embraced the idea that acquired characteristics could be inherited, as proclaimed by the celebrated biologist Trofim Lysenko.) This meant that I would have to smuggle the manuscript across the border.

Transporting "subversive literature" out of the country was a serious offense. I was apprehensive when, after a long drive first south and then west with a stop in Kiev, we arrived at the town of Csap, on the Hungarian border.

Crossing was a nerve-racking experience. The Soviet border guards emptied all of our suitcases. They began by looking for them at the back of our rented Beetle and were surprised when they found the engine there instead. Then they took out the seats and even jacked the car up in order to search underneath it. I was keeping my fingers crossed that they wouldn't come across the manuscript. They did end up finding some of the loose pages—I had interspersed them among other documents—but fortunately, they didn't realize that they contained "subversive" ideas.

After two hours, we were told that we could go. We left quickly, and on the other side of the wide no-man's-land, we were greeted by two smiling Hungarian guards. They were plainly delighted to see us and took only a superficial glance at our U.S. passports. Not many Western visitors passed through this remote border crossing.

In Hungarian, I asked the guards where we were supposed to go, and they told us to go wherever we liked and take whichever route we wished. For our next stop they suggested the picturesque wine-producing region of Tokaj, which wasn't far away, and said we could find many villagers there who would be happy to provide us with food and lodging.

We headed in that direction, but stopped after the first turn. Marjorie and I sat still for a while, tears streaming down our faces. The relief of having left the ironfisted Soviet system was overwhelming. We were no longer considered potential enemies; we were back in the free world. And the free world, strangely (and happily) enough, was now my native Hungary.

♪♪♪

During a visit eleven years later—it was in 1983—I didn't have any problem crossing in and out of the country. I carried a United Nations diplomatic passport (a *laissez-passer*) in my pocket, in addition to a U.S. passport. I was there to participate in a conference on systems theory hosted by the Institute for Culture and the Academy of Sciences.

To my surprise, systems theory and similar topics could be discussed nearly as freely as in the West, and even relatively "sensitive" issues could be debated as long as the dominant economic and political dogmas were not questioned. The younger generation of Hungarian intellectuals was mostly made up of dedicated Socialists who were committed to the humanistic ideas and ideals of the young Marx but were critical of, and often deeply opposed to, the way in which they were applied by the political leadership. Debate and discussion of the issues was intense, stimulated by the contrast between what the young scientists and philosophers held and wanted, and what the government proclaimed and imposed.

At the systems-theory meeting, I met young intellectuals who were at the very heart of this surprisingly independent intellectual movement. They clustered around Ivan Vitányi, whom I had met during a previous visit when I came to interview some of the prominent philosophers in Hungary. Vitányi, one of the editors of *Valóság,* was behind my invitation to contribute to that remarkably independent-minded journal. The group included Gedeon Dienes, an authority on classical dance who served as the international representative of the Institute for Culture; Sándor Timár, founder and director of a famous dance group that spearheaded the authentic folk-dance movement inspired by the research of Béla Bartók; and Gábor Koncz, a social scientist who studied the economics of culture. (Gábor later became the director of the Hungarian Culture Foundation, the institution that hosts the Club of Budapest.)

Maria Sági, later the scientific secretary of the Club, was a principal member of this group, although she steered clear of politically sensitive topics, concentrating instead on the sociology and psychology of art and music. Her major opus was the study of musical creativity in everyday people, a pioneering research on "generative ability" in music. In her sociological work, she employed qualitative analysis and hour-long "deep interviews," which were particularly suited for the tasks of the UN University's project I was involved in at the time. Upon my recommendation, Ivan Vitányi's Institute for Culture became the Central European partner of the UN University's European Identity Project, and Maria was named head of research.

When the UNU research ended, I called on Ivan and his institute to take part in my own Programme on Regional and

Interregional Cooperation at UNITAR. They became a major partner, and helped me engage research institutes in the neighboring countries of Central and Eastern Europe. In December 1983, I asked the participating institutes to come together to review their findings. This was a three-day meeting held at Ivan's Institute for Culture.

The evening of the first day we were treated to a traditional Hungarian dinner. The head fiddler of the gypsy band came to our table to play songs that made us both laugh and cry, and invited us to dance the tempestuous czardas to our heart's content. Dancing was a good idea in any case—it was needed just to digest the delicious but heavy dishes that started with goose liver and went on to include more parts of a pig than I could ever imagine.

The following day at noon, our charming hostesses invited us to lunch, and that meal promised to be nearly as elaborate and heavy as dinner the night before. I was looking for an excuse to slip out when I noticed that Ivan himself was not going to join us—nor were Maria Sági and Gedeon Dienes. I asked Ivan if they were going to skip lunch, but he just smiled and told me to come along.

I went with them and found myself in Ivan's office. Maria and Judit, Ivan's secretary, busied themselves behind an enclosure in the outer office. There were some hot plates there and soon inviting smells began to waft toward us. We were served a type of meal the likes of which I had not known before. Not only was it made up of many different kinds of dishes—so are Chinese meals and those I was familiar with—but the dishes were made up differently for each of us.

Maria, who turned out to be the expert, explained: "This is macrobiotic cooking; it's not just a standardized diet for weight loss. It's custom tailored for each person, according to his or her age and occupation, and also according to the season. This way, it can offer optimal nourishment." Maria knew what was best for Ivan and Gee, and claimed to know what was best for me, too. She must have been right, because I had a highly satisfying meal and felt light and energetic all day.

I had already heard about this style of cooking. I recalled that a few years earlier my secretary Nina came into my office at the UN waving an invitation to a macrobiotic cooking course for members of the Secretariat. She said that she didn't have time for such elaborate cookery, but perhaps it would interest Marjorie. However, when I saw that the young lady who brought the invitation was dressed in a flowing sari and wore flowers in her hair, I suspected that this was some esoteric New Age frill and told Nina that we would pass.

But Maria didn't pass up her chance to learn this culinary art; the year before she had taken an in-depth course in macrobiotics in Vienna. She had become a pupil of the founder of macrobiotics, Michio Kushi, and served as his interpreter when he visited Budapest. In 1995 she edited the Hungarian version of Kushi's principal work, *The Cancer Prevention Diet,* and after our lunch in Ivan's office, she gave me a copy of the English edition to take home—and take to heart.

Regarding the latter, I was willing but skeptical. The sum total of my cooking skills amounted to "creating" scrambled eggs with boiled potatoes on the side. (True, I also had a quite special culinary accomplishment, acquired while living in Switzerland: Swiss cheese fondue. This is a delicate operation, calling for a careful selection of cheeses—I favored the local Gruyère and Vacherin cheeses—and their insertion in a slowly cooking pot rubbed with garlic and seasoned with cherry liquor. The brew requires constant and delicate stirring; otherwise, it could transform its soft creamy texture into the unyielding consistency of a tractor tire. Since this unwelcome transformation could never be entirely ruled out, it was my custom to keep several eggs at hand for a plate of emergency scrambled eggs.)

Maria assured me that even if macrobiotic cooking exceeded my own capacities, it would surely not exceed those of Marjorie, and I was to pass the book on to her when I went home. So I did, and Marjorie soon got the hang of it. From then on, the meals in our home featured a locally grown vegetable-, grain-, and fruit-based variety of the originally Japanese macrobiotic cuisine known for helping people keep body and soul together—into ripe old age.

In addition to innovative cooking techniques, I was also introduced to a form of exercise on yet another visit to my native country. One morning as I was getting out of bed, I found that I could hardly straighten myself upright. I realized that I must have pulled a muscle; my back ached excruciatingly. I called Ivan, who told me not to worry—the same thing had happened to him a few years back, and he knew just what I needed to do. He in turn called Maria, who then took me to see Dr. Géza Kovács.

Géza bácsi ("Uncle Géza," as everybody called him) was a remarkable man with a remarkable history. He was a gymnastics teacher who, in his thirties, had seriously injured his back catching a student who fell off the trapeze while doing his exercises. With his vertebra fractured, his doctor told him that he could be paralyzed for life. This was not the case, fortunately, but he had to spend an entire year in a cast.

Afterward, Uncle Géza was determined to return to a normal life. He devised a series of exercises to reinforce the muscles that support the vertebrae and began to practice them daily. Not only did his back improve to the point where he could move normally, but he could also do even more demanding exercises. He went back to teaching and became renowned for helping athletes. Before long he was training Hungary's national gymnastics team.

Uncle Géza held regular classes at the Academy of Music. Musicians are obliged to sit for hours in positions totally unsuited to the human body: holding a violin under the chin or a cello between the legs, and contorting the spine to draw the bow. Even sitting in front of a piano is not the healthiest of postures, especially when it's assumed for hours every day. Uncle Géza developed an entire series of "soft gymnastics" that, if practiced regularly, corrected a wide variety of posture-based ills. He had kept Hungary's musicians in good shape, and Maria assured me that he would do the same for me.

I met Uncle Géza at the gym of the Music Academy right after one of his classes. He was in a training outfit, as always. With his clear blue eyes and white hair, he was an amazing example of health, fitness, and practical wisdom.

"Young man," he said to me (I was fifty-one then, and he was over seventy), "when you pass fifty, you have to learn that you must take time for body maintenance. Steady exercise for twenty minutes every morning, and five to ten minutes now and again during the day, and you will stay healthy and fit."

I complained of my backache, and he told me that we'd fix it in no time. He first gave me a massage and then showed me the exercises I should be doing, starting with gently stretching my head; then swinging my arms, torso, and legs; and finally flexing my toes.

The "Kovács method" worked. The following day I was able to stand up straight and move around without pain.

After that experience, I consulted Uncle Géza every time I visited Budapest, until he died in his eighties. His longtime associate Dr. Zsuzsa Negyessy is now conducting the Kovács gym classes at the Music Academy.

Eric Blom

On the historic Chain Bridge over the Danube. The spire in the background is that of the St. Matthias Church. The offices of the Club of Budapest are just next to it.

♪♪♪

Since the founding of the Club of Budapest in 1993, I find myself returning to the city more and more. I continue to fuel my romance with my roots through these visits. My sense of belonging to a community of people somewhere in the world has grown, even though I am not a "real" Hungarian anymore than a "real" Italian—or a "real" American for that matter. I am, and remain, just myself, living a life that is still, and always will be, beyond any box.

My ties to my native country have been nourished by the honors some Hungarian institutions decided to bestow on me. In 2001, the University of Pécs, the oldest university in the country, awarded me an honorary doctorate. And in the spring of 2010, the Hungarian Academy of Sciences elected me as a member. I already serve in several august academies, but this distinction pleased me particularly. Membership is normally limited to Hungarian citizens, and most of the members live and work in the country, but there are a few who were born in Hungary but no longer reside there. I have now joined these "external members" and find myself in good company, among several Nobel laureates and world-renowned scientists.

It's often said that you can't be a prophet in your own country, but I am beginning to think that there are exceptions to this. Being an "academician" in Hungary is not exactly like being a prophet, but, as in other European countries, it's not really very far from it.

♪♫♪♫♪♫♪♫

ANNEX

THE WORLDSHIFT NOTEBOOK

When friends first suggested the idea of an "Internet Note-book," I dismissed it with a wave of my hand. I was way too busy to pursue superficial things such as that. But before long, the growth of the virtual culture made me change my mind. Blogging is not something to dismiss lightly—in fact, it's a very effective way to reach many people, especially young people.

When Carl Carpenter, my California software wizard, offered to help me create my own blog, I agreed to give it a try. I began to jot down thoughts and ideas that came to mind and then send them to Carl to post online at the **ervinlaszlo.com** site. I then met Agapi Stassinopoulos at Deepak Chopra's first "Sages and Scientists" conference in Carlsbad, California. Agapi, the sister of Arianna Huffington, told me that I should also post my blogs on her sister's super-popular site, The Huffington Post. So a few weeks later, I began posting my writing there, too, and started to receive dozens, then hundreds, and in some cases, thousands, of comments on what I wrote. My first blogs, organized under four major headings (Why We Need a WorldShift, The Coming of a WorldShift, Mastering the WorldShift, and The New Consciousness) make up the content of "The WorldShift Notebook" reproduced here.

Two other initiatives complement my Internet-based Notebook. One is the "Forum on Science & Spirituality" with contributions from eminent scientists as well as deeply spiritual persons, and the other the WorldShift Community, a networked site that brings together the Club of Budapest–inspired or initiated projects centering on the concept of a timely global transformation—a "WorldShift."

The purpose of the Forum on Science & Spirituality is to overcome the gulf that fragments the contemporary world and produces animosity and tension, culminating at its worst in fundamentalism and violence. Fostering communication between the branches of the contemporary world that British scientist and novelist C.P. Snow dubbed the "two cultures" promotes at the same time the evolution of the broader and deeper vision that my colleagues of the Club of Budapest and I call "planetary consciousness."

The WorldShift Community site in turn aspires to create a weightier and more visible presence for global-transformation oriented projects. Rather than competing with each other and defending our own turf, we aspire to collaborate to reinforce each other in our striving toward our shared goal: to facilitate the changes we so urgently need to avert breakdown and break through to a sustainable, fair, and peaceful world.

♪♪♪

1. Why We Need a WorldShift

This World Is Unsustainable and Unacceptable

Six million children die every year of starvation, while there are 155 million children who are overweight.

Millions in the "developed" world are suffering from obesity, while millions more in the "developing" world go hungry.

Our sustained well-being and even our very survival is in question, but most of us remain preoccupied with making money and holding on to our privileges. Even our political leaders, as I write in reference to the declaration of the G-20, fight for a better place without taking into account that the place they fight for is on the deck of a sinking ship.

We fight cultural intolerance and religious fundamentalism in others, but many of us are willing to subscribe to radical forms of nationalism under the banner of patriotism and national security.

We tell our children to abide by the golden rule, "Treat others as you expect others to treat you," but we seldom treat other people—and other states and other businesses—as we expect other people, other states, and other businesses to treat us.

The problems we face call for long-term solutions, but our criteria of success in the marketplace is the bottom line in annual or semiannual corporate profit-and-loss statements.

The problems we face call for the commitment and participation of every able-bodied person in the human family, but we put millions out of work to cut down on the cost of labor and increase profits for self-centered corporations.

We bring vast herds of sensitive animals into the world for the sole purpose of slaughtering them, a procedure that, apart from its abhorrent ethical implications, wastes an inordinate amount of resources—water, grain, soya, and energy, among other things.

The Earth is bathed in energy—if fully used, 40 minutes of the solar radiation reaching the planet would cover the energy needs of all seven billion of us for a whole year—and there are technologies ready to be applied that would permit us to derive energy from sunlight, wind, tides, plants, and hot subsurface rocks; but for the most part, we still run our economies primarily on the finite supplies of oil and coal.

The ineffectiveness of military means to achieve economic and political goals has been proven over and over again, yet our governments still spend $1.47 trillion a year on the military, developing and stockpiling high-tech weapons that are more dangerous than the conflicts they could possibly resolve.

The Dis-ease of the Western Mind

When someone asked Gandhi what he thought of Western civilization, he replied that it was a good idea. It is indeed a good idea, because it's not really a reality. Western civilization—more exactly, the Western mind that creates the civilization—has a serious disease. It's a "dis-ease" that affects all of us in the West. And now we can have a better idea of what's behind it.

Take these characteristics of the Western mind:

- It sees things as separate, each thing on its own, connected merely by mechanistic relations of cause and effect.

- It is competitive: each individual is on his or her own, making his or her way in an impersonal, indifferent world.

- It disconnects the mind from the body: the mind only "drives" or "manages" the body as it would a car or an organization.

- It best understands the things it has itself created: artificial, synthetic things that can be readily and unambiguously manipulated.

- It disconnects the human from the natural; nature itself becomes the "environment" that humans can manage and manipulate to serve their interests.

- It categorizes and schematizes people and things, viewing them as abstract entities rather than as existing, living realities.

- It deals with the representation of people and things rather than with our living experience of people and things.

- It views all things, nature included, as mechanistic kinds of systems, put together from their parts and capable of being manipulated by acting on their parts.

These traits add up to a dis-ease, to the long-discussed malaise of Western civilization. Other civilizations have their own problems and failings, but the above traits are typically those of the Western mind: of the civilization created by the Western mind.

Are these characteristics purely accidental, just the way in which the typical Western mind happens to work?

A historical analysis can furnish an explanation as to why this particular mind-set came to dominate the West. The main reason appears to be the separation of the world of values, feelings, and spirit from the world of fact and reason at the dawn of the modern age. Following the famous trial of Giordano Bruno, the Catholic Church claimed for itself authority over the world of value, feeling, and spirit and allowed science and scientists to investigate the world of fact through reasoning based on observation and experiment.

The original covenant between science and church, concluded on the part of science by Galileo, was reinforced and made into an unquestioned precept by the radical separation of the two worlds by René Descartes. According to Cartesian philosophy, there is a complete disjunction between the physical world "outside" the mind (the world of "extended substance," *res extensa*) from the thinking, feeling world "within" (the thinking substance, *res cogitans*). Science made great progress by dissecting the outside world into parts and manipulating them; this became the basis of modern technology. And the West fell in love with technology, more exactly, with the powers over people and nature conferred by technology. It relegated the felt "inside" world of value, feeling, and spirit to religion and spirituality, to be celebrated on Sundays and holidays. It made the manipulation of the "outside" world its true concern: the foundation of modern economics and politics, the way relations between people, and between people and nature, are decided and conducted.

This historical backdrop might explain how it is that the West ended up with an impersonal, mechanical, atomized world as its "real" world. But it doesn't say how the Western mind actually operates; why it sees the world as an impersonal, mechanical aggregate of atomistic parts. But cognitive neuroscience can tell us more.

Roger Sperry, Michael Gazzaniga, and other pioneers of split-brain research founded the discipline of cognitive neuroscience. They discovered that we have two brains, not just one. We have the right brain and the left brain—more exactly, the right and left hemispheres of the neocortex. The two brains are dissimilar in their functioning and even in their anatomy. The right hemisphere is wider, longer, larger, and heavier than the left. It's also different in its sensitivity to neurotransmitters and neurohormones, and has a different neuronal structure and organization. It's "tuned" to our experience in an alternate way.

It's important to realize that the world is not perceived in its pristine purity, "just the way it is." Our input from the senses is organized, interpreted by our brain, with the result that the same sensory stimulus can give rise to diverse experiences and interpretations. (Think of the well-known drawing used by psychologists where, when you gaze at it, you can see either an elegant young woman or an old hag.) Our two brains "see" the world each in its own way, and these ways are not the same. The reason we have something like a single world picture is because one of the two brains is dominant. In the West, the left brain is dominant. And here is the clue to the dis-ease of the Western mind.

In *The Master and His Emissary: The Divided Brain and the Making of the Western World*, neuroscientist Iain McGilchrist asked what it would look like if our left brain were the sole purveyor of reality. The whole world would be a heap of bits and pieces; its only meaning would come through its capacity to be used. Our attention would be narrowly focused on the individual bits and pieces, with increasing specialization bringing more and more familiarity with less and less. Information and information gathering would be substituted for knowledge gained by actual experience. And the kind of knowledge we would gain would be rooted in representations of reality, by abstract cognitive schemes that would seem more "real" than the things we actually experience.

Does this world seem familiar? That shouldn't surprise you: the left hemisphere's view of the world is by and large the Western mind's view of the world. There are people and things in this world, but there is no "betweenness"—they are connected only by relations of cause and effect, by how one thing affects another, by what one person "does" to another.

This world is centered upon, and is best when it deals with, the things we ourselves have created. It's a competitive world where everyone is separate and out for him- or herself. And it's an impersonal and uncaring world, where to think that there is meaning, feeling, and purpose is merely to project one's own subjective feelings into an impersonal "objective" reality.

The world of the right brain would be very different. While having only the right brain available to us, our experience would be filled with many positive things. We would be making connections between things, seeing the world around us as a whole in which people and things are organic parts. We would be tending directly to our experience, viewing people and things in their presented uniqueness. We would be living *in* our body, feeling ourselves at one with it and the world that surrounds and embeds it.

The sense of time, the "flow" of things, would be primary, and we would enjoy experiences where this flow is evident, such as in writing, theater, dance, and music. Because of the betweenness connecting us to the world, we would be more empathetic, tuned to compassion and concern for all things in nature. And our empathies would get a powerful boost by our being aware of our intuitions, of our subtle communication with the world beyond the range of our bodily senses. As I shall discuss, this perception is within the compass of the nonlocal quantum receptivity of the subneuronal networks of our brain, but is repressed by the narrow rationality of our left hemisphere.

This right-brained world would seem more familiar to traditional people than to most of us in Western civilization. But to many of us, it might seem more like regress rather than progress, for it would mean giving up much of our technical prowess and manipulative skills. However, this would not be necessary: We could also combine the world of our right brain with the world of the left. We could hand the things and events presented to our world-tuned right brain to the left for analysis, formulation, and communication, and then allow our right brain to place it in context so that we could reach an integral assessment and a balanced way of responding. We would see the forest and still find our way among the trees.

The dis-ease of the Western mind is a product of historical circumstance, but it's not doomed. We could overcome our one-sided heritage of the past. The key is using our brain more fully. This would give us a consciousness where the broad, holistic world of the right brain is linked with the pragmatic, skillful world of the left. Achieving this new consciousness would go a long way toward curing the dis-ease of the Western mind.

A Matter of Vision and Consciousness: Reflections on the Meeting of the G-8 and the G-20 in Canada

The final statements of the June 2010 meetings in Canada of the G-8 and the G-20 make impressive reading ("The G-8 Muskoka Declaration: Recovery and New Beginnings" and "The G-20 Toronto Summit Declaration"). They contain a long list of marvelous commitments through which the leaders of the advanced world can decide to join forces to ensure a better future for all.

All is well, then? Hardly. A closer look reveals major problems.

First of all, the flawless harmony communicated in the declarations was not mirrored in the actual debates. There was little agreement on how to move forward, with the U.S. insisting on additional public spending to relaunch a recovery, and the U.K. and other European nations opting for budgetary cutbacks as the way to move forward. The proposals of the member states also had a tacit "beggar-thy-neighbor" dimension: if implemented, they would serve the given nation's economy, without much regard for the sacrifices incurred by the others.

But the real problem is not the attempt to hide or smooth over internal disagreements—that's normal procedure for international bodies. The problem is that the objectives espoused by the G-8, and the larger G-20 that incorporates the G-8, are one-sided, as if only money would matter, and economic growth of the kind we have known in the past could solve all problems. This suggests a vision that is terminally out of date.

In the G-20 vision, the world is made up of nation-states and groups of nation-states, with national governments in charge of ensuring the national interest. Except for some frills and halfhearted regulations, the national interest is business-as-usual economic interest. The governments are to bring about "recovery," "renewed stability," and "balanced growth" in their national economy; and international cooperation is to rebalance the economic and financial system that the crises of the recent past had unbalanced.

The G-8 and G-20 leaders do not seem to realize that recovering and reestablishing the economic-financial order of the past is to re-create a system that's structurally unstable and no longer sustainable. They do not seem to entertain the possibility that what the world needs is not more of the same, but something radically different: a thorough transformation.

In a world where a third of the people live in abject poverty, and as many people (if not more) face critical water shortages; and where the atmosphere heats up, the climate changes, sea levels rise, and the processes enabling the regeneration of vital biological resources are seriously impaired, a classical economic focus is not just inadequate, it's obsolete. We have seen what reliance on the open market produces: abject poverty for billions, and inequality of the kind where the wealth of a few hundred billionaires equals the income on which half the world's population has to subsist. With the classical vision, the people, at least the poorer and less-powerful elements of the people, will perish.

Evidently, putting more money into humanitarian projects such as reducing infant and under-five mortality is good and necessary. But "recovery"—in the sense of recovering the kind of system and growth that characterized the last several decades—is not. As hardly any serious economist would contest any longer, it would only lead to more and bigger crises, and ultimately to breakdown.

Can we expect the recognition of the need for urgent and deep-seated transformation to dawn in the minds of the leaders of the world's most powerful nation-states? Evidently not. A thorough transformation would—or is very likely to—place in question the legitimacy of the very order that brought them to power and maintains them in power.

Relaunching the kind of growth that the world experienced in the late twentieth century is not the way to go in the twenty-first century. The dilemma is not whether to let states and people undergo imminent crises, or attempting to postpone the onset of the crises; here the choice is clear. The real dilemma is whether to lead the transformation to a more sustainable system or be overwhelmed by it. Leading the transformation offers the opportunity for sustained leadership to those who can still steer the present system, whereas a failure here would surely lead to their demise.

The crux of the matter is that initiating the processes that would lead us to the needed transformation calls for a kind of vision the G-20 doesn't now possess. The type of vision that could solve today's problems demands a new level of consciousness—a consciousness that inspires and motivates cooperation not only by national governments, and not only in the economic and financial domain; but also in the domains of ecology, technology, education, public information, cultural contact, and communication. A consciousness that in today's world the basic precondition of peace and sustainability, and even of enduring prosperity, is wide-ranging cooperation based on a solidarity that embraces transformation. A consciousness, in the last count, of the interdependence and oneness of all the people on this spaceship Earth, and the oneness of our shared destiny.

The "games" the G-20 should be playing are not *inter*national games where either I win and you lose, or you win and I lose. They must be *trans*national games where everyone wins. Because unless all the people win, all the people will lose. Sooner and more dramatically than the G-20 leaders realize.

2. The Coming of a WorldShift

The WorldShift Is a Global Bifurcation

When you exclaim, "That's the last straw!" you express a basic principle that everyone knows but mostly ignores. In science, it's called "nonlinearity." If you load up the back of a camel, you can add load after load and the camel will adjust and cope—until the amount reaches the limit of the animal's carrying capacity. Then, as the expression has it, just one more straw will break the camel's back. A stepwise process that proceeded smoothly, "linearly," suddenly becomes abrupt, "nonlinear." It is a bifurcation in the evolutionary trajectory of that system.

Bifurcation is what happens throughout nature. A living species can cope with changes in its environment—up to a point. When those changes accumulate, the stress reaches a critical point and the species dies out . . . unless, of course, it mutates. In relatively simple systems, critical points lead to breakdown. In more complex systems, these critical points are bifurcation points: they can go one way or another. They do not lead inevitably to breakdown; in fact, they can also lead to breakthrough.

The processes of bifurcation can be modeled by mathematical simulation. Near the state of chaos, the "attractors" that appear in the "phase portrait" of the systems and govern its behavior . . .

shift. Relatively stable point and periodic attractors yield to so-called chaotic or strange attractors, and these are prone to under-going fundamental change.

Bifurcations are also illustrated in the development of human societies. In 1989 a group of East German refugees received permission to cross the Iron Curtain from Hungary to Austria. This proved to be the small but critical shock to the system that broke its back—it was "the last straw." In a matter of weeks, the Communist-dominated East European states seceded from the So-viet Union, and less than a year later, the Soviet Union ceased to exist. The Soviet Communist Party, the most powerful political party in the world, didn't just lose power, it was actually outlawed. The states that made up the Soviet Union did not disappear; after a period of chaos and near breakdown, they managed to transform into more open societies.

In the last 10,000 years, many societies and entire civilizations reached critical bifurcation points; and once flowering cultures vanished—for example, the Babylonians, Sumerians, Mayans, and Easter Islanders. But others met the challenge: they transformed and survived. History testifies that the transformations were often profound. And in the course of time, they became more and more "abrupt." The profound change that first took millennia later took only centuries. Then it took but decades—and now it's taking just years. Then it was just local or regional—today it's global. Meet-ing the challenge of the coming global bifurcation concerns you and me, and everybody on this Earth. And it demands our urgent attention.

The 2012 WorldShift Prophecies

A remarkable number of prophecies speak of the end of 2012 as the period of a worldshift—a global bifurcation. The most fa-mous of these prophecies is that of the Mayans.

The Mayans viewed civilization as a cyclic process, where shifts from one phase of the cycle to the next occur at specific intervals. The cyclic concept of civilization was not an arbitrary invention of the Mayans. Cycles exist everywhere in nature and have been recognized in almost all cultures.

Cycles occur in history as well. In traditional cultures, they were seen as the advent and passing of "great ages." There was the astrological great year, which lasts just under 26,000 years (based on the precession of the equinoxes), and the yugas of Hindu philosophy, a cosmic epoch with a cycle of dark and golden ages. Many myths speak of celestial cycles, and numerous civilizations have attempted to map their principal transitions. Celestial calendars were a major reference for life in many parts of the world. One of the most famous of these calendars is the Tzolk'in calendar, a 260-day Mesoamerican system that was known to the Mayans.

The Mayan calendar itself was completed by priest-astronomers in the year 1479 and carved into the Aztec Mayan sun stone. It details long passages of time and includes mathematical calculations so accurate that modern astronomers are at a loss to understand how a traditional people could have deduced them—for example, the calculation of the length of the Earth's revolution was within a thousandth of a decimal point.

The most famous calculation is encoded in the so-called long count. The "Age of Jaguar," the 13th baktun of 144,000 days, will come to an end on December 21, 2012. That will mark the end of the Fourth Sun (also known as the Fourth World) and the end—and at the same time also the beginning—of the Mayan calendar. This transformative date is written as 13.0.0.0.0 in long-count notation, which is the same as the notation for the first day in the calendar.

Although December 21, 2012, marks the end of the long count in the Mayan calendar (and thus also the end and rebirth of the calendar), it doesn't signify the end of the world. Carlos Barrios, a Guatemalan historian and anthropologist who became a Mayan Ajq'ij, a ceremonial priest and spiritual guide, is certain on the question regarding the end of our existence: "Other people write about prophecy in the name of the Maya," he declared in a series of interviews in Santa Fe. "They say that the world will end in

December 2012. The Mayan elders are angry with this. The world will not end. It will be transformed."

Everything will change: December 21, 2012, will be a date of rebirth, the beginning of the World of the Fifth Sun. The nature of that world is not determined in advance, but the Mayan system suggests that it may be the beginning of a new cycle of ages, starting with the Golden Age. It is likely to mark a fundamental shift in human culture and consciousness.

A global bifurcation at the end of 2012 is predicted in astrology as well. Astrologers have noted that at sunrise on December 21, 2012, the sun will conjunct the intersection of the Milky Way and the plane of the ecliptic, creating a cosmic cross. The center of our galaxy will complete a "cosmic year": a 25,920-year journey around the wheel of the zodiac. According to most systems of astrology, a new cosmic year will then begin, lasting for another 25,920 years. (The reality of this cycle, if not its astrological—or Mayan—interpretation, rests on independent scientific evidence: it concerns the rotation of the Earth on its axis. This rotation is about 23 degrees off vertical: our planet is like a spinning top that is slightly out of balance. In this condition, it takes 25,800 years for the celestial pole to describe a full circle. The conjunction noted by Mayans and astrologers will occur in a 36-year window in time between 1980 and 2016. The Mayans have chosen the winter solstice 2012 as the decisive point, even though it's not in the middle of this window, perhaps because at that point the earth's axis will point exactly toward the "galactic bulge"—the thick central part of the visual image of the Milky Way galaxy as seen from Earth.)

The cosmic conjunction noted by both astrologers and the Mayans was considered a fundamental realignment in a number of spiritual traditions, including the Hopi time-keeping system, Vedic and Islamic astrology, Mithraism, the Jewish Kabbalah, European sacred geography, medieval Christian architecture, and a variety of hermetic metaphysics.

Evidence for a WorldShift: Climate Change

There is significant independent evidence that the 2012 prophecies harbor an important element of truth. Not only will there be an interesting conjunction in regard to the position of our planet in the solar system at the end of 2012, but this conjunction may also actually coincide with a bifurcation for humanity.

One strand of evidence concerns the world's climate. Weather patterns are turning extreme all over the world. There are unprecedented droughts in China and Australia, floods in North America, and cyclones and devastating hurricanes impacting many tropical coastlines. There are threats to health appearing on a scale never before experienced: avian flu and "swine flu," and other tropical diseases, some of which we thought had been vanquished. Global warming creates a widespread and frequent incidence of vector-borne diseases such as malaria and dengue fever, as well as of waterborne diseases such as cholera.

The record shows temperatures fluctuating strongly, and the average is rising. In the summer of 2003, temperature fluctuations averaged 2.3 degrees higher than in previous years. Globally, temperatures have risen over the past century by at least 0.74°C, and the principal causes are still debated. More than likely, both human and natural processes conspire to produce the warming. It is known that greenhouse gases in the earth's atmosphere trap the sun's rays and heat up the atmosphere. This is bound to be a factor in global warming, whether or not changes in the physical processes of the sun contribute to the warming.

Global warming is also produced by natural causes. In addition to the emission of CO_2 and other greenhouse gases; variations in the sun's radiation and sunspot activity and in the earth's orbit and spin; as well as volcanic geothermal activity, all affect and warm the planet's troposphere and stratosphere.

In its 2007 report, the Intergovernmental Panel on Climate Change (IPCC) declared that the warming of the world's climate is now "unequivocal." This is a matter of observed fact. It comes to the fore in the increase of temperatures in the arctic; the reduced size of icebergs and the melting of ice caps and glaciers; the reduction of areas under permafrost; changes in rainfall patterns; and in new wind formations, droughts, heat waves, tropical cyclones, and other extreme weather patterns.

The consequences of global warming include widespread flooding due to tropical storms and the rise of sea levels. The melting of the Greenland ice cap could alter the flow of the Gulf Stream and may deflect it before it reaches the European continent, dropping temperatures in England and the Nordic countries to levels typical of Labrador. If the West Antarctic ice sheet disintegrates during this century, the level of the sea will rise by meters, not centimeters, and human settlements close to sea level will be inundated.

According to *The Stern Review*, commissioned by the British government in 2007, there is a 50 percent risk of global temperatures rising by more than 5°C by the year 2100. In a conservative formulation, this would create a "5 to 20 percent reduction in consumption levels" worldwide. But even a global temperature increase of 3°C would radically transform the flows and balances of the ecology on which animal, plant, and human life are now vitally dependent.

Evidence for a WorldShift:
Population Growth and Resource Exhaustion

Great stress is created by the growth of the world's population. At the end of the twentieth century, population was expanding by about 900 million per decade, equivalent to a new London every month. It passed 6 billion before the turn of the century, and demographic calculations indicate that it will reach 9.1 billion by the middle of the twenty-first century. Urban dwellers number more than half of the world's population, and UN forecasts speak of 60 percent of the global population living in cities by 2030.

Modern cities are the largest conglomerates of humans ever seen on this planet. There are megaconglomerations such as the Greater Tokyo area with 35 million inhabitants and São Paulo with 23 or 25 million. Other cities are rapidly catching up, including Mumbai, Delhi, Mexico City, Dhaka, Jakarta, and Lagos, among others. By 2015 there may be 23 megacities in the world, 19 of them in the developing world and 37 other cities with populations between 5 and 10 million.

Rapid urbanization in developing countries exposes vast numbers of poor people to shortages of drinking water and sanitation, as well as to rising air pollution and airborne toxins. Large cities produce enormous social inequalities, with more than a billion people now living in squalor in slums, favelas, and bidonvilles.

Overcrowding and subminimal living conditions in urban conglomerates are major factors that produce frustration and conflict, resulting in higher levels of violence and unusual forms of crime: mass murders where seemingly ordinary people run amok, renewed suicide bombings in populated city centers, and suicidal terrorism on land and in the air.

The rapid growth of the world's population, especially in the cities, creates increasing problems of resource availability, particularly of clean water and energy. Already a third of the global population lacks access to adequate supplies of clean water, and the share of water-deprived populations is expected to rise to half of humankind within decades. UNESCO and other global organizations speak of the danger of "water wars" as desperate populations become violent in the fight for clean-water supplies.

Urban centers consume three-quarters of the world's energy and are responsible for at least three-quarters of its pollution. The supply of abundant cheap energy has entered a critical end phase. As the world continues to run on fossil fuels, demand for oil rises and supply diminishes. At the beginning of the second decade of the twenty-first century, most of the world's oil producers had passed their peak. The largest oil fields were discovered over half a century ago: the peak of discovery was in 1965. New sources have not been found at the same rate, and as a result global oil production will peak or has already peaked. As the peak is passed, oil becomes more difficult and expensive to extract. The supply of cheap oil drops, and extraction becomes less profitable.

Yet demand for oil is still rising. The International Energy Agency found that in the last few years global demand has been increasing by 2 million barrels per day. If no significant changes in the patterns of energy production and consumption come about, global demand for oil would rise in the next two decades, from the present 80 million barrels a day to 125 million barrels.

Growing demand and decreasing supply drive prices up. Surges in oil prices create an almost instant impact on individuals, enterprises, and economies in every part of the world. Higher prices also trigger conflicts related to discovery and extraction. The Arctic Ocean seabed, which may hold billions of gallons of both oil and natural gas, is becoming a globally contested region. In March 2007, Russia announced that it planned to set up a military force to protect its interests in the region, and in August of that year the Russian flag had been planted on the ocean floor 4km beneath the North Pole to indicate the country's claim to the area known as the Lomonosov Ridge. The U.K. in turn is claiming sovereign rights to more than a million square kilometers (about 386,000 square miles) of the seabed off Antarctica. The opening up of the Northwest Passage due to the melting of Arctic ice is already provoking international contestation and conflict.

Evidence for a WorldShift:
A Critical Cycle in the Sun

Physical changes in the intensity of solar radiation conspire with human impacts to stress the world system and induce major change. Astronomers have noted that since the 1940s, and particularly since 2003, the sun has become remarkably turbulent, with the exception of the last year or so. Solar activity is predicted to peak around 2012, creating storms of intensity unprecedented since the 1859 "Carrington event," when a large solar flare accompanied by a coronal mass ejection flung billions of tons of solar plasma into the Earth's magnetosphere.

The peak will be due to the coincidence of two cycles in solar activity. The number of sunspots (or flares) reaches a maximum every eleven years, while the sun's magnetic energy cycle peaks every twenty-two years. These will occur at the same time at the end of 2012, or at the latest in early 2013.

Solar storms, capable of traveling at speeds of up to five million miles per hour, would knock out virtually every major technological infrastructure on the planet. A NASA report issued in June 2010 stated that a solar storm would hit like a "bolt of lightning" and damage everything from emergency-service systems, hospital equipment, banking systems, and air-traffic control to smaller scale personal devices such as home computers, satellite navigation systems, and iPods.

The solar storm of 1859 was the most powerful event of its kind in recorded history. On the first of September of that year, the sun expelled huge quantities of high-energy protons in a large flare that traveled directly toward the earth, taking eighteen hours instead of the usual three or four days to reach our planet. It disrupted telegraph systems all over Europe and North America. Fires erupted in telegraph stations due to power surges in the wires, and the northern lights (aurora borealis) were seen as far south as Florida.

The second solar storm on record, in March 1989, melted the transformers of the Hydro-Québec power grid, causing a nine-hour blackout that affected six million people in Canada. And the solar storms that reached the earth between October 19 and November 7, 2003, disrupted satellites and global communications, air travel, navigation systems, and power grids all over the world. It also affected systems on the International Space Station.

The solar maximum forecast for the end of 2012 could do greater harm than any before, since human life has become much more dependent upon the global energy grid. It would cause the failure of electric power in most parts of the world, and major cities could be without power for months. People in high-rise apartments, where water has to be pumped up, would be cut off immediately. For most others, drinking water would come through the taps for about half a day, but the flow would then cease without electricity to pump it from the reservoirs. Transportation systems directly or indirectly dependent on electric power (which means practically all systems) would come to a standstill. Backup generators would operate at some sites until their fuel ran out—for hospitals, that would mean about seventy-two hours of essential-care-only services. Without power for heating, cooling, and refrigeration, and with a breakdown in the distribution of medicines and pharmaceuticals, the urban population would begin to die within days.

A National Research Council report issued by the U.S. National Academy of Sciences in the spring of 2009 estimated that the cost of another Carrington event could be as high as $2 trillion, and recovery could take four to ten years.

Scientists forecast yet another disruptive event for the end of 2012: breaches in the earth's magnetic field. In the past this field protected living systems from the effects of solar storms and coronal mass ejections. Lately the magnetic field has diminished in intensity, and holes and gaps have appeared. Scientists in South Africa measured cracks in the magnetic field the size of California, and in December 2008 NASA announced that its Themis Project had found a massive breach that would allow devastating amounts of solar plasma to enter the earth's magnetosphere.

The fluctuation of the magnetic field could also lead to the reversal of the planet's magnetic poles. During the course of reversal, the magnetic field would become still weaker, and the danger to life from solar and stellar radiation would greatly increase.

Another scientific report of relevance concerns the entry of our solar system into a highly energized region of space. This turbulent region is making the sun hotter and stormier and has already caused climate change on other planets. According to Russian scientists, the effects on Earth will include an acceleration of the magnetic pole shift, the vertical and horizontal redistribution of the ozone, and an increase in the frequency and magnitude of extreme climate events.

3. Mastering the WorldShift

Fighting for a Better Place on the Deck of the *Titanic*

The ship is heading into iceberg territory, but passengers in first class squabble among themselves to secure a better place on the upper deck. Does that make sense? To the leaders of the twenty richest and most powerful nations of the world, it apparently does.

The Leaders' Declaration of the Seoul Summit of the G-20* reads like a report of finance and trade managers faced with short-term emergencies. It centers on international trade disequilibria, discriminating exchange rate policies, volatile capital flows, and the threat of financial crises. It ignores the fact that the entire system in which these problems appear is in danger. That system is not just a financial and international trade system, but the system of human communities in the embrace of nature on the planet. It is destabilized by economic, social, and cultural conflict among peoples, and the deterioration of the ecologies that support life on Earth. The international community is equipped to make the worst of these threats: it maintains vast arsenals of weapons of mass destruction on hair-trigger alert. The ship is in danger of hitting an iceberg ahead, but its influential passengers refuse to recognize that it's going the wrong way. They only see the crises that would inconvenience their comfort and threaten their privileges on board.

The Action Plan agreed by the G-20 leaders is a case study in narrowly focused short-term crisis management. It centers on five policy areas listed in this order: monetary and exchange rate policies, trade and development policies, fiscal policies, financial reforms, and structural reforms. Structural reforms are limited to boosting and sustaining global demand, fostering job creation,

---

*The Seoul Summit Leaders' Declaration, November 11–12, 2010. Various sites.

contributing to global rebalancing, and increasing "our growth potential." The effectiveness of such reforms could hardly have inspired the confidence of the leaders themselves: at the conclusion of the Summit, President Obama felt compelled to go on television to address a plea to China and other trade surplus nations to stop growing by exporting to the United States.

The kind of growth that the G-20 treats as a panacea, even when sustained and better balanced, is merely a continuation of the same unsustainable economic system that is now threatening the well-being and even the survival of vast underprivileged populations, altering the planet's climate and degrading its ecologies. Today's looming climate, ecology, energy, and nuclear threats are not isolable into narrow specialty areas, and are not manageable by economic and fiscal measures alone. The world needs leaders who can redesign our societies to become socially, culturally, and ecologically viable. It needs comprehensive structural reform so that people could live in peace with one another and with the ecological systems that sustain their life. And it needs leaders who can address the major threats generated by the reckless orientation of our shared vessel: global warming and nuclear weapons.

If unstopped, the climatic changes produced by global warming will come together with such intense effect that no nation or group of nations will be able to halt or reverse it. According to projections by scientists such as James Lovelock, in the next 100 years more than 80 percent of the human species could perish due to climate-induced catastrophes, diseases sweeping wide territories, and mushrooming conflicts generated by the most massive migration of peoples in history—giant waves of climate refugees moving across the continents. Faced with such dangers, the timely abolition of nuclear weapons is essential for our survival. We need a Nuclear Weapons Convention prohibiting the production as well as the use of all nuclear weapons in all circumstances.

In a world aspiring to democracy, such a Convention must be built on the will of the people. A critical mass of individuals in all parts of the world needs to become aware of the suicidal implications of maintaining vast arsenals of weapons capable of killing the bulk of humanity and destroying most forms of life on Earth.

A critical mass of awakened people is not utopian. In twenty-one countries, *including* the five major nuclear powers, polls show that 76 percent of people support negotiation of a treaty banning all nuclear weapons.

But for now, despite the Internet and the rise of alternative media and forms of communication, the road to building a critical mass is effectively blocked. Nuclear weapons are about power, and governments have not given up what they perceive as a source of their power. Powerful military-industrial complexes are trading on the threat to national security created by the very presence of the military establishments that are called upon to cope with it. In the mainstream media there is a virtual blackout on the subject of the nuclear threat. In the absence of an enlightened leadership, it is nearly impossible to mobilize the will of the people to remove the nuclear sword of Damocles hanging over our heads.

It is ludicrous to squabble over short-term privileges and devise safety nets to ensure the kind of growth that has already brought us to the edge of disaster. The time has come to look the decisive issues in the face, and do something about them. But where are the leaders who are ready to do that? They are not at the helm of the G-20, that is clear.

You Can't Solve a Problem with the Same Kind of Consciousness . . .

It makes sense to paraphrase Einstein's famous dictum in regard to consciousness. Our problem is the unsustainability of the world we have created, and we should be clear that we can't solve this problem with the same kind of consciousness that gave rise to it.

But many people try to do just that, even the leaders of the world's twenty richest and most powerful nations. The November 2010 meeting of the G-20 in Seoul gave indisputable proof of it. Not only did the meeting fail to achieve its main objectives (among them rebalancing international trade and reaching an accommodation between the U.S. and South Korea), the objectives themselves proved to be out-of-date. They centered on restabilizing the same moribund economic and financial system that made the world unsustainable in the first place.

But why is the G-20's failure due to wrong consciousness? Because consciousness in the social, political, and cultural context is the sum total of our view of the world, with its values, aspirations, and background assumptions. It's the "paradigm" that underlies the way we think and the way we set our priorities. The consciousness of the G-20 gives rise to an obsolete view of the world, with faulty values and outdated aspirations. The leaders view the world as the arena for a Darwinian struggle for survival, seen as a competition for growth in the economies of nations. Since assured growth cannot be achieved even by the wealthiest and most powerful nation in the world by itself, the leaders recognize the need for some level and form of cooperation—as a means to an end. The end is for the rich nations to make sure that they remain rich.

If the GDP grows and the trade balance is positive, all is well, nothing more is needed. It appears that the leaders are convinced that all that any person or nation in the world could reasonably ask for is to make money, preferably more money than its neighbor. That the world in which this competition takes place is perilously balanced at the edge of climatic and resource disasters—and that at the same time it's thoroughly equipped with nuclear and other high-tech weapons to make the worst of any crisis coming its way—seems to have escaped their attention.

Consciousness is like a light shining on the objects in which we are interested. It can be a spotlight, narrowly focused, or a floodlight, illuminating a wide range of things together with their surroundings. The G-20's light is a spotlight, focused on their own national economy in the short-term perspective. It doesn't illuminate anything around it, or beyond it.

But this is not the only kind of consciousness people can have, nor is it the only kind that many already have. A new consciousness is evolving in society, enabling people to look beyond the narrow horizons espoused by their leaders. The new consciousness tells them that we live on a planet where we exploit and exhaust our finite storehouses of energy and matter, where we pollute the environment and destroy the systems of nature that support our life. And where continued growth in the world's economy fails to trickle down to more than half of the human population. It tells them that ours is a totally unsustainable situation.

It's time for the consciousness evolving in wide strata of the population to penetrate to the leadership. It's time for concerned and responsible people to speak up. You don't need to have power and wealth to be effective. The Internet and the new media in civil society—among them the Network of IONS and the World-Shift Community of the Club of Budapest—are here to enable you to speak up. And to be heard. It's up to each and every one of us to make good use of the means at our disposal—before it's too late. Because the hour is later than most people seem to think. Certainly, later than the leaders of the G-20 think.

The Challenge of Cooperation

The unsustainable condition of the human and the humanly impacted natural world leads to a global bifurcation, and meeting this calls for global cooperation—otherwise, we could face a global breakdown.

Global cooperation is a new requirement in the history of humanity, and it's not surprising that we are not prepared for it. Our institutions and organizations were designed to protect their own interests in competition with others; the need for them to join together in shared interest has been limited to territorial aspirations and defense, and to economic gain in selected domains. Preparedness for globally cooperative action that subordinates immediate self-interests to the vital interests of the community is lacking both in contemporary nation-states, and in business enterprises.

Globally coordinated action could produce positive results. The world lacks neither the financial nor the human resources for effective emergency action. Abject forms of poverty could be eliminated, energy- and resource-efficient technologies could be made widely available, water could be recycled and seawater desalinized, and sustainable forms of agriculture could be adopted. We could muster the energies to implement such action, and we have the technologies. Even a modest increment in the effective use of the solar radiation reaching the planet could supply the necessary energies, and the reassignment of but a fraction of the funds currently devoted to destructive purposes could finance the principal projects. The reason for the lack of globally coordinated effective action doesn't lie in the condition of humanity relative to the condition of the planet, but in the lack of will and preparedness of the people and institutions of the human world to ensure their survival on the planet.

Gandhi said, "Be the change you want to see in the world." In today's world, this means, "Change your consciousness so that others might change theirs." How can you do that? First of all, get rid of the old consciousness, and the values and beliefs that support it.

Ask yourself: *Do you believe that . . .*

- . . . everyone is separate and rightfully pursues his or her own interest?

- . . . life is a struggle for existence; only the fittest (meaning the wealthiest or most powerful) survive?

- . . . in the ruthless competition for survival, the ends justify the means?

- . . . the more money you have, the better you are (and very likely also happier)?

- . . . people owe allegiance only to one nation and one company—the rest are strangers and competitors?

- . . . if we want peace, we must prepare for war?

- . . . technology and efficiency are the answer, no matter what the question?

- . . . for all intents and purposes the earth is an inexhaustible source of resources and an infinite sink of wastes?

- . . . the environment can be engineered like a settlement or a highway to fit our needs and demands?

- . . . the selfishness and egocentricity that characterize modern people are unalterable expressions of human nature; they cannot and therefore will not change. People were always pursuing their own interests and always will, mitigated at the most by the interests of their immediate family, enterprise, or ethnic or national community?

Given the persistence of such beliefs, the failure of both nation-states and business enterprises to join together in global projects is by no means surprising.

If you hold such beliefs, you are part of the problem. But how can you become part of the solution? Here you must take a further step by adopting new thinking, which means a new consciousness. Einstein said that you can't solve a problem with the same kind of thinking that produced it. You can't shift the world with the same kind of thinking that made it unsustainable.

New thinking is not utopian; it's already emerging at the creative edge of society. In a number of "alternative cultures," people think and act in more positive ways. They share two fundamental beliefs. One is that the ancient saying "We are all one" is not just fiction but has roots in reality. William James was right: we are like islands in the sea, separate on the surface but connected in the deep.

The second belief regards the sphere of human responsibility. If we are one with each other and with nature, our responsibilities do not end with ourselves, our family, our country, and our company; they also encompass the human community and the biosphere. Living up to them is not charity. If we are part of humanity, and humanity is part of life on the planet, what we do to others and to nature we also do to ourselves.

The silver lining on today's gathering clouds is the growing openness of young people to adopt new and more responsible ways of thinking and acting. The "youth culture" and the "alternative cultures" are growing rapidly, but they have yet to produce the globally coordinated action needed to cope with the global emergency. Bringing them together to form a critical mass that has sufficient economic and political weight to implement the worldshift could transform the structures and operations of society and restabilize the cycles and balances of nature. This is arguably the most urgent and important project of our time.

The Two Cardinal Sins—and the Cardinal Virtue

The two cardinal sins and the cardinal virtue of these times of change and transformation are defined by how we ourselves relate to the changes that will come about in the world.

The cardinal sins are *convenient complacency* and *facile skepticism.*

Convenient complacency is born from the convenience of not having to do anything or change anything—things are basically all right as they are. There are problems in our world and occasional crises, but they are being managed by those in charge, or perhaps they will just resolve themselves. The world has seen problems and crises before, and has muddled through them without people like you and me doing anything about them. We don't need to bother trying to change the world—it will take care of itself. Convenient complacency is the sin of the *uninformed optimist.*

Facile skepticism is the reverse of convenient complacency; it's the other side of the coin. It's when we believe that we don't need to do or change anything, not because we think things are basically okay, but because we are convinced that things cannot be changed—certainly not by people like you and me. If we managed to get through problems and crises before, it may have been because we were just plain lucky, or because the issues at hand were not really that serious to begin with. In any case, there is not much we can do about it.

The world has pretty much remained the same, and so has human nature. So if we are still here tomorrow, it will not be because the world has changed and definitely not because we have changed it. Perhaps we are just fortunate, or maybe our problems really are not that bad. And if our problems are serious, and if we are not so lucky, then we won't be here. That will be too bad, but it's the just way it will be. Facile skepticism is the sin of the *uninformed pessimist.*

Why are both the optimist and the pessimist uninformed? Because they ignore the most fundamental fact about our world: it's a complex system that is no longer sustainable. It's on the threshold of chaos. If it doesn't change in time, it collapses. But at the threshold of chaos, complex systems *can* change. They are ripe for, and capable of, global-level bifurcation. At that point they are unstable and supersensitive. In a chaotic system, even small fluctuations can catalyze major changes in structure and behavior (also known as the "butterfly effect").

The choice offered by complex systems at the threshold of chaos is simple and straightforward: transform or collapse. In the sphere of life, it is: mutate or become extinct. In the sphere of society, it is: create reform or lapse into anarchy.

The bifurcation of complex systems near chaos is a well-documented fact; it's not reasonable to question its reality. But optimists who take the stance of complacency don't question the reality of a bifurcation, they just ignore that it's coming. It's more convenient than facing it.

Pessimists are similarly uninformed, because otherwise they wouldn't be so sure that the world cannot be changed. It's simpler to assume that the world is unchangeable—then there is no need to feel guilty for not doing anything about changing it.

The sins of convenient complacency and facile skepticism are sins of ignorance—willful, unnecessary, and therefore, inexcusable ignorance. It's inexcusable because, at least in the industrialized, information-imbued parts of the world, it is practically impossible to remain ignorant of the basic facts of sustainability. More and more, the facts are spelled out in the news, but they are also implicit in the stress we experience in the everyday sphere of our lives. They are equally implicit in changes in the climate: we are unbalancing not just the human world, but also nature. It's absurd to continue to act as if these worlds were not on the threshold of a bifurcation.

Uninformed individuals believe that the world cannot be changed—or that it doesn't need to be changed. Superficially informed individuals see that the world needs to be changed, but they're not sure if it can—at least by them. Truly informed individuals know that the world is supersensitive and prone to change, and that they, and people like them, can do everything that needs to be done to change it the right way.

Truly informed individuals do not lapse into the twin traps of convenient complacency and facile skepticism. They know that the world will change, for it must change. They also know that they can have a role in changing it: a decisive one. Their stance is that of the activist: the informed activist.

Informed activism is the cardinal virtue in our time. It's our best hope for taking control of our destiny: for creating a world we can live in and leave in good conscience to our children.

4. The New Consciousness

Do You Have a Planetary Consciousness?

We live in global times, yet most of us have a tribal kind of consciousness: it's me or you, my group or yours, and whoever isn't with us is against us. The continuation of tribal consciousness is nothing less than a recipe for disaster in a world of nuclear weapons, environmental devastation, increasing population, and dwindling resources.

There can be no doubt: if we're going to live sustainably and in peace with each other, we must all shift from a tribal to a planetary consciousness.

But just what is planetary consciousness? Here is how we defined it in the "Manifesto on Planetary Consciousness" that I drafted with the Dalai Lama and other luminaries of the Club of Budapest in 1996: *Planetary consciousness is knowing as well as feeling the vital interdependence and essential oneness of humankind, and the conscious adoption of the ethic and the ethos that this entails.*

It was our conclusion at the time that the evolution of planetary consciousness was the foundational imperative for the survival of the human species. I remain more convinced than ever that this is the case.

But what do you think? Assuming you agree that we must evolve beyond tribalism if we are to survive, would you consider yourself to have a planetary consciousness? Here are ten questions that I believe, if answered honestly, will tell you whether or not you do.

Ask yourself: *Do you . . .*

1. Satisfy your basic needs without diminishing other people's chances of satisfying theirs?

2. Pursue your own happiness with due regard for the similar pursuit of others?

3. Respect the right to economic development for all people, wherever they live and whatever their ethnic origin or belief system?

4. Live in a way that respects the integrity of nature around you?

5. Work with like-minded people to safeguard and restore your local environment?

6. Require your government to relate to other nations peacefully and in a spirit of cooperation, recognizing the legitimate aspirations of all the members of the international community?

7. Buy from companies that accept responsibility for stakeholders at all levels of the supply chain?

8. Consume media that provides unbiased information relevant to you and your community?

9. Do something to help at least one other person escape the hopeless struggles and abject humiliations of extreme poverty?

10. Believe all young people are entitled to the education they need in order to be productive members of their community?

Answering these ten questions with an honest *yes* doesn't call for money or power. It calls for dedication and solidarity, for the spirit that creates true community, both locally and globally.

The evolution of planetary consciousness is without question an imperative for human survival on the planet. In its absence, it's difficult to see how all seven billion of us will be able to live in peace—or even just survive. To paraphrase Gandhi, "Live consciously, so that all of us may live."

Is Transpersonal Consciousness the Next Step in Our Collective Evolution?

Human consciousness is not static, fixed once and for all. It's the product of a long evolutionary development and is capable of further development. In the 30,000- to 50,000-year history of the species we proudly call *Homo sapiens,* the human body didn't change significantly, but human consciousness did. And it can change again.

In a variety of "alternative cultures," a different kind of consciousness is emerging. The members of these cultures—the green movement, the peace movement, the sustainable-living movement, the movement of cultural creatives, and others—share social values and are open and interactive with society; they don't seek isolation or indulge in promiscuous sex. They aim to rethink accepted beliefs and values, and adopt a more responsible style of living. They shift from matter- and energy-wasteful ostentation toward voluntary simplicity and the search for sustainability and harmony with nature.

A new consciousness is now struggling to be born. Does this mean that the consciousness of humanity itself is evolving? Some famous thinkers have said so. The Indian sage Sri Aurobindo spoke of the emergence of superconsciousness in ever more people, and this, he said, is the harbinger of the next evolution of human consciousness. In a similar vein, the Swiss philosopher Jean Gebser spoke of the coming of four-dimensional integral consciousness, rising from the prior stages of archaic, magical, and mythical consciousness. The American mystic Richard Bucke called the new consciousness "cosmic"; and in the colorful spiral dynamics developed by Chris Cowan and Don Beck, it's the turquoise stage of collective individualism, cosmic spirituality, and Earth changes. For philosopher Ken Wilber, these developments signify an evolutionary transition from the mental consciousness characteristic of both animals and humans to subtle consciousness, which is archetypal, transindividual, and intuitive; and also to causal consciousness and ultimately to "consciousness as such." Psychiatrist Stanislav Grof summed up the characteristics of the emerging consciousness as "transpersonal."

There is remarkable agreement among these visionary concepts. Superconsciousness, integral consciousness, cosmic consciousness, turquoise-stage consciousness, and consciousness as such are all forms of transpersonal consciousness. They transcend the divide between you and me, the individual and the world, the human being and nature. If these thinkers are right, this kind of consciousness will be the next stage in the consciousness evolution of our species.

The New Consciousness Could Be Our Salvation

A new transpersonal, planetary consciousness, using the quantum-resonance based information received by our brain, could be the next stage in the evolution of the human mind. But why would this consciousness be our salvation?

The answer is basic common sense: because a quantum-reception based consciousness gives us a direct, intuitive connection to the world. It inspires empathy with people and with nature; it brings an experience of oneness and belonging. Planetary consciousness enables us to realize that we are one with others and with nature. And thus, what we do to others and to nature we do to ourselves.

The new consciousness will encourage us to join together to cope with the problems we face.

Most of us cooperate with members of our own family and community. But cooperation has now become vitally necessary on the global level: it's in all our best interest to cooperate with our fellows in the global community. Without such cooperation, we'll be hard put to overcome the global threats and problems that face us. Without cooperation, we risk joining the countless species that became extinct because they couldn't adjust to changed circumstances.

With dedicated and purposeful cooperation, we could meet the challenges of human survival: seven billion or more people could live peacefully and sustainably on this planet. We possess the technology, skill, and necessary financial and human resources. And to finance these projects, we only need a small part of the enormous sums of money that we now commit to speculative, self-serving, or downright destructive ends.

When all is said and done, the fundamental need of our time, the precondition of creating a peaceful and sustainable world, is the spread of a new and more adaptive consciousness—the planetary consciousness of oneness and belonging.

When the new consciousness has become mainstream, humanity will have reached a higher stage of maturity. It will have become a species that has not only the technologies and the skills, but also the wisdom and the will to live in the world that it has itself created.

♪♫♪♫♪♫

MILESTONES

- *June 12, 1932:* Ervin Laszlo is born in Budapest to middle-class, relatively prosperous parents.

- *Spring 1937:* Ervin's mother begins to teach him how to play the piano. Whatever his mother plays, he is able to repeat and make into his own piece of music.

- *March 1942:* Public debut with the Budapest Symphony Orchestra.

- *Spring 1944–Spring 1945:* Difficult but ultimately successful struggle for survival under the Nazi occupation and then the Red Army siege of Budapest.

- *Fall 1946:* Abortive participation in the International Marguerite Long–Jacques Thibaud Competition in Paris.

- *June 14, 1947:* Awarded the highest degree ("Artist Diploma") of the Franz Liszt Academy of Music in Budapest.

- *September 1947:* Wins the International Competition of Musical Interpretation in Geneva.

- *Winter 1947–1948:* Lives in Paris with Mother and enjoys a Bohemian lifestyle; falls into the favor of Baroness Alix de Rothschild (the wife of Baron Guy de Rothschild of the great banking family), who allows him to use the piano in her studio.

- *April 17, 1948:* American debut in New York's Town Hall.

- *Fall 1948–Spring 1950:* Embarks on concert tours throughout the U.S. and Canada.

- *1950:* Drafted in the U.S. military and serves as a musician in the USO; later serves as a Goodwill Ambassador of the U.S. Department of State, performing concerts in that capacity in the Middle East.

- *Spring 1953:* Returns to Europe to give concerts in Italy, Germany, Switzerland, and France.

- *Summer 1953:* Resides in Lugano, Switzerland, and meets major influence Wilhelm Backhaus.

- *1955–1956:* Goes on a concert tour throughout Europe and South America.

- *October 1956:* Has first encounter with Marjorie, his future wife, in London.

- *November 16, 1957:* Ervin and Marjorie are married in Paris.

- *March 22, 1959:* First child, Christopher, is born. Laszlo family resides in Munich; Ervin continues to perform concerts throughout Europe and the U.S.

- *January 1, 1960:* Resolves to pursue systematic research into philosophic/scientific questions.

- *Fall 1961:* Meets prospective publisher after performing a concert in The Hague.

- *1962–1965:* Meets Professor Bochenski at the University of Fribourg and moves family to Fribourg, Switzerland, from Lausanne. Works as research associate at the university's Institute of East European Studies, publishes several books and articles, and plays periodic concerts throughout Europe.

- *1963:* Returns to Budapest to interview Hungarian philosophers; first book, *Essential Society,* is published.

- *January 27, 1964:* Second son, Alexander, is born.

- *April 1966:* Performs decisive recital in Bonn.

- *September–December 1966:* Conducts research at Yale and receives offers to teach at numerous universities in the U.S.

- *Summer 1967:* Teaches music aesthetics as a visiting professor at the School of Music at Indiana University in Bloomington.

- *1967–1968:* Moves family to Akron, Ohio, and joins the philosophy faculty at the University of Akron.

- *August 1968:* Returns to Budapest to meet with Hungarian philosophers; joins protests of the Soviet quenching of the Prague Spring.

- *Fall 1968–1973:* Becomes an associate and then full professor of philosophy at the State University of New York (SUNY) at Geneseo; co-edits *The Journal of Value Inquiry* and heads annual Conferences on Value Inquiry; writes and edits numerous books and articles.

- *Spring 1970:* Awarded the Doctorat ès Lettres et Sciences Humaines from the Sorbonne.

- *1972:* Publishes *Introduction to Systems Philosophy* and *The Systems View of the World.*

- *Fall 1972:* Invited as a guest speaker to conduct seminars at the Center of International Studies in Princeton.

- *1973–1977:* Organizes and conducts the Club of Rome's international "Goals for Mankind" project; appointed as special fellow to the United Nations Institute for Training and Research (UNITAR).

- *December 1973:* Vacations with family in Tuscany and acquires the Podere Franatoni (later renamed the Villa Franatoni) in Montescudaio.

- *Spring 1977:* Publishes the *Goals for Mankind* report to the Club of Rome.

- *Fall 1977–1980:* Named director of the UNITAR Programme on the New International Economic Order (NIEO); moves family to New York City.

- *September–October 1980:* The UN General Assembly fails to endorse the NIEO; on request of the Secretary-General, Ervin envisions and begins to work on the Programme on Regional and Interregional Cooperation among Developing Countries (RCDC).

- *1981–1983:* Resides in Rome with family to head the Italian UNITAR project office.

- *1985:* Decides not to return to his teaching position at SUNY and instead lives and works as an independent writer/researcher based in Tuscany; creates and heads the European Culture Impact Research Consortium at the Institute for Culture in Budapest.

- *Summer 1986:* While attending a seminar on the Adriatic coast, has profound intuition regarding the preservation of information in the cosmos.

- *1987–1991:* Heads the European Perspectives section of the UN University's European Identity Project at the Institute for Culture in Budapest.

- *1993:* Proposes the creation of an artists' and writers' club at the Third World Congress of Hungarians; establishes its secretariat in Budapest and names it "The Club of Budapest."

- *February 1995:* While in India, meets with the Dalai Lama, who helps him draft "The Manifesto on Planetary Consciousness."

- *March 1996:* Presides over the first international meeting of the Club of Budapest.

- *October 26, 1996:* Formal signing and adoption of "The Manifesto on Planetary Consciousness" at the Hungarian Academy of Sciences.

- *1997–Present:* Attends meetings and consultations, creates an international network, and publishes numerous reports for The Club of Budapest; lectures and attends conferences in Europe, the U.S., India, and the Far East on the Akashic field and the WorldShift.

- *March 21, 2001:* The Club of Budapest's Planetary Consciousness World Day is held in 29 countries.

- *September 9, 2009:* Launches the WorldShift 2012 Movement at the British Museum in London.

- *Summer 2010:* Co-founds, on behalf of The Club of Budapest, the Giordano Bruno GlobalShift University.

Principal Awards and Honors

- *1989:* Honorary diploma, Institute of Biology, Russian Academy of Sciences

- *1989:* Honorary Ph.D., Saybrook University, San Francisco

- *1989:* Honorary Ph.D., Turku School of Economics, Finland
- *1994:* Honorary diploma, Tecnológico de Monterrey, Nuevo León, Mexico
- *1999:* Honorary Ph.D., International Institute for Advanced Studies in Systems Research and Cybernetics, Canada (awarded in Baden-Baden, Germany)
- *2001:* Honorary Ph.D., University of Pécs, Hungary
- *2001:* Japan Peace Prize (Goi Award), Tokyo
- *2004 and 2005:* Nomination for the Nobel Peace Prize
- *2005:* Assisi Mandir of Peace Prize, Italy
- *2009:* Conacreis Holistic Culture Prize, Modena, Italy
- *2010:* Member of the Hungarian Academy of Sciences

♪♫♪♫♪♫

BIBLIOGRAPHY OF BOOKS, 1963–2010

The following bibliography contains the original editions of my published books listed by the year in which they first appeared. Edited books, subsequent editions, reprints, and translations into foreign languages have not been included.

- [*] indicates a major work—the definitive statement of a concept or theory

- [**] indicates a "life shift" work—marking or triggering a transition between my successive lives as a musician, scientist/philosopher, and worldshift activist

1963

Essential Society [**]
The Hague: Martinus Nijhoff

Individualism, Collectivism, and Political Power
The Hague: Martinus Nijhoff

1966

Beyond Scepticism and Realism
The Hague: Martinus Nijhoff
The Communist Ideology in Hungary
Dordrecht: D. Reidel; New York: Humanities Press

Philosophy in the Soviet Union
Dordrecht: D. Reidel; New York: Humanities Press

1969

System Structure and Experience
New York and London: Gordon & Breach

1970

La Metaphysique de Whitehead
The Hague: Martinus Nijhoff

1972

Introduction to Systems Philosophy [*]
New York and London: Gordon & Breach; Toronto:
Fitzhenry & Whiteside

The Systems View of the World [**]
New York: George Braziller; Toronto: Doubleday Canada

1974

A Strategy for the Future [**]
New York: George Braziller

1977

Goals for Mankind [**]
New York: E.P. Dutton; Toronto and Vancouver: Clarke, Irwin;
London: Hutchinson

1978

The Inner Limits of Mankind
Oxford and New York: Pergamon Press

The Objectives of the New International Economic Order
With R. Baker, E. Eisenberg, and V.K. Raman
New York: UNITAR and Pergamon Press

The Obstacles to the New International Economic Order
With J. Lozoya, J. Estevez, A. Bhattacharya, and V.K. Raman
New York: UNITAR and Pergamon Press

1981

Regional Cooperation Among Developing Countries
With J. Kurtzman and A. Bhattacharya
Oxford and New York: Pergamon Press

1983

Systems Science and World Order
Oxford and New York: Pergamon Press

La Crise Finale (French)
Paris: Editions Grasset

1985

Peace Through Global Transformation
With J.Y. Yoo
Seoul: Kyung Hee University Press

1986

Zene-rendszerelmélet-világrend (Hungarian)
Budapest: Gondolat

1987

Evolution: The Grand Synthesis [*]
Boston and London: New Science Library, Shambhala

1988

L'ipotesi del Campo Ψ (Italian) [**]
Bergamo: Pierluigi Lubrina Editore

The Age of Bifurcation [*]
New York and London: Gordon & Breach

1992

New Lectures on Systems Philosophy (Chinese)
Beijing: Chinese Social Science Press

Management by Evolution
With Christopher Laszlo and Prince Alfred of Lichtenstein

1993

The Creative Cosmos [*]
Edinburgh: Floris Books

1994

Vision 2020
New York: Gordon & Breach

The Choice: Evolution or Extinction
Los Angeles: Tarcher/Putnam

1995

Wissenschaft und Wirklichkeit (German)
Frankfurt: Insel Verlag

The Interconnected Universe [*]
Singapore and London: World Scientific Ltd.

1996

Changing Visions
With Robert Artigiani, Allan Combs, and Vilmos Csányi
Westport, CT: Praeger; London: Adamantine Press

The Whispering Pond [*]
Dorset, U.K., and Rockport, MA: Element Books

1997

The Insight Edge
With Christopher Laszlo

Westport, CT: Quorum Books

Third Millennium: The Challenge and the Vision
London: Gaia Books

1998

L'uomo E L'universo (Italian)
Rome: Di Renzo Editore

Dialogue Across Continents Through the Centuries (Chinese)
With Herman Haken and Wu Jie
Beijing: The People's Press

1999

The Consciousness Revolution
With Stanislav Grof and Peter Russell
Shaftesbury and Boston: Element Books

2001

Macroshift [*]
San Francisco: Berret-Koehler

2002

Holos: Welt Der Neue Wissenschaften (German)
Petersberg: Via Nova

You Can Change the World [**]
London: Positive News

2003

The Connectivity Hypothesis [*]
Albany: State University of New York Press

2004

Science and the Akashic Field [*]
Rochester, VT: Inner Traditions

2006

Science and the Reenchantment of the Cosmos [*]
Rochester, VT: Inner Traditions International

The Chaos Point [*]
Charlottesville, VA: Hampton Roads

2008

Quantum Shift in the Global Brain [*]
Rochester, VT: Inner Traditions

CosMos [*]
With Jude Currivan
London and Carlsbad, CA: Hay House, Inc.

2009

The Akashic Experience [*]
Rochester, VT: Inner Traditions

Worldshift 2012 [*]
Rochester, VT: Inner Traditions; Toronto: McArthur & Co.

Finding Bliss in the Shift (e-book)
With Marco Roveda

Related Publications

World Encyclopedia of Peace (four volumes)
Edited with Linus Pauling and Jong Y. Yoo
Oxford: Pergamon Press, 1986

The Evolutionary Outrider:
The Impact of the Human Agent on Evolution:
Essays Honouring Ervin Laszlo
Edited by David Loye
Westport, CT: Praeger, 1998; London: Adamantine Press, 1998

♪♫♪♫♪♫

ABOUT THE AUTHOR

Ervin Laszlo spent his childhood in Budapest. His life was darkened during the Nazi occupation and the siege of Budapest by the Soviets in World War II. He was a celebrated child prodigy on the piano and made his public debut at the age of nine. Winning the grand prize at the international music competition in Geneva enabled him to cross the Iron Curtain and begin an international concert career, first in Europe and then in the United States and South America.

After shifting to the life of a scientist and intellectual, Laszlo conducted studies and wrote papers for the Club of Rome, of which he was a member. In the late 1970s and early '80s, he oversaw global projects at the request of the Secretary-General of the United Nations. He received his doctorate from the Sorbonne and has held positions at Princeton, Yale, the University of Houston, the State University of New York, and elsewhere. His studies and insights in the 1990s led him to the discovery of the Akashic field, which he has continued to explore ever since.

The author, co-author, or editor of 86 books that have been translated into 23 languages, Laszlo has also written several hundred papers and articles in scientific journals and popular magazines. He is a member of numerous scientific bodies, including the International Academy of Science, the World Academy of Arts and Science, the International Academy of Philosophy of Science, and the Hungarian Academy of Science. He appears in several documentary films, including one based on his theory of the Akashic field. The recipient of numerous honors and awards, he was nominated for the Nobel Peace Prize in 2004 and 2005.

Ervin Laszlo is founder and president of the Club of Budapest. Members of this global think tank, with whom he frequently exchanges ideas about global problems, include: Mikhail Gorbachev, the Dalai Lama, Milos Forman, Jane Goodall, Bianca Jagger, Zubin Mehta, Desmond Tutu, Elie Wiesel, Barbara Marx Hubbard, Jean Houston, and Deepak Chopra.

www.ervinlaszlo.com
www.clubofbudapest.org

We hope you enjoyed this Hay House book.
If you would like to receive a free catalogue featuring additional
Hay House books and products, or if you would like information
about the Hay Foundation, please contact:

Hay House UK Ltd
292B Kensal Road • London W10 5BE
Tel: (44) 20 8962 1230; Fax: (44) 20 8962 1239
www.hayhouse.co.uk

***

Published and distributed in the United States of America by:
Hay House, Inc. • PO Box 5100 • Carlsbad, CA 92018-5100
Tel: (1) 760 431 7695 or (1) 800 654 5126;
Fax: (1) 760 431 6948 or (1) 800 650 5115
www.hayhouse.com

***

Published and distributed in Australia by:
Hay House Australia Ltd • 18/36 Ralph Street • Alexandria, NSW 2015
Tel: (61) 2 9669 4299, Fax: (61) 2 9669 4144
www.hayhouse.com.au

***

Published and distributed in the Republic of South Africa by:
Hay House SA (Pty) Ltd • PO Box 990 • Witkoppen 2068
Tel/Fax: (27) 11 467 8904
www.hayhouse.co.za

***

Published and distributed in India by:
Hay House Publishers India • Muskaan Complex • Plot No.3
B-2• Vasant Kunj • New Delhi - 110 070
Tel: (91) 11 41761620; Fax: (91) 11 41761630
www.hayhouse.co.in

***

Distributed in Canada by:
Raincoast • 9050 Shaughnessy St • Vancouver, BC V6P 6E5
Tel: (1) 604 323 7100
Fax: (1) 604 323 2600

***

Sign up via the Hay House UK website to receive the Hay House
online newsletter and stay informed about what's going on with your
favourite authors. You'll receive bimonthly announcements
about discounts and offers, special events, product highlights,
free excerpts, giveaways, and more!
www.hayhouse.co.uk

JOIN THE HAY HOUSE FAMILY

As the leading self-help, mind, body and spirit publisher in the UK, we'd like to welcome you to our family so that you can enjoy all the benefits our website has to offer.

 **EXTRACTS** from a selection of your favourite author titles

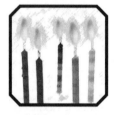 **COMPETITIONS, PRIZES & SPECIAL OFFERS** Win extracts, money off, downloads and so much more

 **LISTEN** to a range of radio interviews and our latest audio publications

 **CELEBRATE YOUR BIRTHDAY** An inspiring gift will be sent your way

 **LATEST NEWS** Keep up with the latest news from and about our authors

 **ATTEND OUR AUTHOR EVENTS** Be the first to hear about our author events

 **iPHONE APPS** Download your favourite app for your iPhone

 **HAY HOUSE INFORMATION** Ask us anything, all enquiries answered

join us online at **www.hayhouse.co.uk**

 292B Kensal Road, London W10 5BE
T: 020 8962 1230 E: info@hayhouse.co.uk